PHOTOSHOP
FOR GAMES

Creating Art for **Console**, **Mobile**, and **Social Games**

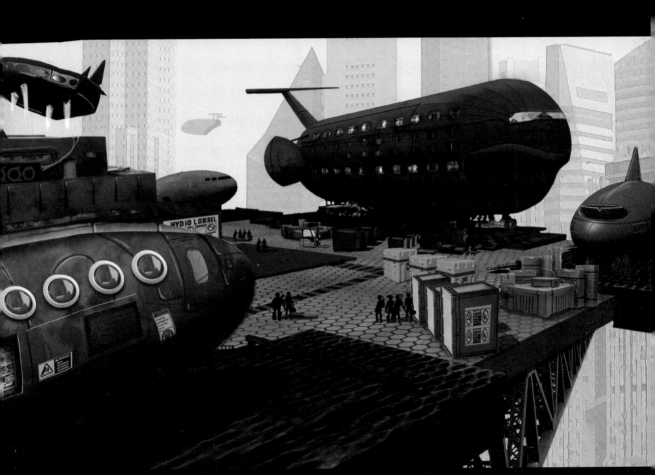

SHAWN NELSON

PHOTOSHOP FOR GAMES

Creating Art for Console, Mobile, and Social Games

Shawn Nelson

New Riders
www.newriders.com

To report errors, please send a note to errata@peachpit.com
New Riders is an imprint of Peachpit, a division of Pearson Education.

Acquisitions Editor: Karyn Johnson
Project Editor: Valerie Witte
Senior Production Editor: Lisa Brazieal
Developmental Editor: Bob Lindstrom
Copyeditor: Patricia Pane
Technical Editor: Jeff Cooperman
Composition: Kim Scott/Bumpy Design
Indexer: Karin Arrigoni
Cover Design: Aren Straiger
Interior Design: Kim Scott/Bumpy Design
Cover Images: Shawn Nelson

ISBN-13: 978-0-321-99020-4
ISBN-10:   0-321-99020-X

9 8 7 6 5 4 3 2 1

Printed and bound in the United States of America

This book is dedicated to my darling wife, Katie,
whose constant support pushes me ever forward;
and to my two crazy kids Blake and Maggie,
who are often confused with eccentric monkeys,
especially in dining situations.

ACKNOWLEDGMENTS

I've been working in games since 1997 and teaching game-asset creation since 2004. I used the very first version of Photoshop and have worked in every update since. That being said, I find that every time I work with a new person or read a new book, I seem to find something new to add to my bag of Photoshop tricks. My hope is that this book does the same for you.

A bunch of people need to be thanked for helping me write this book: Karyn Johnson, the senior editor at Peachpit who helped me present the book and get it going; the fantastic development team who consistently made me look and sound smart: Valerie Witte, Bob Lindstrom, Patricia Pane, Lisa Brazieal, and Kim Scott. Thanks to Jeff Cooperman for making sure I was on the level, and to Lisa Milosevich Matthews for introducing me to the wonderful world of Peachpit.

Of course I need to thank my wonderful family, who gave me the space to put down some words and noodle some images—Katie, Blake, Maggie, Pooka, and Hoola— they are my inspiration and taskmasters, all in the same package. I would also like to thank all the wonderful friends I have worked with over the years who were kind enough to share their secrets of digital art.

For me, being an artist means you are on a never-ending quest to try new things and create new work; and trust me, it is a far more enjoyable journey when you have good people around you.

For more information about me (Shawn Nelson), please visit one of my websites: my work site at http://shaw04.wix.com/snelsondigart or my tiki-themed cartoon site at http://shaw04.wix.com/tikiislandprincess.

CONTENTS

INTRODUCTION

Digital games have been around for years, and although their look has continued to morph with the tide of technology, almost all of them have something in common: They all were built in part using Photoshop. Photoshop has proven to be a game-art juggernaut. Its use is so prevalent that you would be hard-pressed to find a game artist job description that does not include the words "Must know Photoshop." With that in mind, this book features lessons specifically geared to introduce you to some of the most common uses of Photoshop in game development. It's intended to give you the understanding you need to improve your skillset and turn your portfolio into a game-ready package.

ABOUT THIS BOOK

Photoshop is an essential tool used by artists who make games. This book will give you insight into some of those uses and help you enhance the skills you need to create game assets at a professional level.

Who This Book Is For

This book is for anyone interested in using Photoshop to make digital games. Whether you're an experienced artist familiar with all things Photoshop, or you have only a basic understanding of digital art, this book will guide you through the necessary theory and practice you need to use Photoshop when making games.

How This Book Is Organized

This book features a series of lessons, each focusing on a part of the Photoshop interface, a tool, or a technique. Chapters 1 and 2 discuss general concepts used in making games for any format. Chapters 3, 4, and 5 delve into creating assets for specific platforms: mobile, social media, and console. Chapters 6 and 7 explore some advanced techniques that are not often used but are very powerful.

What This Book Covers

This book teaches students how to use Photoshop from its very basic interface to its most advanced tool sets. It also discusses topics such as 3D asset creation, lighting, and batch processing. Some of the theory discussed in this book may be new to you, but the intention is to advance your understanding of how to use Photoshop to create games.

HOW TO USE THIS BOOK

Whether using this book as a guide to self-study or in a classroom context, it is best to work through the lessons of this book in order, because each lesson builds on knowledge you acquire in the earlier lessons.

Each lesson consists of explanatory text and numbered steps designed to introduce you to new concepts and techniques. You should follow these steps precisely to gain the most useful learning experience. Performing steps out of order can produce unintended results and lead to a frustrating experience.

Using This Book for Self-Study

Progress at your own pace. Because you are not limited by time constraints, you may want to reinforce your learning by going through each lesson a second time, trying to do as much of the coursework as possible without specifically following the steps. In fact, as you go through the book, you are encouraged to pursue further experimentation on your own. Use the tools and techniques you've learned to take your art even further the second time around.

Using This Book in a Classroom Setting

This book offers an effective structure for teaching game creation in the classroom. We suggest that the trainer teach the lessons in book order with the students listening and writing down notes. Then the trainer can explain the steps while answering student questions and expanding on the text as necessary.

After a lesson is completed, students may need time to review the same chapter on their own in the classroom, under trainer supervision.

INSTALLING PHOTOSHOP

Although this book was originally written for Photoshop CC, the lessons can be followed successfully using more recent updates or legacy versions of Photoshop. Minor interface and behavior updates may account for slight differences between what the student sees on her screen and in the screenshots in the book.

DOWNLOADING PHOTOSHOP

To download Photoshop, follow these steps.

1. Go to www.adobe.com.
2. Navigate to Downloads.
3. From the product list, choose Photoshop.
4. Click the "Download trial" button.
5. Follow the instructions describing installation for your specific operating system.

ABOUT THE MEDIA FILES

As an added bonus, you can download some lessons that are available in video form. These videos feature step-by-step instructions for creating some of the game assets covered in the text.

Along with the videos, you will also find downloadable image files. These files are the images that I created while writing this book, and many still have the layers intact so you can reverse engineer the file if you need to.

To access the files and install them on your computer, follow these steps:

1. On a Mac or PC, go to www.peachpit.com.

2. If you don't yet have a Peachpit.com account, you will need to create one.

3. Enter the book's ISBN or go directly to the book's product page to register. Once on the book's page, click the Register Your Product link. The book will show up in your list of registered products along with a link to the book's bonus content.

4. Click the link to access the media files for the book. When the download is complete, double-click the archive to decompress it.

GETTING STARTED

This is an introduction to the world of Adobe Photoshop and its uses in the game industry. It takes many different kinds of artists to make a game, and they all have one thing in common: They use Photoshop every day. In the following pages, we will discover who these foragers of fun are and what they do to make their piece of the puzzle sing.

So, whether you are interested in making backgrounds for lost fairy palaces, designing a new HUD for a graffiti gun, or crafting the look of the ultimate destroyer of worlds, you will find a friend in Photoshop. We will discuss the various roles of artists and their places in the game industry, and by the end, you will be itching to become a Photoshop game guru and create your own game assets.

PHOTOSHOP, THE EARLY YEARS

NOTE To access the resource files and videos, just log in or join peachpit.com, and enter the book's ISBN. After you register the book, links to the files will be listed on your Account page under Registered Products.

In olden times (like the '80s and earlier), artists had it rough. "Art materials" were required to create art (**FIGURE 1.1**). In order to sketch something, you actually had to have paper and a pencil.

FIGURE 1.1 In the 20th century, artists used a plethora of art supplies to create a painting.

Creating a painting in color required a pot or tube of goo. Most of the time, you only had one shot at what you were doing—there was no erasing ink—and when you were done, you had to photograph or scan the painting if you planned to use it in a digital medium.

Thankfully, we are now the beneficiaries of years of research into artistic workflow and digital media (**FIGURE 1.2**). You can easily re-create almost any look available in the non-digital world, and you no longer need rooms filled with paint, pens, paper, French curves, T-bars, and so on. This does not, however, mean that you don't need to study and understand how those physical resources work.

It would be hard to say what Photoshop does best. Image manipulation comes to mind, but that is a pretty broad term that includes both photos and illustrations. (You will learn about both types of media in future chapters and even how to combine them.) For now, just know that in today's digital art world, photos are often used as the basis for illustrations (where photos can essentially be painted over) and illustrations are often used to plan out photos and cinematic shoots. The layer system in Photoshop allows you to have multiple versions of the same image, thereby making this type of workflow very easy. Quite a few artists these days also use 3D simulation as a basis to nail realistic perspective and lighting for their illustrations. You have to remember that there is no cheating in art. Anything you can do, and any tool you can use to make your work stronger, just makes you a better artist.

FIGURE 1.2 Modern artists' tools include computers, tablets and software.

Better-Looking Artwork = Better Artist

Photoshop was created by the Knoll Brothers, traditional photographers and computer nerds who based the functionality of the program on how a traditional artist or photographer works (**FIGURE 1.3**).

FIGURE 1.3 The first version of Adobe Photoshop was released in 1990.

As a result, many of the practices in the real world were re-created and purposefully mimicked in the digital space. That does not mean that the traditional approaches to creating art should not be abandoned because the environment is now a digital one. Photoshop is a very powerful tool, but it has a steep learning curve; and if you cannot draw, the software is not going to magically make you a brilliant illustrator. It takes years of practice to become a proficient artist, and you should learn traditional drawing skills because it will only make you a better Photoshop user and more desirable in the workforce.

Photoshop is a huge program with tons of features and tricks that most game artists never fully explore (**FIGURE 1.4**). The industry moves so fast that just learning the techniques you need to get a job done is barely manageable. But after a number of jobs and a variety of peer input, you start to pick up things. The great thing about Photoshop is that it enables you to do things in many ways, and given the ever-changing marks you need to hit as a game artist, that is a good thing. So bring your bag on your game-artist career path, because you will need a place to put all those Photoshop tricks you learn.

FIGURE 1.4 Photoshop, shown here on Adobe's current website, has come a long way since its introduction.

ARTISTS AND PHOTOSHOP

The artistic uses of Photoshop are plentiful. It is utilized in almost every form of digital art. You would probably expect that graphic designers, Web designers, and photographers eat their breakfast with Photoshop, and you would be correct. But that is just the beginning. Many other occupations rely on the software: architects, fabric designers, and even supermodels. The truth is, anyone who needs to draw a digital picture, alter a photograph, or lay out some text will find what they need in Photoshop. It is your one-stop shop for 2D art (and for some 3D art, as well).

But we are here to talk about games, which are (of course) the best of all these occupations, or at least the most fun. Photoshop is the Yin to the 3D Yang. It is the go-to tool for creating 2D assets. You could be the world's best Autodesk 3ds Max or Maya user—stunning your friends with your amazing knowledge and technique—but without Photoshop, you would only have some interesting gray bits running around the screen.

So when we talk about a game artist, we are usually talking about someone who knows Autodesk 3ds Max and Photoshop, Autodesk Maya and Photoshop, Adobe Flash and Photoshop, and so on. In fact, it is often implied that if you know one of the 2D or 3D animation/modeling programs, then you are also quite skilled with Photoshop.

Types of Game Artists

The game industry has room, and need, for many types of artists. Most studios run sort of like a king's court. At the top is, or should be, the *art director*, who unfortunately does not get to do a whole lot of art. Art directors are far too busy taking meetings, and maintaining budgets and schedules. They do oversee all the art being produced, and it is their job to maintain the vision of the game. They establish a game "look" and explain all art decisions to the rest of the managers.

Just below the art director are game generals, the *lead artists*. Lead artists perform a lot of the tasks that the art director initiates, but they are hands-on and actually work on assets. Quite often they will be team leaders and have a number of artists working under them. The lead in their title refers to rank, not the type of artist. You can work in any of the artistic roles used in making a game and still have a lead title.

Next in line is the knight of the game art world, the *senior artist*. The senior description refers to an artist who has been around long enough to be recognized as more experienced than a regular artist. Senior artists generally get better assignments and a higher pay scale.

The game *artists* are the workhorses of the game world, typically given all the worst gigs, and tons of them. They are expected to work like dogs and smile the whole time. This is the job where you pay your dues, and it usually doesn't last very long, either because an artist gets tired of working so much or is good enough to promote.

A team will sometimes have *junior artists* and *interns*, who are basically artists in training. Once junior artists or interns can competently perform whatever task they need to do, they are promoted to artist.

Now that you understand the hierarchy of a game art department, you should also know a bit about the different types of artists that work on games. We'll describe a large studio working on a triple A title, and the kind of project that would be employing the largest variety of artists at the same time. We will organize the talent by their disciplines. Remember that each of these artists can come in lead, senior, regular, or intern; but usually only one art director supervises the team and presumably is a master of all the disciplines.

- **UI artists**—Responsible for the user interface in the game, including buttons, text, info displays, and screens with numbers. They are font masters and really care about each individual pixel.

- **Generalist artists**—Are good in several disciplines and are hired when you need a bunch of work done and can't afford to hire three people.
- **Concept artists**—Specialize in dialing in the look of the game, be it characters or layouts, or backgrounds or mood pieces. The work these artists do usually doesn't make it into the final game but does influence the final look.
- **Storyboard artists**—Create a pictorial run of the script. In games, this work is mostly used for cinematics and cutaways.
- **Cinematic artists**—Create cinematic moments for the game. Sometimes these sequences are pre-rendered and played back, and sometimes they are executed within the game engine and played back in real time.
- **Modelers**—Make digital models for 3D games.
- **Animators**—Make the 2D images and 3D computer models move. This movement makes it possible for a game's elements to have the illusion of life.
- **Illustrators**—Draw anything from concepting to advertising finals.
- **Lighters**—Light scenes in a game engine or a 3D environment.
- **Level artists**—Build levels in a game engine using assets created by themselves or others. They can build anything from towns to jungle forests.
- **Technical artists**—Ensure that art assets are made correctly for implementation into the game engine. Their duties sometimes include programming tools for the art pipeline, and rigging and skinning 3D characters.
- **Texture artists**—Are responsible for the color and patterns on a 3D object and how that color reacts to the game engine's lighting simulation.
- **2D artists**—Work with 2D images.
- **3D artists**—Work in a 3D application such as Maya or 3ds Max.

You may not know yet what kind of artist you are, and that is fine. It sometimes takes years to figure that out. But because you are reading this, you probably have a foundation of skills in some type of art. Whatever your talent is, be it illustration, graphic design, or map drawing, you can find a place to shine in the game world. You just need to practice, practice, practice, and keep learning new things.

LEARNING THE GAME LINGO

As with any profession, game development has numerous colloquialisms that may seem strange but make sense with a bit of explanation. Let's look at some of the language you might encounter in a typical game design meeting, followed by a glossary of those bolded terms. You may feel temporarily lost, as you might in your first game development meeting, but bear with us. Eventually, all will become clear.

The Meeting

You are in an early meeting to design a new game. With you is the head of software engineering, the game designer, and a producer. Because this is an art book the entire art team is present, including a UI artist, a few 2D artists, several 3D artists, and the art director.

The goal is to make a Space Robot Pirate game and the meeting has been called to figure out what needs to be done first. If this is an **agile** project, you will identify the minimum amount of work necessary to create a **demo**. If it is a **waterfall** project, you will create a long-term plan that will place demo creation with a finished project schedule. Agile and waterfall describe polar opposite planning methods. A demo in this instance is a playable example of the game you would like to make, which usually incorporates some sort of proof of concept. This is used to get your project **greenlit**, which means someone will give you money to make it.

The **engineer** begins by helping to determine which **engine** will be used. The **producer** says: "We will need someone who can **code** in **Python**, and we will be using the **Unity engine** with some **secret sauce**." In other words, the team will be using a commercially available game engine called Unity, but the engineers will be modifying it with custom code written in a programming language called Python to provide special features.

The producer asks if there is enough time to open a new **eng rec** and still make the **milestones.** The engineer says the **tools guy** knows Python and can fill in until a new person is hired, but that is going to affect the work being done on the **backend code**. The producer agrees and asks the **art director** if that will affect his **team,** as they were counting on the tools guy writing some tools for **exporting** the **deliverables**.

The art director asks his **lead artist** which **assets** are still outstanding. The lead artist says that quite a few of the **models** are done but need to be **rigged**, **skinned**, and **animated**. He also says that the new enemy robots are not working out and he will need some new **concept sketches** before he can move forward. The art director agrees and asks the senior 2D artist to assemble some **mood boards** and **thumbnails** for a new enemy robot direction.

The producer and the engineer leave and the art department continues with the meeting. The 2D artist who specializes in **UI**, **UE**, and **HUDs** speaks up. Will he need to mock up any new **wireframes** for this demo? The art director says no, but **testing** will need additional help squashing some **bugs** they are finding in the menu.

Everyone is satisfied. Team members leave the room and get back to work. Usually, notes will be emailed to all participants by the producer.

THEY SAID WHAT?

As you can see, the game world is no slacker when it comes to industry-specific terminology. The previous section showcased a lot of the more commonly used game terms in context to give you some idea of their meanings. In future chapters, we will be expanding on these terms, but here is a quick-look glossary for your reference.

- **Agile**—Agile method organizes tasks into small parts with minimal planning for the creation of assets, and does not involve long-term planning.

- **Waterfall**—A long-term planning system that identifies as many of the game's essential assets as early as possible.

- **Demo**—A preliminary version of the game—usually a small part of the game—built to show proof of concept and often referred to as a "vertical slice."

- **Greenlit**—The project is approved for funding and development.

- **Engineer**—A software engineer, programmer, or computer scientist who programs code for video games.

- **Engine**—A software-based, open-ended development system for the creation of video games. An engine can be developed internally or commercially licensed from a third-party engine developer.

- **Producer**—The person who oversees the development of a game, tracking and maintaining schedules, and monitoring the project's progress.

- **Code**—Sometimes referred to as *source code*, it is the lines of programming (written in one or more programming languages) used to create a game.

- **Python**—A type of high-level programming language.

- **Unity engine**—A commercially available game engine.

- **Secret sauce**—A nickname for custom, proprietary code, written by the in-house engineers, that accentuates or alters how an engine, or other licensed game code, operates.

- **Eng rec**—An open requisition for an engineer; an available job, in this case, for an engineer.

- **Milestones**—Markers in the production schedule that identify work and tasks that must be finished by a certain date. Usually payment schedules are tied to milestones.

- **Tools guy**—An engineer who specializes in programming software tools that apply to the engine or other programs.

- **Backend code**—Code that remains on the internal server and is not distributed with the game.

- **Art director**—The director (manager) in charge of the art for the project.

- **Team**—All the people working on the game.

Export—When media assets (graphics, sound, music, and so on) are transferred from the program they were created into the game engine or another program.

Deliverables—Items in the game that are to be delivered according to a schedule.

Lead artist—A senior artist in charge of a project or portion of a project. This is usually a middle manager who reports to the art director.

Assets—Any item used in the making of a game, such as artwork, code, and text.

Rigged—The insertion of a skeletal system into a 3D model with a control structure to allow the model to be posed like a puppet for the animation team.

Skinned—The attachment of a skeleton to the 3D model.

Animated—When an object is manipulated to create the illusion of movement.

Concept sketches—Loose sketches of how a character or object might look. These are used to dial in the look before investing time and assets to create the final appearance.

Mood boards—Mood boards are collages of imagery to establish a visual context for images and models.

- **Thumbnails**—Tiny rough sketches to illustrate some aspect of the game.

- **UI**—User interface.

- **UX**—User experience.

- **HUDs**—Heads-up displays. An onscreen interface element that communicates information to the player, such as a map or power bar.

- **Wireframes**—Rough sketches of what the UI might look like.

- **Testing**—People hired to test the game and look for functionality and performance issues.

- **Bug**—This is a problem of some sort with the game. Bugs are often documented and sent to a team member who can best fix the situation.

SETTING UP A GAME ASSET WORKSTATION

The rivalry between Mac and Windows has been raging for years. The two systems do similar things, but the workflow is very different. Both systems can make wonderful workstations, and your choice of one or the other is really a matter of preference or the work environment you're interfacing with. That being said, there are some things that should be considered.

Configuring a Computer

When shopping for a system aimed at developing game art, here are a few things you should look out for:

- **Make sure you have a good graphics card and a high resolution.** It is very important that you can see what you are creating when making a game. Sometimes every pixel counts, and it would be a shame if you couldn't see those pixels.

- **Buy lots of memory, storage, and processor power.** Let's face it, Photoshop and other game-development software do not travel lightly through your computer. They tend to be resource hogs that will dominate your machine at the first sign of weakness. It is best to go as big and fast as you can.

- **Have plenty of ports.** Always be aware of how many USB ports you're getting. The more you can get, the better. With Bluetooth added to many of the newer Macs and PCs, this is becoming a lesser issue, but many peripheral devices only use a USB connection, such as mice, keyboards, trackballs, scanners, graphics tablets, external hard drives, thumb drives, and TV streaming devices.

Almost all commercially available software is made for the PC, especially Photoshop. There was a time when Adobe and Apple were best buds, but that was a long time ago in a galaxy far, far away. All of the Autodesk products are optimized for the PC and a few of them don't even have installs for the Mac. So you need to make sure that the software you're buying will work on a Mac before you buy it. Of course, there are always emulation programs available to run Windows-based software on your Mac like a PC, but they are not free and may come with some performance compromises.

Choosing a Drawing Tablet

A drawing tablet allows you to use a pen to create art in the computer. When combined with Adobe Photoshop, it puts you in possession of a digital art studio. What is the big deal with having a pen? Most artists have grown up honing their skills using a pen or pencil as the input style of choice. A quality graphics tablet and pen can replicate that artist experience in the computer and leverage that lovingly developed skillset. While early graphics tablets were like writing on large, unresponsive TV trays, modern tablets capture every nuance with sophisticated pressure sensitivity.

Which brings us to the Wacom Cintiq (**FIGURE 1.5**). This is basically a monitor that you can draw on. It has a specialized functionality geared to using programs such as Photoshop. The Cintiq accurately replicates the experience of drawing on paper, airbrushing, or using watercolors or a crayon. It has become the industry standard, and most studios automatically issue one to their game artists.

FIGURE 1.5
The Wacom Cintiq emulates the experience of using conventional artist tools.

Pay Attention to Ergonomics

The furniture in your room might be the last thing on your mind when you are learning how to use Photoshop to make games; but after many tiring hours of toiling in one spot, it may become the only thing on your mind. If you've never experienced back pain caused by sitting at your desk for hours on end, then you are good to go. But eventually, you'll find that anything you can do to make your workspace comfortable is well worth the cost and the effort. Professional studios will go to great lengths to make sure you are comfy at your desk because they never want you to leave. Make sure you get a good chair and properly adjust monitors to suit your eye level (**FIGURE 1.6**). Every little ergonomic bit helps.

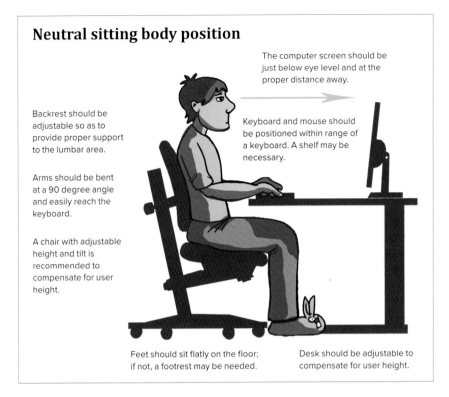

Neutral sitting body position

The computer screen should be just below eye level and at the proper distance away.

Backrest should be adjustable so as to provide proper support to the lumbar area.

Keyboard and mouse should be positioned within range of a keyboard. A shelf may be necessary.

Arms should be bent at a 90 degree angle and easily reach the keyboard.

A chair with adjustable height and tilt is recommended to compensate for user height.

Feet should sit flatly on the floor; if not, a footrest may be needed.

Desk should be adjustable to compensate for user height.

ORGANIZING AND ARCHIVING YOUR ART

Saving your work might seem like a simple thing, but you should keep some very important considerations in mind. Let's get into the philosophy of archiving your work. Ooooh, now it sounds important, doesn't it?

Using Team-Based Network Software

In a professional atmosphere, lots of artists may collaborate on the same work, so it is important to store files in a common place so they can be accessed by other team members. Many software solutions enable this, such as Perforce, Alienbrain, Git, and even Google Docs.

No matter which solution you use, they all apply a system for checking files in and out of storage, and permanently archiving the work in progress. This system works great, but it can be slightly annoying, because all current files must be synchronized before a file can be checked out again. On a team of 200 people all submitting changes to different files, this process can take a bit of time, especially if you've gone days without syncing. When you join a game team, chances are that they will have a system in place to archive files. You will be expected to learn how to use that system. The upside is that someone is generally available to teach you how to use it.

Using Personal Organizing Techniques

If you don't have the money to buy Perforce or the engineering crew to get Git working, here are some simple alternatives.

The easiest answer is a separate hard drive. An external hard drive with multiple terabytes of storage is an inexpensive and easy way to back up files. You can even set the backup process to be performed as an automatically scheduled function. The hard drive must be separate from the rest of your workstation so that if your computer fails, you will have a non-associated backup that you can easily plug into a new computer. If the backup hard drive fails, you can use your computer's internally stored files to rebuild the backup project folder. The point is: You always want to have two copies of your work, just in case.

This method does not provide automatic version control for multiple users, of course; but if you *version up* your files as you save (by adding a version number to the end of each filename (cat_1, cat_2, cat_3, and so on), you can replicate that version-tracking functionality.

Cloud storage is also available, which is Internet-based storage for your files such as Google and Dropbox. Most of them are free for a certain amount of storage, after which a subscription may be purchased for additional storage.

Naming conventions

Photoshop projects can be very complex, and often involve several other programs at once. Keeping track of your files is important, so always make sure that you have a clear naming convention in place that allows you to find your files, even after months of not looking at them.

To create a naming convention, start with the name of the project or an abbreviation of its name and limit it to five characters or less or the filenames become too long to read quickly. Some programs like Perforce cap the number of characters you can use in a name. So if the project is called Ninja Bunnies, the first part of the naming convention could be NinjaB or NB with no spaces. The second part references the category of the art, such as a character or a background. That might give you NB_Chr (for character). The next part should be descriptive of the image. So if it is a bunny ear, your name would be NB_Chr_bunnyear. Finally, add an iteration number in case you've created multiple versions of the subject, for example, NB_Chr_bunnyear1.

File size

File sizes should also be considered when saving your files. If you're working on a project in which the art is 10x10 pixels at 600 dots per inch (dpi), but the end product needs to be 5x5 at 300 dpi, you should archive the original, larger version of your art, as well as the smaller versions that will be used for the game. At some point you may need to rework your file. Keeping both files ensures that you won't have to re-create your work.

UNDERSTANDING FILE FORMATS

Artists deal with many kinds of computer files, generated by many different programs in a variety of *file formats*. A file format is simply a particular type of digital container in which you store graphic data. Fortunately, Photoshop can read and save in almost all formats (FIGURE 1.7). Most of you know some of the more popular formats, such as JPG or PDF, but there are many more.

Here is a breakdown of some of them.

■ **PSD** (Photoshop Document). This is Photoshop's native file format and the file type most game artists use while working. Its layer-preservation attributes allow artists to keep their working files separate and switch in different layers as they work. When finished, the layers are collapsed and saved as a PNG or JPG file, depending on the transparency needs of the image. The original PSD file is always kept in case more work is needed.

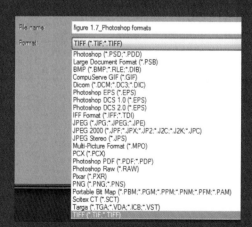

FIGURE 1.7 Photoshop can work with a multitude of file formats.

■ **JPEG** (Joint Photographic Experts Group). JPEG, or JPG, is the most commonly used image format in the world. However, it has issues with image loss due to data compression, so it's not widely used by professionals for finished work. It also doesn't support transparencies or layers. In the game world, it is used for things like mood boards and presentation materials.

■ **GIF** (Graphics Interchange Format). Similar to JPG but much older, this format is limited to displaying only 256 colors and is often used for limited color Web graphics. A GIF also can be animated via a time delay in the display code. Multiple frames are created and reduced to a single file containing a set of images that are sequenced like a slideshow. Animated GIFs are widely used as personal icons and memes, and can be created in Photoshop.

■ **PNG**s (Portable Network Graphics). Originally meant to replace the GIF format, the most important part of a PNG is that it can be saved with transparency. Because of the way games are displayed, transparency becomes very important. Most games are broken up into assets that are reassembled in an engine. If all the assets had white backgrounds—as they would with JPGs—they would not integrate and composite with other images.

- **TIFF** (Tagged Image File Format). This is a lossless compression format that allows you to save photos with the highest possible image quality. TIFFs are similar to PSDs but not commonly used in studios. They are one of the preferred image-rendering file types for 3D programs.

- **EPS** (Encapsulated PostScript). This is a printer's format that carries information on how a printer should reproduce the image during the printing process.

- **PDF** (Portable Document Format). This format includes a complete description of a fixed layout of the document, including the graphics and font information. It also allows you to set the compression and memory footprint. It's a good universal format to use for general distribution. It's also used for sending out promotional information such as a *deck*, a concise representation of what a game is like and used in marketing and sales. A deck contains pictures and documents, and a PDF stores those elements exactly as formatted, no matter what device you are displaying it on.

- **BMP** (Bitmap Image File). This is a raster graphics file format used to store bitmap digital images, independent of the display device. It is quite often used in Microsoft Word.

- **TGA** (Truevision TGA). Also known as TARGA, this raster graphics file format was created by Truevision, Inc. TGAs were the computer graphics rendering file format of choice for many years, but were replaced by TIFF. TGAs are sometimes used for creating alpha masks, which are great for making dirt maps and stenciling for 3D textures.

How can you tell what kind of file you're dealing with? One way is to look at the filename extension or filename suffix. This is an extra set of (usually) alphanumeric characters appended to the end of a filename to allow computer users (as well as various pieces of software on the computer) to quickly determine in which format data is stored in the file. Note that this may be hard to find on a Mac, as OS X and compatible apps do not always display extensions.

Folders

Folders may seem like a trivial topic to talk about, but once again, keeping track of your files gets harder as you generate more files and the project length expands into months or years. It's a good idea to store your files by category using conventions similar to those you use for the files.

This means that you would have a folder called NB_Bunny, and in it would be the bunny ears, eyes, tails, and the like. You needn't make folders for all the different bits of the bunny, one for each is fine. The folder structure tree would look something like this: Project > Ninja Bunny > characters > NB_Bunny.

If you're combining multiple images to create a single image, it's best if all of the source files for the single image are stored in one folder along with the image master. This technique gives you quick, one-location access to all the parts of the master if you need to alter or swap out an element.

Adobe Bridge

Adobe Bridge is an individual program that brings all of your assets together and, in the darkness, binds them (**FIGURE 1.8**).

Oops, that's a different movie. Adobe Bridge is a program that allows you to access all your creative assets from a single viewport. You can search, organize, and even run batch processing on any of the stored files. You can create what are called "favorites," which are links to your file directories allowing you to customize your workflow for each project.

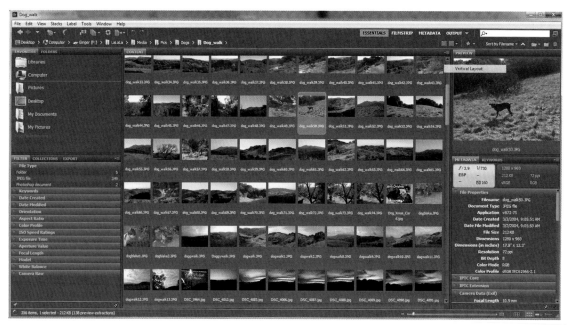

FIGURE 1.8 Adobe Bridge gives you access to every creative asset within a single view.

Bridge has an extensive search engine and can easily find a specific image file or all image files of a certain type. You can run the standalone program, or what is called the Mini Bridge, which is part of Photoshop.

Getting Help from the Photoshop Community

Considering the huge number of people using Photoshop, when you type a question about Photoshop into your browser, you'll probably find more answers than you can read. This enormous community generates tutorials, videos, podcasts, and many other resources to help you use Photoshop more effectively, and locate information on almost any Photoshop-related topic. You can even learn new techniques that you never knew you needed. Here are some of the Photoshop helpers you'll find online:

- As you might expect, after years of fielding support calls, Adobe has developed a system for providing copious information about Photoshop. On the Photoshop website, under the Adobe's Support and Learning tab, you will find the user forums, links to official Adobe training and tutorial videos, and many other handy resources. This section can be accessed from Photoshop by clicking the Help tab at the upper-left side of the workspace.

- DIY demos, such as the ones found on Youtube.com and Vimeo.com, are a great source of information. Not only do they supply you with the answer to your question, but they may also offer alternative solutions. Yes, you may have to suffer through some pretty bad dialog, but the tech is described and that is what you came for.

- Professional tutorial sites feature training led by terrific artists with years of experience. Most of them require a subscription fee (usually very reasonably priced) and the linear nature of the tutorials means that you will not have to go searching for subjects you would like to cover. There are some great Photoshop tutorials at www.safaribooksonline.com, including this book and many other books and videos.

- Let us not leave out blogs and personal websites. Many terrific artists have their own sites devoted to Photoshop. Many of them have video demos and visual examples of their work accompanied by explanations of how they were executed. In some cases, artists will list tour dates where you can catch them live.

- Conventions are also a great source of Photoshop information. Adobe exhibits at a number of Photoshop-related conferences (such as Adobe MAX, one of the largest Adobe-run shows), and other great conventions include the Game Developers Conference, Comic-Con, and E3 (Electronic Entertainment Expo). They often offer many workshops, training sessions, and symposiums, in addition to all the product demos presented on the show floor. Conventions can keep you informed on the cutting edge of Photoshop and games.

CHAPTER WRAP-UP

This chapter may have been your first introduction to the game industry, and to some of the aspects of it that you will encounter throughout this book. As the chapters progress, the topics covered here will come up again, and now should not blindside you. You also should have an understanding of who does what in a game company's art department and their responsibilities. Finally, you should know how to organize and save your files, their file formats, and how best to store them.

You are ready to get into the nitty-gritty techniques of game art development. Get your stylus ready, and warm up that DigiPad because you have some art to do.

2

PIPELINES FOR GAMES

Games are made in many different genres—social games, role-playing games, word games, shooting games, racing games—but the process of building a game is similar regardless of whether it thrusts the player into a world of mythical dragons or just asks you to fill in a puzzling number grid.

Building a game is similar to building a house. All houses have a foundation and walls and a roof, and are made of similar materials, yet every house built from these common materials can look very different.

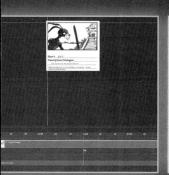

Shot # ___007___
Description/Dialogue: _____
NB - I must recue the princess but how?
Wide shot with hero in view. Evil Dojo in the distance. Slowly

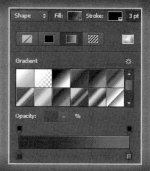

NOTE To access the resource files and videos, just log in or join peachpit.com, and enter the book's ISBN. After you register the book, links to the files will be listed on your Account page under Registered Products.

When building a game, the idea is your foundation, the concept drawings are walls, and the story is your roof. All these areas of development have different people collaborating on a finished product, all made out of programming and graphics and similar digital assets.

In this chapter, you will learn about processes and workflows that are universal to all game making.

IT STARTS WITH AN IDEA

Sometimes coming up with a good idea for a game is the hardest part. If someone were to give you unlimited funding to make whatever game you wanted, what would you do? What genre would you choose? Zombies, horror, military, and bunnies? How would it play? Would it be for a console or iOS? With a universe of gameplay ahead of you, you have many first choices to make. Fortunately, we have methods in place for developing your initial idea.

The first thing to do is to narrow your choices. Even if those choices change later on, you will at least have a general context for your game.

It is always good to start with genres or concepts that you like or are comfortable with. Say that you're fascinated by ninjas (ever since that trip to Japan where you were stalked by a stealthy, masked shadow of a figure), so you choose to build your game concept around ninja stealth and fighting. This is great. You have now moved in a purposeful direction, and with one decision, have answered a slew of questions about your game's setting and activities. Images start floating through your head and forward movement begins.

Using Mood Boards

Mood boards (**FIGURE 2.1**) are collages of preexisting imagery that suggests the overall "feel" of your game.

Mood boards are great tools for getting your idea out of your head and onto the screen. By collecting "inspirational" images, you create a visual overview of the various aspects of the game you are trying to build. You can then distill the images to create the one image that is close to the style you want to achieve. You can also show mood boards to other team members to start aligning everyone's vision and realize a consistent look across a project.

To create a mood board, open a large Adobe Photoshop file. A 10x10-inch canvas at 300 dpi should give you plenty of room to drop in randomly sized pictures from the Web. Mood boards are traditionally collections of images from whatever sources you want to draw. The items you place on that board needn't all depict the subject that you are researching, but can also include colors and styles, and lighting and shapes. Almost anything fits, as long as it leads your brain down the road you would like it to go and helps establish a "big picture" creative vision.

FIGURE 2.1 Mood boards for a Ninja Bunny game.

Sticking with our example of a ninja-themed game, you might want to start like this: Begin by collecting photos of various Japanese temples, maybe some tribal tattoo art, perhaps some images evoking Japanese culture, a few panoramas of beautiful sunsets on the beach, and some serene stills of Asian gardens. Put them all together on your mood board and see which colors and shapes are repeated in the different pictures. It is a fair bet that if you replicate those common elements, your game will suggest the "ninja feeling" you are trying to achieve.

Once you're done with your mood boards, you should discuss them with your team. Find out what aspects of the images have hit a nerve. Because game design and development is a constantly changing process, the look of your original mood board may not reflect the look of your final game. What's important is that a well-executed mood board exists as a visual signpost that points everyone down the same creative path.

Creating Conceptual Drawings

Conceptual drawings pin down the "big picture" concepts of the mood boards into visual specifics. They are rough to finished sketches of a character, object, or environment that defines and develops a design before it is finalized and put to use in the game.

Generating concept drawings is one of the more hands-on jobs you can have in a game development studio. It requires you to be a good illustrator, a great idea

NOTE Game artists secretly believe in a law of concepting. (Not a real law, but it is funny.) It is almost always guaranteed that the one image you think is the best will not be selected for follow-up development, and the image you hate the most will be the one that everyone else loves.

person, and have the ability to bring any whim to light with a minimal amount of work. It usually requires many iterations on a single theme and the ability to produce loads of redrawing.

EXERCISE 1: CONCEPT DRAWING

NOTE This demo requires a computer with Photoshop. A drawing tablet is recommended, and although the exercise was developed using a Wacom Cintiq, none of its special functionality is used, so you can perform the exercise with any tablet or even your mouse.

In this step-by-step exercise, you will learn one of the methods for creating the concept art while developing a game character. Your character may not turn out exactly like the one being concepted, and that is OK. Learning the workflow is far more important than duplicating the image shown in the exercise.

By the end of this exercise, you will understand how to create a professional concept drawing (**FIGURE 2.2**). Although you may need to practice your illustration skills, knowing the correct method of creating a concept is a large part of making your work look professional.

FIGURE 2.2 The beginning of a concept drawing, including roughs.

The assignment

Concept out a mutant bunny bad guy for a 3D ninja-themed arcade fighting game. You do not need to copy the bunny as shown. In fact, it is preferable that you work on your own design. Creativity is a large part of what makes this exercise fun.

The steps

If you wish to be a successful concept artist, it is a good idea to come up with a methodology to your work. Because you will most likely need to repeat the method again and again, you will want to realize the same high-quality results every time. Many artists even keep logs describing the steps they took, and use the logs to evaluate how effective the steps were as a means to improving their process. Here are some of the steps commonly used in the workflow:

- Create a set of character **silhouettes** and choose one for further development.
- Rough in the sketch with a light outline tracing of the silhouette shape to identify key points in the illustration.
- Lay down a **base tone** pass giving the form volumetric quality.
- Add **shadow** and **light** to further define the form.
- Add **color.**
- Refine **color.**
- Finalize **image.**
- Add **background** if desired.

Creating the silhouettes

Begin small. If you are starting from nothing, it is a good idea to draw some thumbnails just to see what kind of shapes you can come up with. These might take the form of a silhouette or a cat scratch or any number of drawing forms. The point is to come up with a shape that reads well and is in character for the rest of the piece.

Draw your sketches small so you are forced to concentrate on the whole image instead of getting caught up in details. You will find that creating an interesting silhouette helps create a good pose, which helps define the body mass, which helps decide the lighting, and on and on as each step feeds into the next step.

1. In Photoshop, choose File > New, and create a new image.
2. In the popup menu, set Width to **10 inches**, Height to **10 inches**, and Resolution to **300 Pixels/Inch** (FIGURE 2.3). Or, navigate to the Resources folder, and open Bunnyrough.tiff.

FIGURE 2.3 The file size options window.

3. Choose Layer > Create a new layer and name it *b_ silh* for bunny silhouette.

 Now there are two layers showing.

4. Select the lower layer.

5. From the toolbar, choose the **Paint Bucket** tool, and assign it a **medium gray** color to fill the workspace.

 This produces a neutral background that will help you to work looser. All white or all black backgrounds require too much contrast and will push you toward working on the details.

6. From the toolbar, choose the **Pen** tool, and set Opacity to **70** and Flow to **55**. Use a dark color or black.

7. Return to the transparent layer, *b_ silh*, above the new layer, and begin sketching (**FIGURE 2.4**).

 Try to stay small. Start in one corner and work your way across.

FIGURE 2.4 Sketching out various concept drawings.

8. Do four sketches across the top, and then drop down and do four more and repeat so that you have a total of 12 images, commonly called a *proof sheet*.

This method should give you a good sampling of characters to choose from, and ensure that the size of each is relatively small. In truth, it really doesn't matter how you organize the images just as long as you are working fast and small.

In a studio setting you will be required to create many concept sketches quickly, so figuring out ways to do this is paramount. Keep track of the steps you take to create a sketch, and when you're done ask yourself, "Could I have done anything better or faster?"

Approving sketches

When you're working in a game studio, some of the aforementioned steps may be gated by an approval system.

For example, after executing your first several concept drawings, you'll usually have your first review. You, or the art director, or your team picks a few images—or maybe just the one that they like the best—and you talk about how you might refine it.

Ask loads of questions at this time, because this is when you need to nail down the person in charge to a specific direction. If you do not, you'll almost certainly have loads of redraws in your future. It is not uncommon to hear, "I don't know what I want, but I will know when I see it." These early discussions help ensure that all the pertinent team members are on the same page and that there are no surprises.

Depending on the team and the studio's accepted workflow, it is a good idea to email your images at every stage. This is a good way to protect yourself from office shenanigans and get feedback from your fellow team members who may not be involved in decision meetings. It also generates a discussion trail. People tend to change their minds less when they have made their decisions in writing, and when someone has written that an image is *approved*, it is officially approved.

So far, your drawings represent a variety of shapes, styles, and levels of details. Usually, you would stick to one style: the silhouettes, the loose sketches, the slightly tighter sketches, or a mixture of the three. It is your choice. Once you have established your particular drawing style, then you would build out from that. However, in the spirit of showing you various drawing options on one page, each line is a different style.

Roughing in the sketch

Now you'll take the approved sketch and begin working with it further. Our goal here is to create a piece that will be used by the team as a beacon for where the game's look and feel are going. It could be used in pitch meetings, it could be handed off to a modeler, and it might end up on a T-shirt. So the importance of the drawing should not be underestimated.

1. Copy the image off the proof sheet, and paste it to a new layer. Name the layer *rough sketch* (**FIGURE 2.5**).

2. Hide the proof sheet layer and scale up the image until it fills the space.

3. Knock the layer opacity down to **50%**, and create a new layer.

4. On this new layer, rough in the landmarks of your bunny silhouette (**FIGURE 2.6**). Define the eyes, nose, mouth, and such. If, while you are working, you get an idea for better posture or a stronger pose, do not hesitate to incorporate it into your work. Those hunches are usually right. Just make sure that you duplicate the layer you are working on and hide it. Then you can work on the new layer

FIGURE 2.5 A rough image, separated, and placed onto a new layer.

and have the original if you need to return to it. As you can see in the image, the bunny has been adjusted to a better pose and the silhouette layer has been hidden.

FIGURE 2.6 Line art pass of a concept character.

Laying in the base tones

Now it's time to lay down the *base tones*, which are the darkest value on an object, not including light or shadow (**FIGURE 2.7**). It is your middle tone. Laying down base tones first will give you an idea of how the light will work on your concept and suggest what will happen with your image with the addition of lighting and color. If you can get your image working in tone, then later passes will be much easier to do. It might be of some benefit to hide your silhouette now that you have an outline. By doing so, you can lay down the tone fresh; but it is not required.

FIGURE 2.7 Base tone pass on a concept character.

1. Create a new layer and name it *base tones*. Move this layer below the rough sketch layer in the layer stack.

2. Select the **Brush** tool, and with a **medium gray** color, paint in all the skin area of the character while leaving the eyes, nose, teeth, and clothing blank. You can also set the layer to multiply and have it above the pencil layer to help hide lighter brushstrokes.

3. Select a **lighter gray** and paint in the clothing, eyes, nose, and the tail.

4. If you have drawn outside the lines, go back now and clean up your edges. It is also a good idea to temporarily change your background to a **red** color. This will allow you to see any holidays (places where you missed filling in.) Return the background to **gray** when you are done.

Adding shadow and light

Next comes light and shadow. First, pick a direction that the light source is coming from. Then start in with the shadows. If it helps, you can set up a light source and take a photograph of a physical object—such as a stuffed animal or an action figure—posed in a matching light source as a reference image (or just find one on the Internet.)

1. Open a new layer and name it *shadow*. Then pick a very dark tone (but not black) and work it into the areas that would have shadows. Depending on the volume of your object, you may need to pick a slightly less dark color and blend the edges (**FIGURE 2.8**).

   If you are concepting a character to be realistically rendered, or perhaps built in 3D, it is a good idea to think about your image as a sculpture rather than a flat image. This will help you understand how the shadow and light wraps around the form. Another method is to pick a black color and paint out the shadowed areas in total darkness. Then reduce the opacity until you reach the desired tone.

2. Whichever technique you use, continue working the darker tones until you feel that most of the shadows are laid out.

3. Pick a tone that is slightly brighter than the background's medium gray and start working the highlights (**FIGURE 2.9**). You will have to switch back and forth many times.

   Do not think that just because you have finished the shadows you can't go back and make changes, you should be adjusting things as you notice that they need adjusting.

FIGURE 2.8 Shadow pass on a concept character.

FIGURE 2.9 Highlight pass on a concept character.

4. Once you have developed your shadows and highlights to the point that you are happy with them, create another layer and name it *touchup*. Use this layer to blend any shadows or highlights that might be too sharp. This is done by selecting a soft brush with 50% opacity, and then with the Eyedropper tool, select thin tones in the art and painting passes to blend or accentuate the edges of the shadows and highlights (**FIGURE 2.10**).

FIGURE 2.10 Tonal blending pass on a concept character.

Adding and refining color

With the tone pass finished, you can move on to adding color. Adding color is a bit easier, as you do not have to think as much about the lighting. The hardest part is getting a color scheme that fits your character.

1. Open another layer, and name it *color*. Change the layer type from Normal to **Color**.

   It is a good idea to figure out what your character is about and choose colors that you think would be representative of that character. For instance, an Ice Creature would not be red, a hot color that is not great for suggesting cold. Our creature is a mutant sumo bunny so we will use green, a traditional mutant color (**FIGURE 2.11**).

FIGURE 2.11 Adding color to a concept character.

2. Begin adding color and, again, try to stay loose and block in portions to show representative colors in sections where you want it.

TIP As you add color, you may want to create a different layer for each color so you can adjust each color individually.

Don't go too tight, too early. If you need to adjust your brush to a different flow or opacity, feel free to do so. Don't worry about the outlines because you will get back to that. This is when the job you did on the base tones either sinks or swims. If you were too light or too dark with the base tones, the color you may have wanted to use might not show up correctly. If this is the case, don't fret. Just go back to your tonal layer and adjust the tone in question to better suit your needs.

3. Open yet another layer. (I know. It never ends, but you will be grateful later on.) This will be your final layer, or one of them.

TIP Basically, whenever you start a new pass or you want to try something out, you should start a new layer.

4. On this new layer, you should be applying the finishing touches to your drawing. Now is the time to go in tight and work on the eye, the mouth, the teeth, and all those details. If you are realistically rendering your character, you should also eliminate all those black sketch lines (**FIGURE 2.12**).

On a real object the edge lines would be shadows—not a single color but all various colors and tones from the surrounding light. If you leave the edge lines black, it results in a very cartoony look. So be sure that is what you want. Both are perfectly fine for a concept drawing; it just depends on the type of game you are making and which style is appropriate for the content.

FIGURE 2.12 Finished concept character.

Creating a background

Finally, you can create a background for your character. It is a good way to further sell the mood of the piece to the team. If you are short on time, a photo from the Internet can sometimes fill in. Generally, these pictures will never be sold, so original art is nice but not necessary.

1. Create a new layer and call it *Tbackground* (for themed background). Move it down to just above the gray layer you made when you began this image.

2. Fill the layer with any color that complements the character and makes it stand out (**FIGURE 2.13**).

If your image is primarily green, then you might try a light yellow or a soft purple. I recommend the purple if you'd like to play up the villain thing. If you can't decide, a light pale blue is always a good fallback color for a background.

3. Not enough? Then go into the blending options and, from the pulldown menu, choose **Gradient Overlay**. Pick one of the gradient's dark colors at the top (**FIGURE 2.14**). If your ramp is reversed, you will need to rotate the image 180 degrees.

FIGURE 2.13 Single-color background.

FIGURE 2.14 Gradient background.

4. Still not enough? Create a new layer above the one with the gradient. Go into the blending options of the layer and choose **Bevel & Emboss**. Leave the default settings in place, and return to the image. Select the **Brush** tool and open the Brush options (**FIGURE 2.14A**).

FIGURE 2.14A The options flyout for the Brush tool.

5. Choose one of the scatter brushes, such as **Chalk**, and set a large brush size of around **400 pixels** to **900 pixels**. Select a color from the background and stamp it around, making an abstract yet interesting pattern (**FIGURE 2.15**). You may need to adjust the opacity so it is not too overwhelming.

FIGURE 2.16 shows the finished character with a theme applied to the background.

FIGURE 2.15 Gradient background with interest added.

FIGURE 2.16 Finished character with themed background.

FIGURE 2.17 shows the progression of the concept. You can see that the beginning stages were quite rough, and even though the image was not fully rendered at the end, the final result gets the point across.

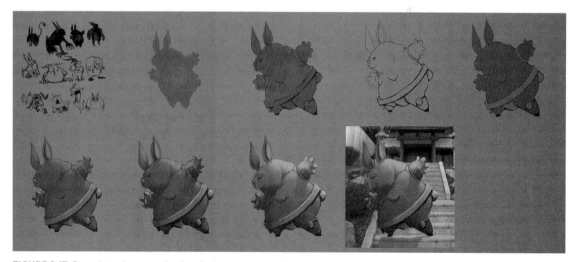

FIGURE 2.17 Snapshot of process for developing a concept character.

THE WORLD OF FILM AND THE CAMERA

Since you are going to be working in a filmic arena, it is important to understand some film terms.

Aspect ratios—This refers to the dimensions of the box you are drawing in and the pixel size of the screen the viewer will be looking at (FIGURE 2.18). Think of it like a motion picture screen. The more common aspect ratios in video and film are 1:1.33 for TV, 1:1.85 for film, and 1:2.35 for widescreen. What does that mean? The 1:1.33 ratio refers to an image that is 1 unit high by 1.33 units wide, a unit being a square in this case. So, if you were to stack a square next to a vertical slice that is 0.33 of that square, you would get this aspect ratio. In games and on the computer, we tend to speak of images in terms of pixel sizes, but these are set up to emulate the filmic ratios: 640x480 pixels, 1024x960 pixels, and so on. Another set of ratios/pixel sizes exists for mobile, and yet another set for tablets. You'll learn more about those later in the book.

Over the years, camera compositions have been named according to commonly used types of shots (FIGURE 2.19). When someone talks about a "two shot," film professionals know what they are talking about. Here are some of the more common types of shots used in the industry:

- **Close-up**—The camera is close to the subject, focusing on a certain portion of that subject, which fills the whole frame.

- **Medium shot**—The camera is at a medium distance showing a larger part of the subject.

- **Long shot**—The entire subject is visible in the frame, as well as some of the surroundings. Also called a *wide shot*.

- **Down shot**—A shot with the camera placed above the subject looking down.

- **Upshot**—A shot with the camera placed below the subject looking up.

- **Low angle**—The camera is pointed at the horizon but from a low angle.

- **High angle**—The camera is pointed at the horizon but from a high angle.

- **Two shot**—A shot of two people, usually a mid-shot sometimes used for shooting conversations.

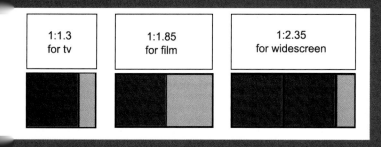

| 1:1.3 for tv | 1:1.85 for film | 1:2.35 for widescreen |

FIGURE 2.18 Common aspect ratios for TV, film, and widescreen.

- **Over the shoulder**—Looking from behind a person at the subject.

- **POV (point of view)**—An angle set up as if the viewer is the camera.

Camera shots often take place while the camera is motionless, but the camera can and does move. Below is a list of camera move terms used in the industry. In the world of storyboards, these are suggested by various graphic means (usually arrows).

- **Arc**—The camera moves in a rough semicircle around the subject.

- **Dolly**—A dolly is a cart that is used to move a camera along a rail, providing a parallel movement or zooming view in relation to an object. The term describes a shot that does this movement.

- **Dolly zoom**—This is the same dolly movement, but the camera moves its focus closer to or farther from the subject as it travels.

- **Follow**—The camera follows the subject, either with a handheld camera or a camera on a dolly.

- **Pan**—The camera swivels left or right from a fixed position.

- **Tilt**—The camera swivels up or down from a fixed position.

- **Trucking**—Similar to a dolly, except the camera moves in a left or right direction only.

- **Zooming**—A camera move closer to the subject that is executed as a function of the camera lens and not an actual movement.

Close-up   Medium shot   Long shot   Down shot

Up shot   Low angle   High angle   Two shot

Over the shoulder   Point of view   Extreme Close-up   Extreme long shot

FIGURE 2.19 Types of camera shots, as seen in storyboards.

MAKING STORYBOARDS

Quite a few, if not all, games are based on a story that is usually the driving force behind the game's action. *Fight your way out of the underground lab and get to the surface to warn the world about zombies,* or *avenge your brother's death in the old west.* Whatever the plot, games tell stories exactly as films do—maybe a little more interactive than a film, but certainly in the same way. It only makes sense to use the tools developed in the film industry to tell the game story.

Storyboards are often the first steps in making cinematics. They can also be the first steps in creating a comic book or a flow previsualization for a website. They are very useful tools in seeing how a directed narrative plays out over time.

Generating Storyboards

Storyboards are essentially little illustrations depicting elements of a narrative in sequence over time. They're kind of like the picture books your mom read to you when you were little.

Each artist's storyboard style can vary greatly, and although some commonly used visual devices exist for conveying various directions, the rules seem to vary a bit. A film project tends to establish a set of visual storyboard rules to follow, but those rules don't necessarily translate to a game cinematic.

Storyboards are not animation. They do not illustrate each animation frame. They are more like a snapshot of each key action in a movie scene, often showing a particular camera angle and movement. That's among the reasons why film-styled storyboards don't work so well in games.

Because the player controls the camera in most games, in-game cinematics are often used. These are a series of animations featuring in-game characters that use the engine to create a real-time movie. They can unfold from any angle, so all the drama normally gained by using a particular angle is lost.

This is not true of canned cinematics in games, which are movies that take control from the player and are shown to advance the story. Generally, these look much better than the in-game movies, as they can utilize higher-resolution models and better special effects. In either case, the storyboard is the best tool for illustrating to higher-ups what you plan to do with a scene, an encounter, or what have you.

The art of creating storyboards is a profession on its own, with its own visual language and culture. Because it has come to the gaming community via the film industry, the conventions used are mostly filmic and may be confusing to people who've never had a film class or worked on a film production. In fact, it is nearly impossible to be a storyboard artist without those filmic skills. Fortunately, most computer software interfaces also use filmic conventions for their camera movement tools, so you might know a little more film theory than you think.

Consulting the Script

The script contains all of the details of what you will be drawing in the storyboards. It is a great idea to read the entire script before you begin to get an understanding of the entire game design. Even though you may only be boarding a few scenes, knowing what the characters are like and what they have been doing will keep you from making mistakes that might result in redraws.

A script can vary in format from writer to writer, but as with camera shots and angles, script writing has developed established formats over the years that are common to most projects.

FIGURE 2.20 is an excerpt from a game cinematic script. It is just a scene or two about the mutant ninja bunnies for which we previously did a concept drawing. The boxes indicate how to read the script and what the directions mean.

Using Storyboard Sheets

Reading a storyboard sheet is fairly easy. Each sheet has a number of little boxes that contain the images and a few lines below for direction and dialogue. The written dialogue does not have to be the entire dialogue of the scene, but it must include enough to identify which part of the scene is depicted. Other information could include the shot number, a camera direction, or various other notes.

The storyboard template shown in **FIGURE 2.21** is filled out with information from the script. In this case, each bit of dialogue occupied just one frame. This may not always be the case, and that is fine. It sometimes takes a few frames to get your point across.

As you can see, the images in the frames are based on a mixture of the dialogue, camera notes, and the storyboard artist's interpretation of what the scene should look like. A storyboard artist contributes greatly to a finished production, and in some cases, can provide alternate interpretations of a shot and even influence the way a scene is ultimately shot. This is the reason that directors tend to stick with storyboard artists that they like.

To save space on the sheet, the initials of the speaker precede the dialogue. The camera directions are written out below the image. Arrows in the image frame can be included to denote actions within the shot and camera movements.

NOTE Animation can have a specialized type of script, called an X-sheet, that breaks down the dialogue to individual frames; however, storyboard artists do not usually need to deal with it.

How the scene starts —— Fade in:

Where and when action takes place —— **EXTERIOR, EVIL NINA DOJO – DUSK**

Short description of the scene —— A quiet lake with a very historic-looking temple/dojo sitting atop a hill. The shot is from below near the lake.

The description follows the first time the character appears —— **NINJA BUNNY**
A supernaturally altered bunny who has ninja powers and is fated to save the world from the evil powers that created him. He is on a quest to save his beloved Princess.

Character that is speaking ——————— NINJA BUNNY

Dialogue ——————— I must rescue the princess, but how?

Camera or scene direction —— *Wide shot with hero in view. Evil Dojo in the distance. Slowly push in toward the Dojo*

                              NINJA BUNNY
                    Aha! I will use the trees to hide my
                    attack.

Bunny dives out of frame and into bushes. Exit screen right

Ninja Bunny jumps from tree to tree

Tracking shot as NB jumps from tree to tree and then out of frame screen right.

                              NINJA BUNNY
                    Now evil one, I will surprise you and we
                    will do battle.

Close up of NB in tree he jumps out of frame down, camera tilt follow.

INTERIOR, EVIL NINJA DOJO

                              NINJA BUNNY
                    Now I have you, evil one

Camera on internal of the evil dojo. NB drops into the camera view from above.

SUMO BUNNY
A supernaturally altered bunny with Sumo powers. He is very large and evil.

                              SUMO BUNNY
                    Ha, ha, ha, little one. Now we will see
                    who the greatest ninja is!

Pull back to show Sumo Bunny standing just out of frame and ready for battle.

FIGURE 2.20 Dialogue from a game cinematic script.

Title: Ninja Bunny

Storyboard Sheet # D14

Shot # 007

Description/Dialogue:

NB - I must rescue the princess but how?

Wide shot with hero in view. Evil Dojo in the distance. Slowly push in towards the Dojo

Shot # 008

Description/Dialogue:

NB - Aha! I will use the trees to hide my attack.

Bunny dives out of frame and into bushes exit screen right

Shot # D09

Description/Dialogue:

Ninja Bunny jumps from tree to tree - Tracking shot as

NB jumps from tree to tree and the out of frame screen right.

Shot # 01D

Description/Dialogue:

NB - Now evil one I will surprise you and we will do battle.

Close up of NB in tree he jumps out of frame down, camera tilt follow.

Shot # D11

Description/Dialogue:

NB - Now I have you evil one

Camera on internal of the evil dojo. NB drops into the camera view from above.

Shot # 012

Description/Dialogue:

SB - Ha, ha, ha, little on. Now we will see who the greatest ninja is!

Pull back to show Sumo Bunny standing just out of frame and ready for battle.

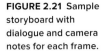

FIGURE 2.21 Sample storyboard with dialogue and camera notes for each frame.

EXERCISE 2: STORYBOARD EXERCISE

Creating storyboards requires a mixture of drawing and camera blocking. In the following exercise, you will create a storyboard sequence for a segment of a script. You will devise the best way to express the emotions of each frame, and through illustration, lay out the plan for the actual construction of the scene.

The assignment

Using the script segment we have provided and the storyboard blank, you will create and draw six story frames and fill out the dialogue portions of the boards.

Starting your storyboard

Creating a storyboard sheet in Photoshop is not difficult. You will first need a template page to work with. Many free options are available on the Internet, and if you are working for a studio, it will most likely have a template for you to use. For this exercise, you will make one of your own, and you will then have the PSD (Photoshop Document) file to work with later.

Making a storyboard blank

1. Create a new Photoshop file with a size of 8.5x11 inches at 300 dpi, and name it *Storyboard Blank*. We use this size because storyboards are often printed out and distributed to the team. Using a standard printer-size page means you will not need special paper. Some artists prefer to draw on the paper printouts and then scan them. This method is fine, but because this book is about using Photoshop, we will stay in the digital realm.

2. Create a new layer and name it *pic_frame*. In the View section of the Photoshop menu, turn on **Rulers** and **Grid**. You will use this to align your boxes (**FIGURE 2.22**).

FIGURE 2.22 The View/Show Grid pulldown menu.

3. You are going to create frames that are 1:1.85 ratio. The easiest way to do this in Photoshop is to choose the **Rectangle** draw tool and change the fill color to **white** and the stroke color to **black**.

4. Size the stroke to **3 pt.**, create a rectangle of any size, and size it to 1035x560 pixels. This is the correct aspect ratio for this layout. You could also use the Create Rectangle options box to create the rectangle.

5. Using the grid as a guide, place your box 2 grid units from the right and 4 units down from the top of the page, that is, **0.25 inches** from the right side and **1 inch** down from the top.

6. Create a new layer and name it *Lines*. Below the rectangle you just created and the layout grid, draw four black lines using the Line drawing tool at about **10 px**. Use the grid lines to offset the line placement and make sure they are no longer than the width of the box.

7. Create another layer below the Lines shape layer and merge down the lines. This allows you to cut the top two lines for text. With those cut, you can now type the words *SHOT #*, and on another layer, *DESCRIPTION/ DIALOG*. Move those into place, as shown in **FIGURE 2.23**.

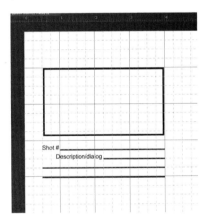

FIGURE 2.23 Frame layout of a storyboard.

8. Select all the layers except for the background, and gather them into a new layer using the "New Group from Layers" function. Duplicate this layer.

9. Press **Shift-Left Arrow** to move the layer to the left until it is 2 grid units from the left side. Holding down the Shift key makes the move faster.

10. Now select and duplicate the two layer groups. With the new layer groups selected, press **Shift-Down Arrow** to translate the images down the page so the top of the new box is 1 grid space below the bottom of the four lines from the previous set of lines. Do this one more time to create the lines for the text or dialogue.

11. Create a new layer at the top of your stack. At the top of your image, use the Line drawing tool to stripe a line that goes from the upper-right corner of the right box to the upper-left corner of the left box. Create a new layer under this layer and merge the shape down so you can edit it. As before, use the Marquee select tool to select and cut parts of the line out and add the text, as shown in **FIGURE 2.24**.

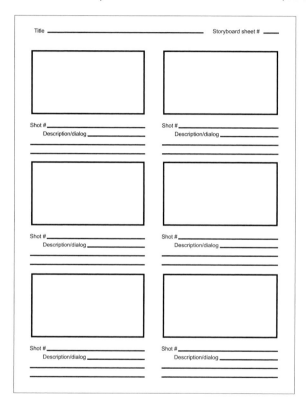

FIGURE 2.24 Full layout of a storyboard.

Now that you have your template, or blank, you can get to work. Just make sure that you don't save over your original blank because you will need it again and again. It is a good idea to save this file as a JPG image and work from that. You will not need all that layer info for what you have to do in the future.

12. Create a folder on your desktop called *NB_Storyboards*. Place your storyboard blank file in it. This will be the repository for all your work. You can store your temp work, and all your finals, and anything related to the storyboards here. Later on when you get into animatics, it will be important to have all of your files in the same folder, so it's best to start some good organizational habits now.

Drawing your storyboards

Here is the second page of the script that you will be breaking down.

1. Begin by reading the entire script to get a good understanding of who the characters are and how they operate in the story. Make thumbnail sketches of what comes to mind as you read. Factor in the stage directions and make sure that you have an idea of the continuity from shot to shot. You can use the storyboard blank you created, but keep everything on layers so you can clean it up later.

    The first things to identify in the script are camera cuts. These are natural breaks that should correspond to a new frame in a storyboard.

NINJA BUNNY SCRIPT

Page 2

Camera cuts to a two shot and pulls back slowly:

INTERIOR, EVIL NINA DOJO

A large square room, with a three story roof. Each side of the square has another smaller square room off of it. These rooms are filled with weapons and practice equipment.

> NINJA BUNNY
> I believe the advantage is to me oh
> Warrior of too many dumplings?

Camera cuts to a close up of NB

> SUMO BUNNY
> Mmmmph, let us hope your sword is
> sharper than your wit!

Camera cuts to a close up of SB. SB squints his eyes and charges forward

Cut to NB who also squints his eyes and charges forward out of frame

Cut to wide shot (slow motion) of two characters in midair about to clash. The characters hit and real time is restored. They exchange sword play.

The two characters retreat to a defensive pose in a two shot. Slowly pull the camera back

> NINJA BUNNY
> I am amazed that you have the speed of
> one warrior but the stomach of two.

> SUMO BUNNY
> Appearances are deceiving, my friend. I
> am not fat I am merely big boned.

---

2. Separate the script into frames by selecting the dialogue and pasting it into the blank Photoshop file you created.

   If after doing this, you find you would like to insert a story frame, just slide all the other frames forward. This is one of the reasons you keep everything on layers. It sometimes helps to have multiple blanks open for just such an event. You should end up with something that looks like **FIGURE 2.25.**

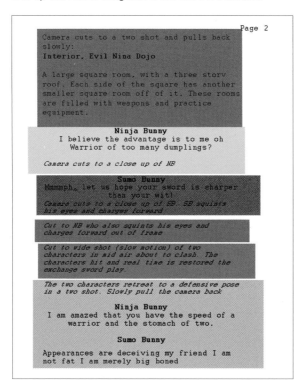

FIGURE 2.25 Script breakdown by story frames.

The color portions of the image indicate the shot breakdowns. These could have been broken down further, but for the purpose of this exercise, this is what you will work with.

In **FIGURE 2.26**, you can see that the text from the script has been added to the storyboard blank. This gives you a pretty good idea of what you should be drawing. It's up to you to decide the exact details of the image, how far to push in, and what angle to use. You might want to collect the text into its own layer group and lock it, as Photoshop and text are notoriously funky.

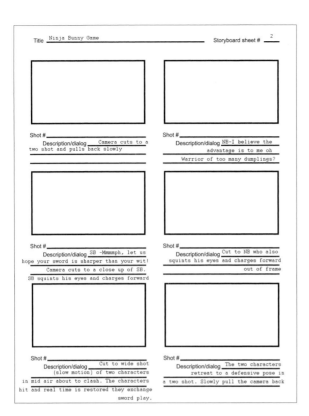

FIGURE 2.26 Script breakdown by story frames.

Title Ninja Bunny Game   Storyboard sheet # 2

Shot #
Description/dialog Camera cuts to a
two shot and pulls back slowly

Shot #
Description/dialog NB-I believe the
advantage is to me oh
Warrior of too many dumplings?

Shot #
Description/dialog SB -Mmmmph, let us
hope your sword is sharper than your wit!
Camera cuts to a close up of SB.
SB squints his eyes and charges forward

Shot #
Description/dialog Cut to NB who also
squints his eyes and charges forward
out of frame

Shot #
Description/dialog Cut to wide shot
(slow motion) of two characters
in mid air about to clash. The characters
hit and real time is restored they exchange
sword play.

Shot #
Description/dialog The two characters
retreat to a defensive pose in
a two shot. Slowly pull the camera back

3. Finally, you can begin to draw your images, as shown in **FIGURE 2.27**. Start on the first frame and rough in your first pass. As when creating concept drawings, it pays to be zoomed out and working small. Getting a good silhouette and a nice distribution of positive and negative space is key. When you get something you like and it matches the description, you are ready to take it to the next step.

FIGURE 2.27 Storyboard with dialogue and image added.

Shot # *007*

Description/Dialogue:

NB - I must recue the princess but how?

Wide shot with hero in view. Evil Dojo in the distance. Slowly push in towards the Dojo

4. You can work a few different ways. You can work on each frame individually, taking each to final, or you can rough in the entire page to see what the visual flow is like. You can then make adjustments and take the images to final. Both ways are fine, but with the first method you have to keep the continuity of the scenes in your head.

    FIGURE 2.28 shows a roughed-in example of the storyboard sequence. It gets the actions across and shows what the shots look like. A great storyboard artist will be able to put down the minimum amount of content to get a dynamic and quick example of what the scene is about. It's not enough to just be a good artist; you also have to be able to capture the feeling of the scene.

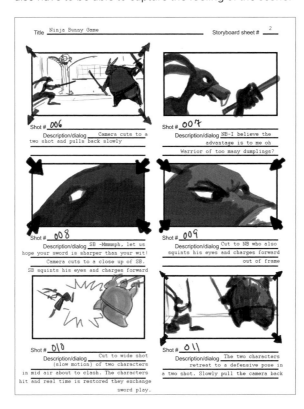

FIGURE 2.28 Roughed-in example of the storyboard sequence.

5. When you are happy with your work, you can go in and polish up the frames as needed.

    This polish pass process is similar to what you previously did with the concept drawings, except this time you should focus primarily on character, lighting, and form. The character part is not so hard because you have been working with only two characters; but if the script had an army of ninja bunnies, you would need to visually indicate which one was our hero.

    The actual size of the image will also dictate how much work you need to put into it. Photoshop is capable of tremendous detail. Unfortunately, your eyes are not, and seen among several hundred other storyboards, the work you put into a frame may be lost, not to mention the time expended on unnecessary refinement.

A good way to find your sweet spot is to look at other artists' work. People have been doing storyboards for a long time, and you will easily find loads of references on the Internet. That being said, every game or production is different, and it is always a chore to dial in just how much work you should do for a sequence to make your colleagues happy. You will have to work that out with your director or producer. Showing early is always advisable.

The final pass on your digital storyboard is to collect the image and the text into a new layer group so you can move the frames around, if necessary (**FIGURE 2.28A**). Often, when working out a story, segments are moved around to adjust the pace of the narrative. In traditional productions, the storyboards are on 3x5-inch cards and, therefore, easy to move around. To mimic this digitally, we collect the work on layers.

FIGURE 2.28A
Traditional storyboard meeting.

6. In the Layers editor, select all the layers that pertain to the one frame. That would be the image for that board, the picture box, the shot, the dialogue lines, and anything else that you might have added. Choose "New group from layers." Make sure you name this group for the number of the particular shot, such as *shot 1*, *shot2*, and so on, so you can track it.

7. You can also collapse the file, and then marquee select and paste the frames to separate them out. This will make for a smaller file to send to people. Just be sure you save a PSD of the original file in case you need to edit the text at a later date.

CREATING ANIMATICS

Animatics are the slightly more exciting brother of the storyboard. While a storyboard is used to dial in a story, the animatic is used to see how the dialogue and the story work together. It is also good for establishing the pacing of a scene.

Creating animatics in Photoshop is not as hard as you might think. You have already done most of the hard part by creating the storyboards. Animatics are "filmed" storyboards strung together like a slideshow to give you an idea how the scene plays out for timing. If you are lucky, you also have the edited voice recording cuts, i.e., the dialogue. This will allow you to go into an editor program and cut your animatics together to fit the audio dialogue.

Animation-Building Software

There are so many digital-editing software packages available today that you could use a different one every day for a long time—or at least until you forgot why you were downloading all that software. They all do pretty much the same thing but in slightly different ways.

The meat and potatoes of an editing package are that it allows you to combine movie footage, still images, and audio files on a timeline in the order and timing of your choosing. Most will let you edit and remove sections of the movie or audio file and add transitions, alter volume levels, and so on. Still images can be set to display for as long as you like and can be processed with all the transitions available to the movie-editing side.

A few packages allow you to create and integrate content such as text and shapes. Some also have the ability to animate the footage around the viewing frame.

The combined and altered footage is then assembled into a single file, called a *render*, and output in a video file format.

FIGURE 2.29 shows an animatic in Adobe After Effects (AE). It has an MP4 sequence called Dog Sled as its source footage. It is pretty representational of an editor program. It has a bin, or a library, in which footage is stored. It has a timeline where you edit the footage and other elements in your animatic, and a view window where the project is viewed. It has a set of DVR-style controls, and displays the video frames or timecode values (depending which you prefer to work in) to sync up and time out your work.

FIGURE 2.29 A scene in Adobe After Effects.

FIGURE 2.30 A scene in Camtasia Studio.

Camtasia Studio, shown in **FIGURE 2.30**, is also a very good editor. Although it does not have the range of special effects available in After Effects, it is very easy to use and great for cutting footage together. It also has one of the best screen-capture modules available. As you can see, its layout is similar to AE, with a media library, an editable timeline, and a viewing window. It also produces a final render and exports to many formats.

In addition to AE and Camtasia, other editing software packages for Windows and Mac OS X are worth investigating, including Adobe Premiere®, Final Cut Pro, Vine, Windows Movie Maker, and iMovie.

Any of these are excellent for cutting together your animatic and many of them come with a one-month trial period. But since this is a book about using Photoshop, you can guess what software we are going to use in the following exercise.

EXERCISE 3: ANIMATICS EXERCISE

"What, what, what?" you say. "Photoshop has an animation module?" Well, of course! The Timeline window in Photoshop may not be the most efficient editor, but it borrows a lot from the excellent Adobe After Effects timeline. However, as you grow more familiar with the Photoshop timeline, you learn to appreciate its functionality and the cleanliness of its menu system. The best part about it is that you do not have to open another program to create your animatic. In fact, you don't even need to close your storyboard file. Just flatten the layers and you are good to go (**FIGURE 2.31**).

FIGURE 2.31
Photoshop timeline mode.

Adding Audio

Photoshop accepts a number of audio formats, including MP3, MP4, and WAV, but if you are not savvy to the ways of audio editors and recording equipment, have no fear. You can do what all professionals do when they have a script but not a final mix of the dialogue. You can record what is called a temp track on your mobile device. This is not a special function. You can just record a movie as you would if you were at your cousin's birthday. Except, instead of shooting cake and scary relatives, you will be reading the script's dialogue. Then transfer that movie clip to your computer and you have your roadmap for making an animatic.

Reading dialogue does not require years of acting classes. For animatic purposes, just reading the words out loud should give you a fairly accurate timing. Even William Shatner couldn't change the timing that much. Just read each line as clearly as possible so you can easily identify the words in the playback editor when you are *scrubbing*, moving back and forth through the timeline content.

Here is the complete dialogue for both of the ninja bunnies' scenes:

```
Page 1
                              NINJA BUNNY
                  I must rescue the princess but how?

                              NINJA BUNNY
                  Aha! I will use the trees to hide my
                  attack.

                              NINJA BUNNY
                  Now evil one I will surprise you and we
                  will do battle.

                              NINJA BUNNY
                  Now I have you evil one

                               SUMO BUNNY
                  Ha, ha, ha, little one. Now we will see
                  who the greatest ninja is!

Page 2
                              NINJA BUNNY
                  I believe the advantage is to me oh
                  Warrior of too many dumplings?

Camera cuts to a close up of NB

                              SUMO BUNNY
                  Mmmmph, let us hope your sword is sharper
                  than your wit!

                              NINJA BUNNY
                  I am amazed that you have the speed of a
                  warrior and the stomach of two.

                              SUMO BUNNY
                  Appearances are deceiving my friend I am
                  not fat I am merely big boned.
```

Collecting Media

Now that you have your dialogue recording, you can bring in the storyboards. You have multiple ways to do this. You could cut out all the storyboard frames to remove the text, and save them as individual files. But that can be a lot of files to manage. You could also collect those files into a single layer and hide the layers you do not want shown. Or, you could just flatten the images into a JPG image, which is what you will do now.

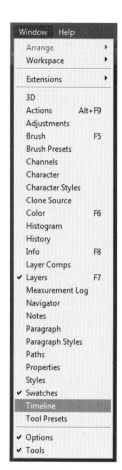

FIGURE 2.32
Timeline option under the Window pulldown menu.

Save the two JPGs of your storyboard and the dialogue file into a folder on your desktop, and call it *Animatics*. Saving files to your desktop enables your computer to access them faster than saving them on a standalone drive or on the cloud. Although access speed is not so important for this brief exercise, when you have an hour of recorded dialogue and hundreds of drawings, you'll appreciate the speed boost.

Working with the Timeline

In this exercise, you'll get to know your timeline editor. You'll set timeline keyframes and learn how the timeline editor works.

1. Close any open windows in Photoshop, and open your first storyboard sheet. Your file should be 8.5x11 inches at 300 dpi. If it is not, then please convert it as necessary.

2. In the Layers editor, duplicate your base layer and delete the bottom one. You do this because sometimes the base layer is not editable or is locked.

3. Open the Timeline editor (**FIGURE 2.32**). In the menu bar, choose Window > Timeline.

   A new bar, most of which is grayed out, will open on the bottom of the screen.

4. In the middle of the timeline is a little pulldown menu that either reads "Create Video Timeline" or "Create Frames Timeline." Choose "**Create Video Timeline**" (**FIGURE 2.33**).

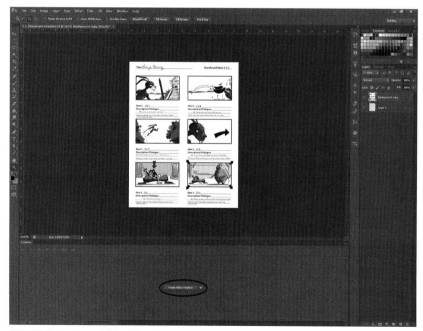

FIGURE 2.33 Create Video Timeline button.

Your video group will open. It is the long bar that stretches across the screen. The left is the video group's name, which should be the same as the layer, and a little arrow. If you click the little arrow, you should now see three categories: Position, Opacity, and Style. These are the animation keyframe controls. They allow you to put keyframes down, marking how you have altered the files above.

NOTE A keyframe is a marker on the timeline that represents an action you have performed on the file, such as translation, rotation, opacity, and many other actions.

5. Make sure the frame indicator in the timeline is on frame **0**, at the far left of the timeline, shown in **FIGURE 2.34**. This tells you where you are in time, and as you move to the right along the timeline, time progresses. Next to the word "Position," click the clock icon (keyframe options) once and a small yellow dot appears on the timeline to indicate that you've added a keyframe. On the left, a yellow diamond shape will appear to indicate that it has recorded the translational information of the image at a certain time.

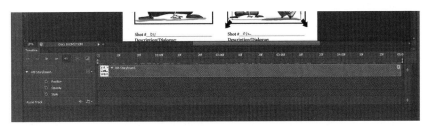

FIGURE 2.34 Set the frame indicator on frame 0, at the far left, and then progress through time as you move to the right along the timeline.

6. Advance the time indicator to frame **10** by clicking the blue handle on the red line and dragging it to frame **10**. Click the diamond between the two arrow icons (which are the Move to Next keyframe buttons), which will now be gray (or empty). Now, using the Move tool, slide your image slightly to the left. YAY! You have just animated your image (**FIGURE 2.35**).

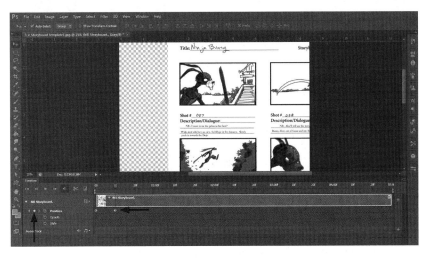

FIGURE 2.35 Setting a keyframe in Timeline mode.

7. Move the time indicator (the blue handle on the red line) back to frame **0** and click **Play** in the timeline movie control area to watch your image move to the side.

8. If you like the results, click the second keyframe icon to select it, and press **Delete** on your keyboard. This should erase your key and move the image back to the original position.

Placing audio on the timeline

Now that you have a basic understanding of timeline use, let's add the dialogue (**FIGURE 2.36**).

FIGURE 2.36 Adding audio to the timeline.

1. In the audio track bar, just below the area we have been working in, click the **Add Audio** icon (the music note button), and from the popup menu, choose **Add Audio**. Navigate to the audio file you previously created with your phone.

2. Select the file to load it as an audio clip.

   The audio clip is probably too long to fully display in the default timeline window. Don't worry. It's all in your timeline, just off the screen at the moment.

3. If you want to verify that you opened the entire audio file, at the bottom of the timeline window, you'll find a zoom slider. Drag it right and left to zoom in and out of the timeline, and finally adjust it so you can see your entire audio clip.

Animating the clip

This might seem like a lot of work just to make a hopped-up slideshow with audio, but the flexibility of this technique will carry you miles in your career. You are ready to put it all together... almost. You need to make one more adjustment to the storyboard JPG.

Because you previously flattened the storyboard image—and you now want to display only one board frame at a time—you need to make a visual mask. There are plenty of different ways to do this in Photoshop, but we are going to "cheat."

NOTE The 1100x1000-pixel dimensions only work if the master image is 8.5x11 inches and 300 dpi.

1. From the menu bar, choose Adjust > Canvas Size. In the Size window that appears, set Width to **1100 px** and Height to **1000 px**. Click through all the warnings (remember, we are cheating) to close the window.

2. With the mask adjusted and a keyframe placed at frame **0**, use the Move tool to align the image with the new view. The first frame and the entire dialogue should fit perfectly in the window.

After the positioning is set to your liking, you need to make sure you can hit that mark every time.

3. Set up a couple of guidelines to cross at the corner of the image frame. This provides a registration mark to go to with each new frame. If you just eyeball the registration, the frame may jump all over the place, which is a bit distracting (**FIGURE 2.37**).

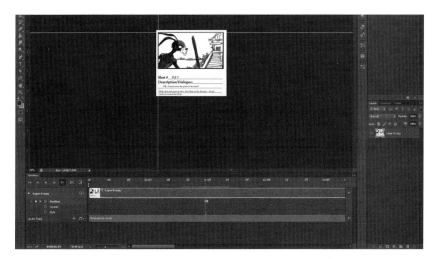

FIGURE 2.37 Setting up registration for animating the image.

4. Now play the scene, and note the timecode where the first line of dialogue ends, "*I must rescue the princess but how?*" Where you hear the word "how," set another keyframe.

5. Move the time indicator forward **1 frame/tic** on the timeline, and set another key. Then move the storyboard so the second frame is now showing in the canvas. Drag the time indicator left and right and watch the frames change. (This is the scrubbing process mentioned earlier.)

6. Repeat this technique for all six frames:

    Find the dialogue cue.

    Set a keyframe, and move the board into the canvas.

    When you finish, you can move on to the next board because the appropriate dialogue is already queued.

7. With your storyboard frames synced with your audio dialogue, you're ready to render out the animatic. Choose File > Export > Render to Video. Use the settings shown in **FIGURE 2.38**.

    The settings you really need to worry about relate to the type of file, or *format*, which in this case has to be QuickTime. Also, pay close attention to the location of the file being rendered, so you do not lose it. Don't laugh, it happens all the time.

FIGURE 2.38
Rendering settings
for the timeline.

Storyboards and animatics are used in games and film every day. They are the first steps toward locking down the overall story and pacing of a piece. No matter what the game or film, every cut scene, every encounter, and every intro movie was story-boarded. It is an inexpensive way to previsualize scenes and the go-to method for most directors to visually convey their visions. We took it a step further by animating it, but, hey, we are just those kinds of guys.

CREATING A USER INTERFACE

In the game world, user interface (UI) is the text, virtual buttons, gauges, knobs, sliders, and a whole host of other elements that allow the player to control and interact with the game. A skillful UI artist needs a strong background in graphic layout: knowing the ins and outs of constructing an appealing page, which fonts read the best, what colors work well together, and how to lead the eye.

Here are the job requirements for a game UI artist as they might appear in the want ads:

- Education in Graphic Design or related discipline, such as Illustration or Fine Art.
- Commanding skill of Photoshop and Adobe Illustrator.
- Organized and detailed.

- Understand limitations of information display and interactivity on today's game consoles.

- Ability to respond elegantly to difficult creative changes, often late in the process.

- Self-motivated, with a talent for solving creative problems.

- Ability to communicate with other artists visually using quick thumbnail sketches.

- Practicing knowledge of Autodesk Maya (or equivalent), modeling, After Effects, Flash, 3D animation, or any combination of these for prototyping is a huge plus.

- 2+ years of game industry experience using archiving program.

As you can see, many talents are needed to create something that seems simple.

In addition, you should have skill in structuring the user experience (UX). This involves knowing how to anticipate how a player might interact with the UI, and designing it for maximum functionality, speed, and convenience. Very large game studios have both a UI and a UX designer, but most of the time the UI artist is also expected to be a UX authority.

As if that weren't enough, UI artists are also responsible for working with the game designers to create comprehensive wireframes. What are wireframes? We thought you'd never ask.

Understanding Wireframes

Wireframes are the storyboards for the design and function of an interactive page (**FIGURE 2.39**). They are most commonly used in the production of Web pages where buttons and tabs and popups roam freely, jumping from page to page with reckless abandon. However, they are also used in game design as a way to set a UI. It is a way to roadmap the flow of button presses and enables rapid prototyping.

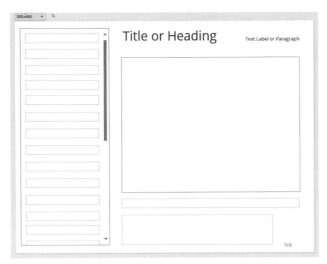

FIGURE 2.39 Sample wireframe.

Wireframes are most often black-and-white drawings or images that represent where page information will be placed. They are not generally interactive but sometimes have notations to indicate what a button press might do. The main goal of a wireframe is to map UI functionality and not to display your artistic prowess. It is best to keep them as simple as possible. Chances are, if you were to incorporate color and images, you would find that the people who evaluate your work become obsessed with the unfinished design of the buttons, and are not sufficiently concerned with the button locations on the page.

Because Photoshop is a great drawing tool, it is obviously well-suited for creating wireframes. Many UI artists create a library of often-used boxes, lists, windows, and buttons that they can place Lego-like on a page to speed up the design process. Furthermore, with this technique, they don't have to worry about duplicate boxes being of variable pixel ratios. (The other way to get around this is to numerically create your box objects.)

A boring font is also recommended for the same reason that you use outlines to indicate buttons. Team members are easily sidetracked if you apply a cowboy font to a space game UI, even if they know the font will be replaced later. As a result, it is always best to go with a neutral font such as Comic Sans or Palatino.

EXERCISE 4: PRODUCING WIREFRAMES

In the next two exercises, you will be given a list of screen assets to assemble into a wireframe homepage design for the ninja bunny game; then you will use that wireframe as a guide to create the final UI and cover art (**FIGURE 2.40**).

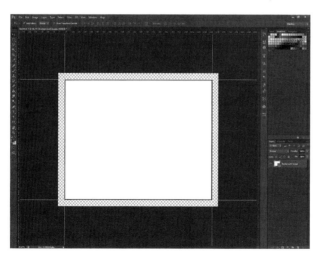

FIGURE 2.40 Creating a workspace for the wireframe.

Building a Wireframe

First, let's build the wireframe using elements that you downloaded with the other media files for this book.

1. Choose File > New > Preset > Web. Choosing the Web preset gives you access to a host of Web options.

2. Set Size to **1280x1024**. The 4 by 3 ratio is the most common Web standard. Click **OK** and a new file is created.

3. With your new file open, make sure the rulers are visible in your work area. If they are not, choose View > Rulers, and check the **Ruler** option box. Once the rulers are visible, right-click the ruler bar to change the measuring unit to **Pixels**.

   Now that your workspace is set up, we need to talk about the elements that will go into your homepage. A homepage is the first screen that appears once a game has loaded. It usually has a picture, a logo, and then various other buttons and icons, and some creator credit information. It most likely will also have a button to proceed to the start of the game and a menu button for changing gameplay options. It sometimes serves as a hold screen while the game is loading, and if this is the case, the page will also need a loading bar of some sort.

   In a professional game studio, you would have received a list from the game designer, who also might have some idea of the page's look and functionality. You smiled at him, took the list, and said, "Let me take a crack at it." Your job now is to combine (sometimes "cram") the following elements into a single wireframe page:

   - Main artwork showing a representative shot of the game
   - A menu button
   - A play button
   - Logo of your company
   - Logo of distribution company
   - Loading bar
   - Game logo

   The largest element you need to create is the background picture. It will usually occupy the entire page. But for this project, your game designer wanted a black border, so let's add a 50-pixel border and earn some brownie points.

4. The easiest way to figure out how large your background shape should be is to do the math. Our overall image is 1280x1024 pixels. You need a 50-pixel border surrounding the background image, so subtract 100 pixels from the height and width to arrive at the dimensions of the background image: 1180x924 pixels.

5. Once you have your area sized out for your border, choose the **Rectangle** tool, and make the shape. Make the fill color **white** and the border stroke **black**. Also set the stroke to **3 pixels**.

6. Strike a rectangle on the page, and set the width to **1180** and the height to **924**.

7. Use the Marquee tool to select your entire background image.

8. With your image selected, choose the **Move** tool and, on the top menu bar, you will find the align tools (**FIGURE 2.41**).

FIGURE 2.41 Alignment options in Photoshop.

9. In the main menu bar go to the align tool, and choose **Align Verical Centers** and **Align Horizontal Centers**. If you have trouble telling which one is which, you can hover your mouse above the icon and the text info will appear.

   Now that your image is centered in the screen, you can add guides so that if you need to move a layer, you have a visual reference with which to do so.

10. Shift-click on your side ruler bar, and drag until your pointer changes to a bracket. As you drag out of the ruler area, a blue guideline will appear to help you align your buttons.

11. Drag to align one guideline and drag another to align with the right, top, and bottom of the background image.

    These guidelines outline your safe zone, more often called a *safe frame*. All of the work we do should live in this area. Stay within the lines; the lines are your friends.

    Why do we do this, you ask? Because your game will be played on (or converted to) a variety of hardware devices, monitors, TVs, consoles, and other devices, all with their own display resolutions (**FIGURE 2.42**). Defining a safe frame, and keeping all of your interface elements within it, will guarantee that players will see every bit of your UI, no matter who is viewing your game.

FIGURE 2.42 Screen-size popularity across the country.

12. Create a new layer and place it below the layer you just created. Fill it with **white**, and name it *BG*.

13. Create a new rectangle shape above the background image layer, and name it *sponsor logo* (**FIGURE 2.43**). Because your sponsor's logo is a square, make sure that the shape you create is **140x140**. Name the layer *sponsor logo*.

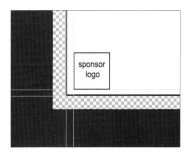

FIGURE 2.43 Sponsor logo positioning.

14. Using the Type tool, type *sponsor logo* in the square you just created. Combine the text and the shape in a layer group, and also name it *sponsor logo*. Now move the whole element so it is aligned **25 pixels** from the bottom of the background image and **25 pixels** from the rightmost side.

15. Now create another box (or duplicate the previously created layer group), and place it **25 pixels** to the left of the box you just created (**FIGURE 2.44**). Name the group *my logo*, and change the text layer to also read *my logo*. If your logo is a rectangle instead of a square, you may also want to adjust the shape parameters.

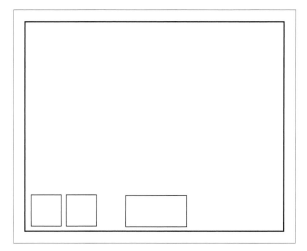

FIGURE 2.44 Duplicated and modified button shapes.

16. Using the same method, you will create the menu button. In the layer group, change the size of the shape object to **280x140 pixels**. Align it with the far-left side of the safe zone, and then move it back **25 pixels** back toward the right.

17. Once again duplicate this layer group, and name the copy *start button*. Use the Marquee tool to select the layer group. Then with the Move tool, align the new button to the horizontal center of the page at the same height as the other buttons.

18. With the Rectangle tool, create a rectangle that is **560x30 pixels**. Align it to the page horizontally and about **100 pixels** above the top of the start button.

    Finally, you will create a space for the game logo. This is the most important part of the page and should take up a good deal of real estate.

19. Create a new rectangle shape of **1024x512 pixels**, and center it to the page horizontally. Then move it down **50 pixels** from the upper edge of the safe zone.

20. Add the text Main Logo and put the layers in a group using the method you have learned in this exercise.

Your laundry list of UI elements is completed. The results should look something like **FIGURE 2.45**:

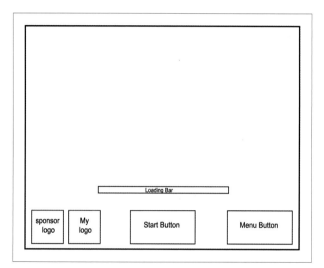

FIGURE 2.45 Finished wireframe for Ninja Bunny screen.

EXERCISE 5: FINALIZING THE UI AND COVER ART

In this exercise, you will produce the final UI and cover art for your homepage.

With your wireframe, the one you just designed, you know exactly where UI elements will appear on the page. Now you just need to dial in the look and feel of the text, the supporting buttons, and the imagery.

Normally when manipulating or designing text, you would go straight to Adobe Illustrator with its extensive set of text tools. But we are working with Photoshop and it is no slouch in the text department. Most of the time in a game studio, any assets you create in Illustrator would be brought into Photoshop for final implementation anyway. Think of this exercise as skipping the middle man.

Creating the Main Logo

The first part to tackle is the game logo. This text will set the tone for the rest of the page and give you clues to which colors to use and what treatment the text should receive.

When creating a logo, it is a good idea to first do research. Find text that is conceptually in the same vein as the logo you are trying to produce. That inspirational image can come from anywhere—old movie posters, toys, and even food containers. Again, you could create a text mood board, taking bits and pieces and putting them together until you have something you like.

Of course, you could also download a font pack and use it, but most custom-created fonts charge a fee and require a license for commercial use.

Since you're working on a ninja bunny-based game, it would probably be a good idea to do a logo that includes the color red and suggests a Japanese style.

1. Begin by going into the main logo layer folder and typing the words **NINJA BUNNIES**. Select the text to highlight it, and from the Fonts menu, select a font that is bold and to your liking. The font pictured one is called Ash.

2. Scale the font to fit in the area defined by the box you made earlier. This one is 190 pt.

3. With the Text tool still selected, in the main menu bar, from the Create Warp Text pulldown menu, choose the deformer called **Flag** (**FIGURE 2.46**). Adjust the warp by dragging the sliders, and when you're done, click **OK**.

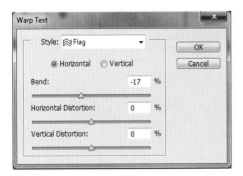

FIGURE 2.46 The Warp Text setting for the main title.

4. Make sure you have the layer selected, and then choose Options > Blending Options.

5. Check the **Stroke** check box and click on the Stroke options tab to open its properties (**FIGURE 2.47**). Set the Size to **3 px** and the Opacity to **100**. Set the Color to **black**.

FIGURE 2.47 The
Stroke option under
Blending Options.

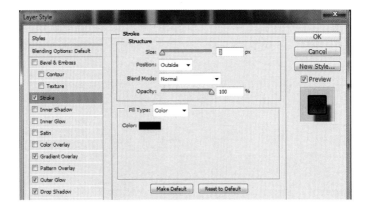

FIGURE 2.47 The
Stroke option under
Blending Options.

6. Remaining in the Blending Options menu, go to the *Gradient Overlay* tab and
check the box. Select the **Gradient Overlay** tab to get to the options and double-
click on the gradient itself (a black-to-white bar). When the new menu pops up,
choose the **red and green** preset from the gallery (**FIGURE 2.48**).

Down below is a red bar the blends into a green color. Click the **Stop** box under
the green box and change it to a shade of **red** that is lighter than the red in the
Stop on the other side of the gradient. This should give you a fairly subtle red
gradation.

FIGURE 2.48 The
Gradient Editor and
Layer Style windows.

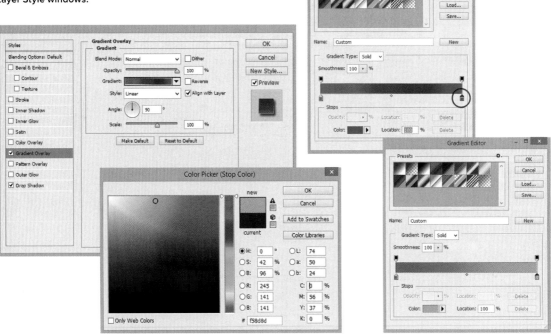

Because Photoshop allows only one external stroke in the Blend Options Editor, we are going to use Outer Glow as a second stroke line (**FIGURE 2.49**). It takes a bit of wrangling to do so, but it will look just like the built-in stroke when we are done.

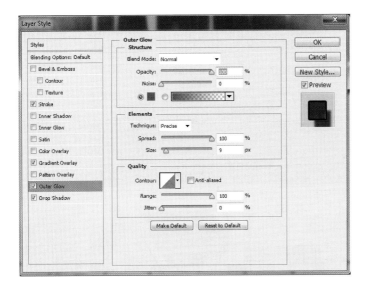

FIGURE 2.49 Blending options: Outer Glow.

7. Select the **Outer Glow** check box. Select the Outer Glow tab and go into the options. Change the Blend mode to **Normal**, set the Opacity to **100%**, and select a **gold** color. Now change the Technique to **Precise** and the Spread to **100%**. Set the Size to **9 px** and the Range to **100%**. This should give you a sneaky solid outer glow, or as far as anyone can see, a second stroke.

8. Lastly, select the **Drop Shadow** check box, and extend the Distance to **20 px**. Set the Spread to **8** and the Size to **5** (**FIGURE 2.50**).

FIGURE 2.50 Finished Ninja Bunnies title art.

That should do it! You are done with the main logo for now.

Developing a Background Image

In a game studio, you would usually have a whole game to draw inspiration from. There would be screenshots and illustrations, and a whole host of artwork to spur your creativity. You would know the story and the characters, and creating a single defining image representative of the entire game wouldn't be done in a vacuum.

If the studio were large enough, one person would be designing the UI and another would be drawing the background illustration, and the homepage would just be a matter of dropping the background file in and making sure it jives with your UI design. But you do not have that, so you'll have to leverage what you've done on your own.

1. Open a new Photoshop file at 1280x1024 pixels. Think about the assets you have already created. There are lots of images in the storyboards you can use. So that would be a good place to start.

2. Take the very last frame of the storyboard, and clean it up. With your sumo bunny concept cleaned up and a little finishing work tossed in, the ninja bunny image from the storyboard frame can be refined.

3. Combine the sumo and ninja bunny images on the page with the storyboard frame in the background (**FIGURE 2.51**). Arrange and modify the sumo and the ninja bunnies until you have something you like.

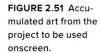

FIGURE 2.51 Accumulated art from the project to be used onscreen.

4. You now have the characters in place, but they are going to need a background. Begin by doing an Internet search for a dojo interior or an ancient temple. Find one that matches the scene and has the correct perspective.

    Generally, the images you'll find on the Internet are copyrighted and cannot be used commercially without proper licensing. But there is no law that says you can't use these publically posted images internally as reference for an original image you will eventually draw.

5. Using that image as inspiration, draw a somewhat loose version of the scene. Remember, the characters are the main focus.

6. Bring the two characters and the background together and drop the image in as a background (**FIGURE 2.52**). Then check to see that the colors work with the title.

FIGURE 2.52 Main titles and background image.

Understanding UI Buttons

Next, we will focus on the buttons at the bottom of the wireframe. Usually, game buttons and any interactive portions of the UI are constructed in Adobe Flash or Illustrator because they have more options for vector drawing than Photoshop; and if the game needs to scale to fit on a tablet or mobile device, the UI element will need to scale too without losing resolution. Flash has its own programming language called ActionScript and an animation system that makes it a one-stop shop for button creation. The code and animation from Flash also can be directly ported into many game engines.

Adobe Illustrator also has several button types in its presets (**FIGURE 2.53**). If you were to browse through the Illustrator Symbols Library, you would see a lot of familiar button designs.

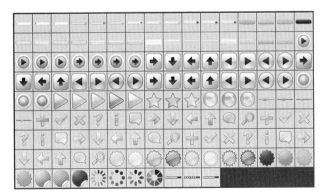

FIGURE 2.53 Premade buttons in Adobe Illustrator.

Illustrator works great for creating vector buttons, but just like Photoshop, you need some coding to place them into a game, and most of the time those vector buttons are exported as a SWF (Shockwave Flash movie) or PNG (Portable Network Graphic) files.

A button consists of several images because you need to represent the various interactive states of that button. The two most obvious are the *neutral* and the *engaged* *states*. The neutral state is displayed when nothing is happening to the button. It is the default state. The engaged state appears when the button is clicked. Generally speaking, the neutral state is in full color and should be designed to fit in with the page. The engaged state is either dimmer or far brighter, and more or less saturated in color. This is a convention used to indicate that a button has been pressed or engaged in some way.

Buttons may have a third state, sometimes called the *rollover state*. This is applied when the button changes color or saturation, because the mouse pointer passes above or hovers over the button without triggering that button's interactivity.

Choosing the Color of a Button

You already know the approximate size of the buttons from the wireframes you developed, and you can use the shape you created as the basis for the button. Remember, buttons first need to be vector images so that they can be scaled. But you should ask some questions before you start. What style of button do you want to make? What shape of button do you want to make and, of course, what is the color scheme?

The button colors should fall within the established palette. Since your main title is a red ramp and the BG elements are mostly green and brown, you should go with one of those colors. If you are unsure of your choices, you can always create a color palette (**FIGURE 2.54**).

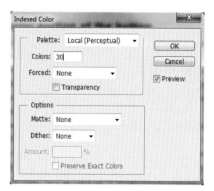

FIGURE 2.54 Indexed color mode.

1. To do this, first save your file. Then choose Image > Duplicate to copy the file in your window.

2. With the new file selected, choose Image > Model > Indexed colors, and flatten and reduce your image. A dialog box will open with options for converting your image. Set Palette to **Local Perceptual**, and in the color dialog box, set the number of colors to **50**. Set Forced to **None** and Dither to **None**, then click **OK**.

   Your image is not looking so colorful anymore. It is a good thing you duplicated it.

3. Choose Image > Mode > Color Table to view the colors selected from your image (**FIGURE 2.55**). You need to save the table, otherwise you'll lose the new palette when you close the file. To load the new palette with your new swatches, open the **Swatches** palette, and from the dropdown menu, choose **Load Swatches**.

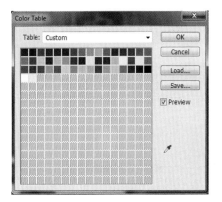

FIGURE 2.55 Indexed colors from scene.

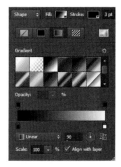

FIGURE 2.56 The Gradient picker.

4. Browse to the folder where you saved your color table, and open the new palette. You will see the predominant colors in the scene. Any of these would be okay for use as a button. But you are going with red so it pops off the green background.

5. In the layer group Menu Button, find the layer with the shape called *menu button*, and duplicate it. Hide the lower original shape by clicking the eye icon (visibility toggle).

6. Select the layer and then go to the Shape tool. At the top of the menu, double-click the fill color. Switch it from a color to a gradient by selecting the gradient option icon from the menu that pops up (**FIGURE 2.56**).

7. Change the gradient to match one of the reds in the BG image. Set the color stops on the ramp (the little boxes under the bar) to **red** and a **dark red** (**FIGURE 2.57**).

   Make sure that the two reds you pick are somewhat close. Subtlety is the key to making a superior UI. If your ramps are too drastic, it will be distracting. A good UI design is attractive and useful, but doesn't call attention to itself. A garishly designed UI sticks out like a poorly colored sore thumb.

8. Return to the layer, and create a new empty layer above it. With the Marquee tool, select the upper half of the button. Select a **white** color and a soft brush around **50 px**. Using only the top half of the brush, stripe a white line across the bottom of the selected area. Your button should look something like **FIGURE 2.58**.

FIGURE 2.57 Choose a red color from the Gradient picker.

FIGURE 2.58 Menu Button with gradient.

9. Reduce the Opacity to **85%**, and using the Transform function, scale the edges to be within the red portion of the button.

10. Return to the red button layer, and select the **Shape** tool again. This time, click in the stroke color area, and over at the upper right, click the rainbow icon to bring up the Color Picker. Use the Eyedropper tool to select the darkest red in your button gradient.

11. In the color field, select an even darker version of that red, and click **OK**. Select your red button layer again, and right-click to open the Options menu.

12. Select Blending Options and select the **Inner Glow** check box (**FIGURE 2.59**). Change the color to the same color as the stroke. Change the blend mode to **Normal**, and set the Size to **35 px**.

FIGURE 2.59 Blending options: Inner Glow.

Making Button States

When setting the text for a button, you do not necessarily want to use the same font that you used for the main titles. Because the key to a good UI is subtlety and clarity, it is a good idea to pick a font that is easily read—even on a mobile device—and one that may be used royalty free.

1. Select the **Text** tool, and over in the layers, select the text layer that reads **Menu Button**. Delete the word "Button" while leaving the word "Menu."

2. With the text still selected, change the font to **Tahoma/Bold** at **70 pt**. Change the font color to **white**.

3. Go to the layer again, and open the blending options. Select the **Gradient Overlay** check box, and in the overlay, change the first color to **orange** and the second color to **yellow** by once again selecting the stops under the gradient bar and altering the color (**FIGURE 2.60**).

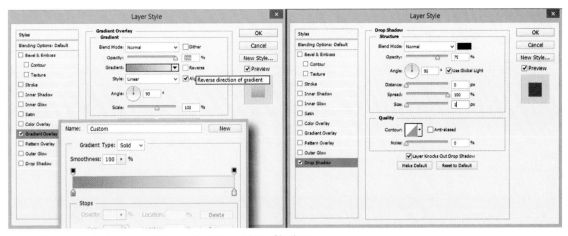

FIGURE 2.60 Blending options: Gradient Overlay and Drop Shadows.

This should reflect the treatment of the main title. The color yellow will be associated with text for this game; and if you would like to establish an overall visual language (and you do), you are now on your way. Just remember to include some form of yellow in your text for navigation from here on out.

4. To make the text pop a bit more, we are going to add a shadow, so select the **Shadow** check box. Set the Blend mode to **Normal**, and select a **dark red** color. Set the Angle to **90**, the Distance to **0**, the Spread to **100**, and the Size to **1**.

   These settings essentially put a stroke around and a bit behind the text, which works better for this purpose than a stroke would.

5. One last thing: Select the **Inner Sha**dow check box, and set the Blend Mode to **Multiply**. Set the Opacity to **48** and uncheck **Use Global Light**.

   These settings change the direction the shadow is cast without messing up the drop shadow that you just finished.

6. Set the Distance to **5**, and the Choke and the Size to **0**.

   The resulting menu button should look like the one in **FIGURE 2.61**.

   FIGURE 2.61 Menu button with text.

   Now after all that work, you have a finished button, right? Nope. Remember, each button has at least two stages: the neutral state, which you just created, and the engaged or active state, which you'll create next. The good news is that once you have the first state done, the second state is a breeze.

7. Duplicate the entire layer set called Menu Button, and name it *Menu Button Active*. Hide the original so you don't accidentally work on it.

8. Open the group, and go to the red color gradient layer. Double-click the layer to open up the gradient fill control. Click the darker color stop, and change the color to a more intense red by sliding up and to the right on the Color Picker.

FIGURE 2.62 The two states of the red part of the Menu button.

9. Select the other stop, and slide it to the left to produce a pinker color. Click **OK** to leave the picker (**FIGURE 2.62**).

10. Return to your layers, and unhide the original layer. Now click **Visibility** on and off to compare the states and make sure you didn't go too far with the colors.

11. If you're happy with the results, save your file and hide the original layer again. In the text layer, open the Blending Options for the text that reads "Menu." Turn off **Inner Shadow** and turn on **Outer Glow**. Change the Blend Mode of Outer Glow to **Normal** and the color to **yellow**. Set the Opacity to **32**, the Spread to **24**, and the Size to **8px** (**FIGURE 2.63**).

FIGURE 2.63 Blending options: Gradient Overlay and Outer Glow.

FIGURE 2.64 The two states of the text in the Menu button.

12. In the gradient color tab, adjust the color bar just as you did with the red color. Make the left stop a **true yellow** and the right stop a **whitish yellow**. Click **OK** and exit. Return to the layers and unhide the original.

    If everything went well, this two-cycle animation should give the impression that the word "Menu" illuminates when the button is clicked (**FIGURE 2.64**).

13. Collect the two layers into a new layer group called *Menu Button*.

14. Turn off **Visibility** on the active state (the eye icon in the layers), so you can see what the default state looks like as you work on the other buttons.

Creating a Start Button

Happily, the Start Button just happens to be the exact same size as the menu button. Can you see where we are going with this?

1. Copy the Menu Button set, and name it *Start Button*.

2. Move the new group over the top of the Start Button wireframe layer.

3. Move the old Start Button layer into the new group, and hide it.

4. Select the text portion of the layer. Using the Text tool, click the word "**Menu**" on the new button, and change the word "Menu" to "**Start**." Make sure that you are in centered-text mode so that you keep you alignment when you type.

5. Repeat this for the active layer.

6. You'll also need to change all the layer names to "**Start**" or things will get very confusing. You can repeat this for all buttons of this size.

For buttons of a different size but the same style, the process is a bit different.

7. Duplicate the button group as you did before, and with the button group selected, transform/scale the button to the new size (**FIGURE 2.65**). This works great except that the kerning on the text also gets scaled and looks bad.

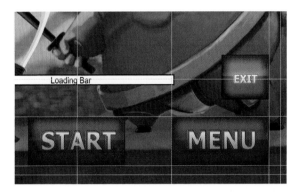

FIGURE 2.65 Copying the layer style to the other buttons.

8. To fix this, delete the text layer in the scaled button. Go to one of the other non-scaled buttons and copy the two text layers. Drag them into their respective layers.

9. Realign the text to the box, and under font size, reduce the font (do not scale). This method is slightly faster than redoing or copying all the blending options you have already set.

Creating the Loading Bar

A loading bar is a device that indicates information is downloading to your device. Once again, this is one of those elements that Adobe Flash was made for, but Photoshop can handle the task with no problem.

You already made the required shape when you made the wireframe. That long, skinny box is exactly what one would expect from a loading bar. So let's start by creating the inside color.

1. First, make two duplicates of the shape in the loading bar layer group. Name the first one *Loading Bar Color* and the second one *Loading Bar Seat*. This should give you three layers: Loading Bar, Loading Bar Color, and Loading Bar Seat (**FIGURE 2.66**).

FIGURE 2.66 The loading bar broken out into its components.

2. Select the Loading Bar layer, and then choose the **Shape** tool. In the options bar, remove the fill from the shape and leave only the stroke.

3. Select the Loading Bar Color shape layer, and then choose the **Shape** tool. Go up to the options again and turn the stroke **off**.

4. Double-click the Fill color box, and choose the **Gradient** option. Change the stops to match the gradient that you used on the text. Make the first stop **orange**, and the second stop **yellow**.

5. Create a new layer below the color bar you just made, and merge the two layers.

   At this point, you have to go raster for this to work.

6. Use the Marquee tool or the Magic Wand tool to select the color bar. Cut the shape from the scene by pressing **Ctrl+X**.

7. Create a new layer below the Loading Bar Seat layer, and merge the two layers. Choose the **Magic Wand** tool, and click the white part of the box.

8. From the Photoshop main menu, choose Edit > Paste Special > Paste Into. You should now be able to move the color bar within the frame, as pasting this way creates an automatic mask to be created.

9. On the Loading Bar Seat layer, lower the Opacity to **50%**. If you like, you can open the animation window and animate the color bar in motion (**FIGURE 2.67**). This will preview how it will look in code.

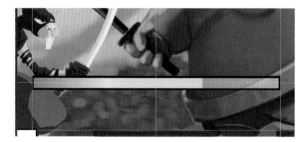

FIGURE 2.67 The loading bar with gradient.

Adding Logos

Adding logos seems like a simple thing to do, and for the most part, it is. But one big fat issue always comes up—resolution. The issue is that when you try to crush a beautiful intricate logo with words into a 128x128-pixel space, you end up with a compressed visual mush. What can you do?

Many companies have several sets of logos: one logo with text that is suitable for high-definition environment, and one with just the bare essentials to appear in the corner of an iPhone game. Sometimes this smaller logo is just a recognizable portion of the main logo.

The smarter companies like Adobe and Autodesk (to name two) use a very simple logo that works well large or small. For our purposes, we are going to drop in two types of logos. One logo is very simple, and one will have to be cut down (**FIGURE 2.68**).

FIGURE 2.68 Adding in the custom logo art.

As you can see, the ME logo should reduce pretty well. It has a ramp on the text, but for the most part, it is fairly bold with good contrast.

The sponsor's logo, however, will have a few issues. The text is already cramped together and the background is very subdued. The whole logo is slightly off square, and the fire logo will stretch poorly if you scale it as a whole.

Because this is someone else's logo, you would need to have a conversation with them about changing it. Quite often they will be able to supply you with a version of their logo that you can use. Companies often have multiple versions of their logo designed for clarity at different sizes. But let's pretend that they said, "Um, can you fix this?" Your task then becomes a matter of seeing if you can reconstruct the logo to work at a low resolution.

You would start by eliminating the portions of the image that will drop out when reduced: the background, the highlights, the shadow. Keep the stroke. To address the possibility of the text blending together, you could lose the logo, or if you have the room, extend the text out and place the logo at the side.

FIGURE 2.69 shows the original logo alongside four potential solutions. The first solution was to extend the area and eliminate the noise on the text and in the background. The second version included all of the above and eliminating the icon. This solution got closer to the square size that would suit our page. In the third version, the amount of text was reduced to let the more important text have a little breathing space. The fourth featured just the icon, which, if it is popular enough, can work okay. These are all very simple answers to the problem. A professional UI artist working in the industry would most likely have to work on this issue for a while.

FIGURE 2.69 Adjusting art to fit the space better.

FIGURE 2.70 shows the finished Homepage/Loading Page/Start Page. A few things got altered along the way, but that is how art for games works. As you can see, some issues pop up, even with the best-laid plans. Being flexible and a good problem solver are essential to working in the games industry.

FIGURE 2.70 Final game screen.

CHAPTER 2 WRAP-UP

In this chapter, you learned some processes that are not tied to any particular game medium. These skills will be useful no matter which area of games you want to go into. Photoshop is obviously a very powerful tool capable of many things. The variety of work in just the few topics we covered would take four or five people of different artistic backgrounds to resolve professionally. That is a lot of folks with different backgrounds using just one tool (**FIGURE 2.71**).

FIGURE 2.71 The art from all of the projects in the chapter.

GAME ASSET CREATION FOR SOCIAL MEDIA

Social games are just games that have a social component on the Internet. It has more to do with where the game will be seen than networking with other people to play. For example, any game you find on Facebook is considered a social game. It is also a way for developers to identify what size the game will be and what technology skills will be required.

NOTE To access the resource files and videos, just log in or join peachpit.com, and enter the book's ISBN. After you register the book, links to the files will be listed on your Account page under Registered Products.

A social component brings people together on a single site and enables them to interact with each other in some way. This could include dating sites, gambling sites, food review sites, eBay, Facebook, and even Amazon to a certain extent. The interaction does not have to be a videoconference or real-time communication. It could be as simple as leaving a review of a product or liking a friend's photo of a cat falling on grandma's head.

In this chapter, you will learn some of the ways that assets are created for social games using Adobe Photoshop, explore the crazy world of casino games, and learn how to leverage your art.

WHAT IS SOCIAL MEDIA, AND WHO MAKES IT?

A huge gaming market exists for the social scene and its users, often called *casual gamers*. Unlike so-called hard-core gamers who may play for hours at a time, casual games often only play for around 5 minutes. However, this statement is a little misleading because a casual gamer might play for only 5 minutes but at many times throughout the day.

Loads of money is being made catering to these casual social gamers. Most of the social games are free and can be played on a social site's Web page. This business model, called *free to play*, depends on *microtransactions* to survive. That is, players are charged for purchasing instant improvements to an in-game factory, or adding time to their candy wall, or acquiring new levels of play. To support an ongoing stream of purchasable features and improvements, the developer needs to create a constant stream of new content in order for the game to survive. Microtransactions on a healthy game earn, on average, about a nickel a day per person. That may not sound like a lot of money, but multiply that nickel times 2 million users, seven days a week, and it adds up.

Quite a bit of social content is autogenerated. The artist makes graphic assets that are put into an engine, which spits out asset variations in arrangements and colors and sizes that give the players new levels to conquer. That being said, there is still a lot of asset creation going on at a social game company.

The Social Game Team

The teams that produce social games have traditionally been on the smaller side of around 10 to 20 people. However, some social games boast teams of more than 100 people, even though it is harder to maintain a team that size on profits from microtransactions.

Most game teams have the same employees running around, no matter what kind of game they are making, and working in four departments: Management, Production and Design, Programming, and Art (**FIGURE 3.1**).

PROGRAMMING

DESIGN

ART

MANAGEMENT

- **Management** includes all the people who keep the business side of the studio running. It usually includes the CEO, the CFO, a lawyer, some office managers, and maybe some accountants. They handle payroll and new business ventures, and renting a building, and buying pens, and recording your vacation, and tracking the game, and making sure it is running on time. Sometimes art directors and technical leads are included on the management team.

- **Producers** are a liaison between management and the rest of the studio. They track and report project progress, and keep everybody chugging along. They coordinate to-do items, lead scrums, and if you have a good producer, help your department avoid being overwhelmed by requests.

- **The game designer** in a social game studio usually numbers one person per game who figures out all the intricacies of the gameplay. This individual works on story, page layout, social interactions, monetization, character development, level design, and everything that does not need to be drawn or programmed. The job is also about making sure the game is fun by tuning the mechanics in a way that keeps players engaged.

- **Engineers** for a social game work in a variety of areas: front end, back end, tools, and graphics. Front-end programmers make sure that the game runs. Back-end programmers make sure that the game runs on servers, and websites, and social outlet media portals. Tools guys write tools for the rest of the company that enable a more efficient workflow. Graphic programmers concern themselves with making the game look good by writing code that allows the art to run quickly and display as attractively as possible.

- **Art** usually is headed by an art director who runs the show and takes responsibility for developing and maintaining the look of the project. He and his graphic designers will take endless meetings trying to guide a game in a visual direction. He is in charge of assigning work to the other artists, and may also be in charge of outsourcing some of the work.

The other artists on the team fall into several job titles, ranked like this: lead, senior artist, junior artist. There are no hard and fast job descriptions or qualifications for these titles. Usually, these artists have years of experience in the industry, but there are plenty of second-year lead artists who have art directors as friends. On a social game, you are most likely working in 2D and outputting to Adobe Flash or some other custom game engine optimized for pushing 2D around.

THE PIPELINE FOR CREATING SOCIAL GAME CONTENT

We've just discussed who all the players are in a game company. Now we will learn how they interact and work together.

Games are created in many different ways. They always start with an idea. Sometimes an individual has an idea for a social game. She then gets her friends together, they create all the assets and do all the engineering, and then they release it through one of the many outlets for selling a game. Most original-looking games were created this way. If the game does so well that the money starts to flow into the project (either through investors or through the sales associated with the game), the company generally expands and tries to repeat the process with a new game.

The other way social games come into being is via a think tank at an existing game company. Tank members come up with a concept and a team is assigned to it. The game is put into production using the company's revenue from other projects. Unfortunately, this often results in employees having to work on a sequel or a clone of a different company's game, because investors see sequels and clones as a better bet to gain a return on their money. Of course, when too many games are too similar, that genre gluts and kills the market until another original title comes out to dominate the market and attract a new horde of imitators. It is the circle of game life (**FIGURE 3.2**).

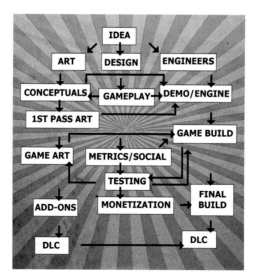

FIGURE 3.2 A game flowchart.

The Demo

Out of everyone on the team, the engineers have it the worst. They have to cobble a game atmosphere together without any art or design direction. Usually at this stage, the engineers will work on functions that are not specific to the game. They work on things like profile creation, and saving, and a rudimentary system for handling art assets. Most of the time there is some existing code to build on or an engine that will need modifying, and that keeps them busy until art and design catch up.

It doesn't take long for art and design to create some assets and catch up to engineering. Once this point is reached, the goal of the team is to create a demo, sometimes called a first playable. This is a very rough version of the game that hopefully proves the game can be made, and should continue to be funded.

To create the demo, a designer begins by sorting out the gameplay defining the attributes that the game will need, such as leader boards, doobers, possible themes, characters (if any), rewards, in-game money or points, and anything else that may be useful to realize in a demo (**FIGURE 3.3**).

The main priority at this stage is to get the demo up and running so that its systems can be tested. To serve this goal, the art department must create a lot of temporary art that may or may not be cleaned up later for inclusion in the actual game. Artists will also generate conceptual sketches of various aspects of the game (**FIGURE 3.4**). The art director reviews the concepts, makes asset lists, creates a schedule for the artists, fleshes out themes and colors, and most likely looks worried because the engineer is asking for art assets ahead of time.

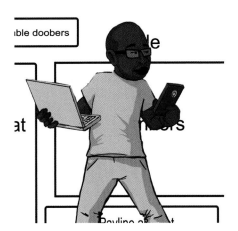

FIGURE 3.3 The game designer.

FIGURE 3.4 The harried artist.

Once the demo is done, everyone should have a pretty good idea of what the game looks like and does, including management and/or the publisher, who at this point, will need to review the game for additional funding. Most games are funded on a milestone schedule that pays in installments based on the completion of a previously agreed-upon amount of work. The first playable is usually the first major milestone, based on whether the publisher decides if the game should move forward or not. If yes, then great, you have a green light to finish the game. If no, then the game is stopped right there and the team is reassigned or let go. All of the assets are archived and the idea is lost. It is very sad.

In our case, the publisher has given us the green light, which means we are good to finish the game. Whew! The next steps are to polish and iterate. This means final art is now created for all assets, and final task and asset lists are compiled so that everyone knows what needs to be done to finish on time. That milestone system is still in place, so the deadlines need to be met.

Post Green Light

The publisher green-lit us to create a social slot-machine game, so the designer is now working on game balancing and making sure the game is fun to play. He also needs to develop a plan for how to monetize the game. With a slot machine, the monetization is pretty simple. It is a gambling game and people are used to putting money into them. In this type of social game, you buy credits with real money.

In addition to buying credits to play the game, the player will also have the option to purchase new themes and new skins, so the designer feeds the art team with asset requests that will enable those monetization elements.

Stylistic Choices

Part of generating a revenue stream is establishing who your audience is and what kind of genre they are into. The science of trying to figure out what kind of games people want to play has grown tenfold in the last few years. Companies now have whole departments dedicated to watching, logging, and hypothesizing game-playing habits.

Based on all the data collected, who is playing social games the most? Why, it's 43-year-old women (**FIGURE 3.5**). Yep, it's your mom, and as a game artist it's your job to create game visuals that will attract your mom to play. Some choices are self-evident for this audience.

You should stay away from camouflage, decapitated aliens kidnapping bikini models, and demons unless they are terribly handsome or hopelessly cute (**FIGURE 3.6**). You can see where this is going. Traditional male icons should be shelved for most social games. Although men are playing social games, they represent less than half the market share, so we don't care so much about them.

So how do you devise a visual design that targets people you know almost nothing about? You get into their heads. You buy magazines that are geared toward them, and you look at the colors being used. You watch *Ellen* and *The View*, and see what

FIGURE 3.5 Yep, it's your mom who's playing the social games.

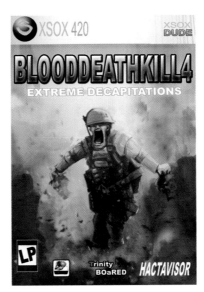

FIGURE 3.6 This is not a game for your mom.

topics they cover. And, of course, you examine the most popular game among those people and borrow from it. This process is exactly what the mood board is for. Start collecting images that you think would work for your social group and you will find that, when you get a body of images together, certain styles keep rising to the top. This is your subconscious helping you out. Listen to it, it's probably right.

Size and Formats

Because this game is going to be on a social website, it needs to adhere to the format rules for that medium. This means that the same size constraints that apply to website building apply here.

A great place to start is determining the most commonly used screen size and pixel resolution for your target group. This information changes all the time, so it's a good idea to follow the latest information on the Internet. Plenty of websites do nothing but publish the findings of nationwide surveys on hardware and software use. Because the size of the screen dictates the size of all of the assets you will need to create, it is very important to define that parameter before work begins. Just to be clear, when we are talking about screen resolution, we are talking about a window that pops up in your browser that you do not need to scroll in order to see the whole game. It is perfectly feasible to make a game that is 1024x3720 pixels and will be played on 1920x1080-resolution monitors. However, players would constantly (and inconveniently) have to scroll through the game to see it all. In the game world, this is just not done. In general, you don't want to create any inconvenience that might give players an excuse not to play your game.

According to many of these sites, an average screen resolution is 1366x768 pixels. So, any art assets that you create should be optimized for this resolution. If, for instance, you wanted to make a game that would take up half the screen, you would create your assets for a 1366x384-pixel high-resolution screen (**FIGURE 3.7**). If you wanted to make a character that was about a quarter of the screen height, you would make him around 200 pixels high.

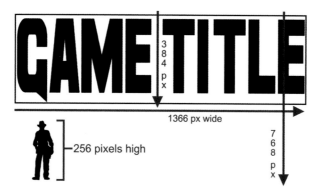

FIGURE 3.7 Comparison of screen sizes.

Scaling

Because you can't know every screen resolution on which your game will be played, you always have to account for *scaling*, that is, resizing your art smaller or larger to accommodate every possible screen context. You can do this in a few different ways in Photoshop, but most artists use the *transform* or the *free transform* tools. This allows you a visual reference while scaling, whereas some of the other options only allow for a numeric input.

When something is scaled, its dpi doesn't usually go with it, and that is what's called a breaking point. This is the point where Photoshop gives up and you lose visually clarity. In essence, when you scale something up, you are stretching the same amount of pixels over a larger area, and although Photoshop works quite a bit of magic to hold your image together, it can't get blood from a turnip, and you get a visual breaking point (**FIGURE 3.8**). Of course, scaling vector art is a different story, because it is code-based it scales far better and with no errors.

FIGURE 3.8 This image shows the word SCALE scaled up and down at the same resolution. Notice what happens to the edge of the lettering.

Photoshop produces the best scaling results when resizing a higher resolution down to a smaller resolution. In fact, the visual benefit of going from larger to smaller is a rule of thumb in game graphics, which is why most artists work at a higher resolution than is necessary. Doing so also provides the higher-resolution images required for magazines and promotional material.

In our example of a screen size of 1366x768, an artist might work at double or triple that resolution and then scale down the image for the final commit. The only caveat (as you learned in Chapter 2, "Pipelines for Games," with the corporate logo) is that sometimes what is legible at a larger size is not readable at a lower size.

For games, it is common for the engineers to scale the art in the code on the fly. Sometimes this is the best way to resolve memory issues or format changes. It falls to the art director to evaluate whether the engineers' scaling programming produces aesthetically acceptable results.

Graphics Formats

Most artwork for social games is saved in a PNG format because of its ability to maintain a transparent background. This allows you to overlay your work onto other assets without a background border. However, most art assets for social games are actually created in PSD or TIFF formats because they support image layers that are much easier to work with than a flat image. Unfortunately, the two formats have larger memory needs than PNG, and are therefore not suitable for the memory footprint of most games.

Photoshop has a special save function just for producing assets to be used on the Web, called "Save for Web" (**FIGURE 3.9**). We used it a bit in the last chapter to make a button palette. We did not, however, discuss the fact that it eliminates as much extraneous info as possible. By default, a normal Photoshop file saves with a few bytes of information that is extraneous for game use. You can view that information in the options menu of a file if you open a saved file and look in the details section of the properties. Select *Remove Properties and Personal Information* on the bottom of the windows, and you will get another popup that lists particular pieces of the save (**FIGURE 3.10**).

"Save for Web" gives you the option to remove some of this information when saving. Getting rid of a few bytes of information might not seem like a lot of savings in a single file, but multiply that by tens of thousands of assets in a game, and it starts to add up.

"Save for Web" also allows you to change formats and preview the results. You can also apply image optimizing, percentage scaling, and color indexing. "Save for Web" is great when you have to ensure that all your files are compatible. With numerous artists working on images, this Photoshop feature enables one person to examine the properties of each art asset and make sure that it is suitable to be committed to the game engine.

FIGURE 3.9 The Save for Web window in Photoshop.

FIGURE 3.10 The Save As Properties popup menu.

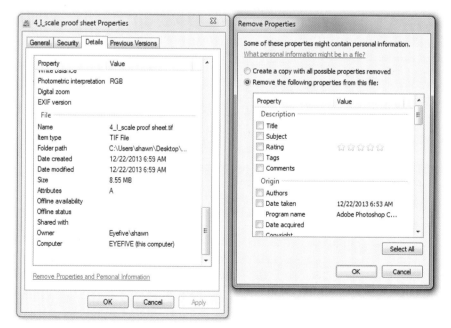

Characters for Social Games

Over the years, social games have definitely distinguished themselves as a unique entertainment form. As console games become more and more realistic, the social space seems to go more toward the cartoons of the '50s. Large heads and tiny bodies are common, and pastel palettes and simple lines can be found throughout the net. Make no mistake—more than a few games out there have hard-core rendering styles; but for the most part, cute 1950s-style cartoon characters seem to be the target style.

Characters in social games (and other aspects of the art world) are sometimes measured in *heads*. So, a character that is two heads high would be divided into two parts of equal height: his head and an equally tall body. A character only two heads high gives you a character with a giant head and a tiny body. You most likely have seen characters like this as farmers and frontiersman, maybe knights. This ratio gives the viewer a good look at the face, and if you are all about showing emotion on the character, it is a good way to go. It also saves on animation. If you can't see legs moving very well, executing a walk cycle becomes much less complicated.

The main problem with the two-head ratio is that it's hard to sell costumes to players in a microtransaction when the players can't see them clearly on the character's body. So, you tweak the ratio a bit to a three-head ratio. You still get the big head feel, but you can see the body much better, thus encouraging players to dress their characters in many wonderful add-on costumes. Many companies have switched to a larger character body for this reason alone. Computers have also evolved to provide much higher resolution, which allows you to create characters with more detail.

In **FIGURE 3.11**, you can see three different ratios for the same character. It almost looks like father, teen, and baby. The head in all three images is exactly the same height, only the bodies have been stretched out. In traditional art terms, a normally proportioned human is eight heads high: three heads for the torso, four for the legs, and one for the head (**FIGURE 3.12**). In Photoshop, you can use the guides and the ruler to show these divisions. In social games, you will most often be asked to design characters in the one-, two-, and three-heads high range.

With the ever-changing social market, it essentially will be up to you to decide which ratio you would like to use, and that is why you should do extensive research before you start designing characters for your project. You don't want to have infant-size characters in a war simulation or realistically proportioned bikini babes in a farm-simulation game. Or maybe you do?

At this point, the art team is chugging away on assets. The animator is animating, the UI guy is UI–ing, the illustrator is illustrating, concepts are being visualized, and finished assets are integrated into the game. The refinement process happens on the fly at this point. As features are implemented and tested, decisions are made to keep or change assets as needed.

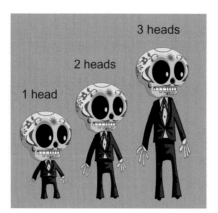

FIGURE 3.11 Characters in social games are usually designed using three different ratios, measured in heads.

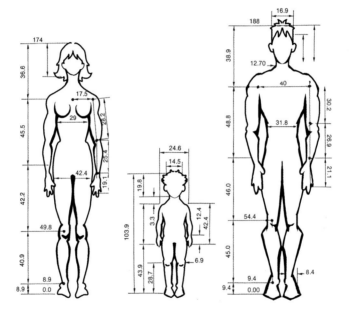

FIGURE 3.12 Realistic human height ratios.

Toward the end of this cycle, the art director will start to limit changes in order to maintain his schedule and avoid what is called *feature creep*. During development, team members inevitably think of additional features that could require a lot of new work. Sometimes these additional elements are approved if the game needs a little extra kick because it is underperforming or is just not fun. However, uncritical approval of new features means a game can't reach completion, development costs skyrocket, and it can fall victim to feature creep, eventually collapsing under the weight of its never-ending ambitions.

Going Live

When a social game is fully programmed, it has been tested, the bugs are cleared, and it works on the server, it can then go live and be made available to the public to play on the social media website. Going live is a very nervous time for social game makers. Every little click is scrutinized, group usage is tracked, and spending habits of players are analyzed.

Assuming no serious issues surface, the art team gets a little break as the producer and the designer determine how the game is doing through the dissection of the metrics.

Downloadable Content

With a social game, everything in it is downloadable, but the term "downloadable content" (DLC) specifically refers to add-ons and features that are made available (usually at additional cost) after a game is released.

For a social game, DLC is very important because in a free-to-play business model, most of the money is made through microtransactions after players install and start using the game. Because DLC often constitutes new characters, new graphics, new levels, and in the case of our slot machine, new graphic themes, the art department carries much of the responsibility for producing those DLC assets. Sometimes when a social game lasts for years, a whole team does nothing but continue to make assets for that game just to provide players with tons of add-ons to keep them interested and paying that nickel a week.

ART FOR WEBSITES

Art for websites may seem like an unrelated topic, but because social games play within a website, you need to be aware of the art and design conventions that should factor into your game's art style.

When you go to a Country Western bar, do you feel more at home in a tuxedo or a pair of jeans and a Stetson? The tuxedo could be fun, but if you are trying to fit in, the jeans and hat are better choices. It is the same with social games. You do not want to stray too far from the conventions used in websites because doing so will confuse people. The general public has spent years learning where things usually are on a website, and they get confused and frustrated when you switch things up too much.

When previously discussing wireframes, we talked a bit about layout and some of the reasons for the user-interface choices we made. Most of these choices reflected those made for most contemporary websites. We just switched out the content to make a game screen. When you are in the process of creating game assets, and you know a UI element will be needed onscreen, you should take inspiration (and design decisions) from Web designers. After all, you are in their Country Western bar.

Consider using *Format Responsive Layouts* for a website. This means that when you are looking at a website on your 17-inch laptop and then switch to viewing the same site on a phone or tablet, the layout changes to accommodate the different screen sizes. For games, this presents some interesting challenges because so much of the gameplay is usually dependent on the screen size. When you change the formats of some games, it also changes the way the game plays.

As you can see in **FIGURES 3.13** and **3.14**, when made playable on a mobile device, the game has to be radically changed to accommodate the smaller screen. The UI was also adjusted to the new format. The nuts and bolts elements are still there, but wouldn't you rather play this game on a laptop? Hell, yeah, but to hit a wider market and allow people to play whenever and wherever and however they want, both formats must be considered and the art optimized for both. A whole host of things must be done to realize this level of flexibility. You learn what to do later in this book, but for now it's enough to realize that this might happen.

Most websites these days offer multiple versions of their sites depending on whether you access it with a computer, a tablet, or a mobile phone. You can force your browser to view any Web page on your phone as a full-sized computer-optimized Web page, but the page will run faster if you accept the mobile version, and you'll have to do a heck of a lot less scrolling.

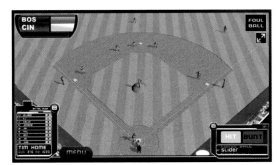

FIGURE 3.13 Screen with a horizontal orientation.

FIGURE 3.14 Screen with a vertical orientation.

EXERCISE 6: CREATING A CASINO GAME SKIN

In this exercise, you will produce and assemble assets to make a casino slot-machine game skin. You'll make various UI elements based on an existing wireframe, and then work on several assets to theme the piece. In the end, you should be able to make dozens of these if you wish.

The Assignment

Using the slot machine wireframe provided in the Resources folder and the chosen theme, you will create your own Dias de los Muertos Casino Skin named Loco Dinero.

What Is a Casino Game Skin?

The layout of our game is everything you would expect from a classic slot machine: three windows and a button just like in Vegas. But in social games, it makes sense (and makes money) to revisualize a game you've already made and give it a new look. You may have seen this in Vegas, as well. The Cleopatra slot, the cute little fish slot, and the wolf slot are the same game hardware and software with just a different appearance. That appearance is called a *skin* in the game world.

The skin you are going to create is "Dia de los Muertos," the Day of the Dead— a traditional Meso-American holiday that celebrates people's ancestors, and honors both death and the cycle of life. It is filled with beautiful painted skeletons and wonderful colors.

In a game studio, when a theme has been chosen for a game, the artist can focus on any portion of the theme and incorporate it into the game. He can also put his own spin on the theme. For instance, "Dia de los Muertos" is a somewhat dark theme dealing with the death of loved ones; but if the images are happy skeletons and beautiful flowers, it loses the dark mood and celebrates the happy fun part, which is what you are going to do.

Mood Boards, Again

Whether you grew up celebrating the holiday or you have never heard of it, it's always *a great idea to put some ideas together in a mood board.* This helps you organize your ideas and will give you a tool to explain to others what you would like to do. **FIGURE 3.15** is a mood board I threw together on the current subject.

Wireframes

Because this is a re-skin of an existing game, you already have wireframes. Unfortunately, for an imaginative person like you, the code was finished and the mechanics worked out a long time ago, so you have limited creative freedom. If you were

FIGURE 3.15 A mood board that will be used as inspiration for a Dia de los Muertos-themed game.

FIGURE 3.16 Slot machine wireframe.

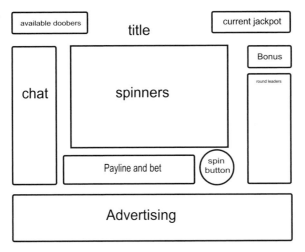

to come up with a great idea for this particular skin that required some framework restructuring, however, it might not be impossible (**FIGURE 3.16**). You would just need to verify the possibility with the engineer, sell management on the concept, and determine that you have the time and budget to execute your innovation.

In the wireframes, you can see where all the game elements need to go, along with the kind of assets that will be needed and in what sizes. Since this is not the first time around for this game, you are simply switching old assets from the following list for new ones:

- Game background
- Game title
- Game title decorations
- Main spinner window
- Main spinner window background
- An available doobers box
- A current jackpot box
- A bonus box
- Current win status box
- Advertising
- Round leader boards
- Spin button
- Pips (10 points on each side)
- Three numeric symbols
- Three alphabetic symbols
- Three character symbols

Begin with a Concept Drawing

Just as when you were drawing the character concept, now you're going to rough in the look of the skin using Photoshop. In a professional atmosphere, this would allow the colleagues involved to see the direction you are going and make comments before you final your work.

There are no rules when concepting, but speed is the name of the game. As you learned, you can use whatever you want from the Internet because this concept image will never be published. So if you find a piece of UI you would like to use, throw it in. If you find a character you would like to use, grab it. If you find backgrounds or numbers or letters or anything, use them. Just remember that before you final, you must replace those assets with original assets, or some lawyers will be sending you a nice letter.

The concept drawing for this re-skin is going to be a little different because you will be tracing over the existing wireframe. In this way, you will have your layout all set to go.

1. In Photoshop, from the Resources folder, open the "Chpt 3_casino wireframe" image, or create your own image to match the one shown previously.

2. Start a new layer and name it *titles*.

3. Pen in the title *Loco Dinero*, and place it in the middle of the page just above the spinner window. Open the Blending options, and tag Stroke.

   With the main title in place, you can go crazy. Well, sort of crazy. You know that the boxes can't change, but they can be dressed up; and you know that you will need pips on either side of the spinner window for the payout line. But how they look is up to you. Sometimes it is beneficial to slug in a color blob when you're not sure what you will place there. This gives you a size and color reference when you final it later.

4. Work like this until you have a very basic idea of where things go. When you are happy with your concept, and would like to start refining some of the ideas you've come up with, collect all of the concepting layers into a single layer group so you can reference it while working on the final assets (**FIGURE 3.17**).

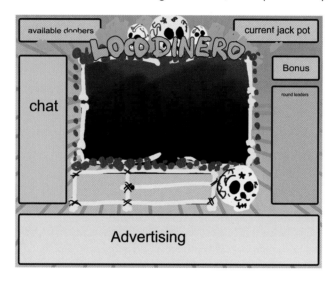

FIGURE 3.17
Concept and
color sketch.

Start Creating Final Assets

In a game studio, before you can progress, you would have to obtain *approval* from your art director, a go-ahead to clean up (finalize) your rough sketches. Let's pretend you got that, and you can begin working on the assets you will need to fill out the page.

Also in a game studio, you would have to create items from that list of assets in a particular order, so that the people you're working with can integrate the assets into the engine according to their standard workflow. This kind of collaboration looks great on paper, but being an artist is a touchy-feely thing. Sometimes when you're having a hard time getting your head into a project and the first thing on your task list isn't working for you, it's a good idea to skip right to the dessert and do your favorite part first. You may want to clear this with everyone, but they will probably understand because they've been there, too. So if you would like to do funny characters instead of leader board squares, go ahead. Just know that at some point you're going to have to come back and work on ALL the stuff on that list.

Creating the Background

Now that you've come to terms with your project, and drawn a lot of inspirational characters to get your head in the game, you're ready to address those list items. Let's start by creating our Day of the Dead background.

1. Open a new layer at the very bottom of the stack and name it Background.

   This will be the furthest backplane in the layout, and is usually not animated. It must not visually compete with the rest of the layout, so no bold colors or sharp dark lines.

2. Lay down a color ramp or use a fill, and then apply a color ramp in the Blending properties (**FIGURE 3.18**). Hide all the layers except for the background image. Pick two colors that are bone-colored—one light and one dark—and make sure that the darker one is at the bottom. The colors shown are 208, 177, 157 and 199, 178, 153.

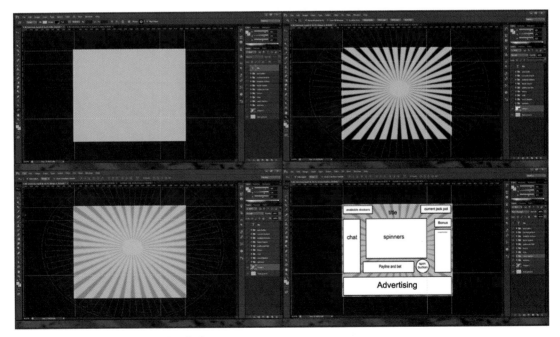

FIGURE 3.18 Adding a background to the layout.

3. From the Shape tool, pick the Registration Target II shape that looks like some radial lines. Set the fill to a **dark red**, and the Stroke to a **brownish-gray** color with a stroke size of **5 pts**. Scale the shape such that its outer edge is beyond the edges of the image frame.

4. Now adjust the Transparency of the layer to **30%** (**FIGURE** 3.19). Hide all the layers, and check your work to make sure you've executed what you wanted. If you have, then you can move on to the next stage.

    Know that you aren't locked into that background for the project. If you have a better idea later or find that the image just isn't working, you can change it. For now at least, you have something that would work.

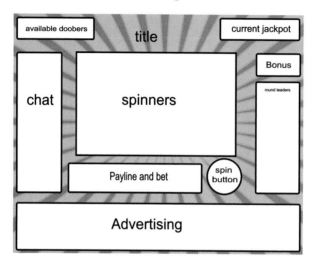

available doobers   title   current jackpot

Bonus

chat   spinners   round leaders

Payline and bet   spin button

Advertising

FIGURE 3.19 Layout with background.

Main Titles

No single graphic element can make or break your game like the main titles. It's the first thing players see when they open the page, and the thing they will remember when deciding whether to continue playing. Suffice it to say the titles better be good.

As you've learned, titles are usually drawn in Adobe Illustrator, a really good tool for working with vector-based text. The title of our game is Loco Dinero, which roughly translates to Crazy Money.

Oftentimes in the game world, you have to take what is given to you and make it fantastic. So what do we know about our game? It is going to be a cartoony Day of the Dead game. The colors associated with the holiday are mostly white, black, and red, which will work well for the UI and the background. Bones and skulls factor into the style, so some text made out of bones might be a good place to start. Gold also factors into the casino style and Mexican heritage, so that color might also work. Colorful flowers could also be a good addition. So many choices.

1. Begin by selecting the Text tool, and typing *LOCO DINERO*. Choose a bold, fat font to start with.

    Generally speaking, if you were to research fonts that made you think of Mexico, you would come up with two types: The first would be a very ornate script-like font that suggests the lace and floral images often used in Mexican art. Such a font is beautiful but sometimes hard to read. The second font would evoke the rough, hand-painted folk art script, which looks great, but might be hard to incorporate into this theme while maintaining a professional look.

2. With the words entered, you can apply different fonts and see if you can locate something that works for you. Keep the color of the font black for now so you're not distracted by too many choices.

FIGURE 3.20 suggests that we have five likely choices: ASH, ALLEY OOP, COFFEE HOUSE, DAMN NOISY KIDS, and GHOST WORDS. These were created by various artists, and their licensing information is available online. Fonts that you do not make yourself may need to be purchased for commercial use. The layers have been named to match the fonts' names, so they can be looked up easily.

FIGURE 3.20 Choosing a font.

FIGURE 3.21 shows the font we chose to use—Alley Oop by A.J. Paglia—and the author requests a donation for the use of his font. It's a nice compromise between the folk and the script styles and also has a cartoon feel so, all in all, it's a pretty good fit. Now let's work on color.

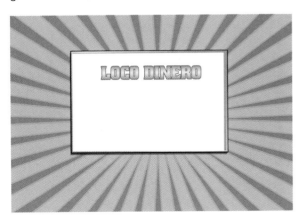

FIGURE 3.21 Color added to the font via the blending options.

3. Select the text layer, and open the Blending properties. Choose the Gradient Overlay option, and click the gradient. This opens the color bar.

4. Change the black to a **dark red**, and the white to a **full red**. Now click the Stroke bar, and size the stroke to **8 px**, and choose an **orange-brown** color. This color will help settle the eye while you dial in other choices. Check out how this looks on your frame.

   This actually might work, but you should explore at least a few more options (**FIGURE 3.22**).

FIGURE 3.22 Exploring color variations.

5. Duplicate the layer and change the color of the ramp to an **orange-yellow**. This will look like gold, and it is also a preset gradient in Photoshop. You can add another color stop into the ramp, if you like.

6. Now repeat this process one more time using the colors from the background. Flip through the layers to see which one is working the best for you.

7. When you've made your color decision, hide the other two layers and begin to adjust the text layout. Choose the Text tool and highlight the text. Choose "Create warped text" > Arch. Set the Blend to **+7** and the rest of the settings to **0**.

8. Adjust the text so it breaks at the top line of the spin window. Unhide the rest of the windows, and scale down the text so it does not clip into any of the other windows.

9. In the layers blending options, add a stroke and a bevel emboss.

   As you can see in **FIGURE 3.23**, we chose the gold color, so as the piece progresses, you will want to reinforce the impression that the text is made from solid gold.

FIGURE 3.23 Adding stroke and emboss to the title text.

As powerful as it is, Adobe Photoshop is not the master of manipulating text; but only a poor UI artist blames his tools, so we're going to do a bit of strong-arming to get the results we want. By this, I mean we are going to use functions in Photoshop in ways they weren't exactly designed. Dum, dum, dummmm!

10. Create an inner stroke between the dark orange and the color ramp. You can do this by going into the Blending options and selecting Inner Glow (**FIGURE 3.24**).

    You might also have used Inner Shadow, but we're looking for an even stroke, and a shadow has directionality parameters that make it a bit harder to set up.

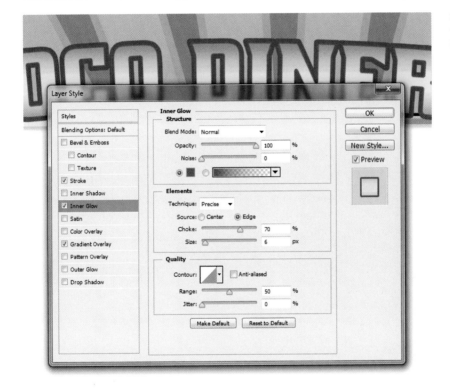

FIGURE 3.24 Adjusting the inner glow in the blending options.

11. After selecting Inner Glow in the Blending properties, change the color to **red**. Change the Blend mode to **Normal**, and set the Opacity to **100%**, Technique to **Precise**, Choke to **75%**, and Size to **6 px**. Leave the other parameters at their default values.

    What you've done is turned the normally fuzzy glow function into a hard shape, which in this case, makes the lettering look a bit more embossed.

12. Speaking of embossed, click the Bevel & Emboss tab, and change the Style to **Outer Bevel**. Set the Depth to **100%**, and the Direction to **Up**. With Size set to **8 px**, you should be good. As you can see in **FIGURE 3.25**, the titles are starting to pop.

FIGURE 3.25 Adding bevel and emboss to the title.

Now for the fun part. You're going to customize the font a bit by using skulls to replace every letter "O" in the title, but you want them to have the same treatment as the text (**FIGURE 3.26**).

FIGURE 3.26 Creating little skulls to add detail to the title.

13. Select the text layer, and with the Magic Wand tool, select an O in the word "Loco." Create a new layer, and fill the selected shape with a **red** color. Fill in the middle.

14. Copy and paste the layer style from the text layer to the new layer with the red O. Doing so should give you a copy of an O from the title. Open a new layer and draw a little skull face using the darkest color in the title. Group the layers, and copy and place them over every O in the title. It should fit pretty well, but you may need to clean up the edges and scale and rotate things a bit.

15. Duplicate and merge the three skull O layers and the original title text file layer. Drag the new layer below the title text layer, and name it *shadow layer*.

16. With the "shadow layer" selected, in Hue/Saturation, drag the Lightness sliders all the way to dark. Select the same color that you painted the skulls, and use it to fill the new black shape. Then, slide the new layer up and behind the text to give the appearance of thickness.

17. Using the Perspective tool, pinch the bottom of the shadow layer a little. Use the Brush tool to clean up the edges and erase where necessary (**FIGURE 3.27**).

FIGURE 3.27 Adding
a shadow layer to give
the appearance of
thickness.

18. To create the effect of light on the titles, select the text layer again, and using the
Magic Wand, select the text (**FIGURE 3.28**). Create a new layer above all of the
title-oriented layers, and fill it with a **white** color.

FIGURE 3.28 Adding
lighting effects to the
title.

19. Using the Elliptical Marquee oval selection tool, select the bottom portion of the
white layer in a large arch that extends across the middle. Cut that selection. In
the layer properties, lower the Opacity of the white layer to **30%**.

20. Create a new layer, and name it *glare*. You are now going to make a glare, flare,
sparkle shape to highlight the text. Use the Polygon Lasso tool to create an
8-point star/snowflake-like shape, and fill it with **white**.

21. Deselect the object. Choose the Brush tool with a soft brush that is big enough
to obscure the middle of the star. Give the star one tap of the brush, and you are
good to go. Translate that up to the text and—Whoo-hoo!—instant lens flare.

22. Select all the layers and collect them in a group called *LocoDineroTitle*, as shown
in **FIGURE 3.29**.

TIP Don't ever delete
the layers after you've
decided not to use
them. Simply turn off
their opacity. You never
know what will happen
down the road, and if you
decide you would rather
go with the red font
rather than the gold one,
it is much easier if you
do not have to recreate
the red layer. Game artist
rule #124: The second
after you throw some-
thing out permanently
is the second you will
need it.

FIGURE 3.29 Grouping
all layers into a new
group.

The Spinner's Background

The spinner's background is the space behind the little spinning dials. Traditional slot machines used three cylinders because that constituted the mechanical limitations of the times. But our game will have five areas for spin cylinders. This is how the code was set up for the previous game, and it is one of the constraints you have to work within. Your background will not spin, but your spinner icons will appear to spin. This means that the background image must not compete with the spinners.

The team agreed on a lace pattern for the spinner background (**FIGURE 3.30**). Besides being a key element in Mexican culture, lace is often a tablecloth, so players will be used to seeing things on top of it. You can create your own lace pattern in Photoshop, but it is once again useful to find a reference lace image on the Internet.

FIGURE 3.30 Skull image worked into the lace pattern.

1. Open a new file. The next task will get too large memory-wise to create it in the same memory-heavy window you've been working in. Make the new file the size of the spinner window—1200x670—and name it *spinner window*.

2. You can use Photoshop premade shapes if you like. Photoshop installs with some very lace pattern-like shapes, or you could trace over your reference image. We have worked a skull into our lace pattern just to personalize it a bit.

   As you can see, in **FIGURE 3.31** we used the Freeform Pen tool to create a floral pattern. There is no stroke and the fill is a whitish color on a dark gray background.

FIGURE 3.31 Enlarged area of the lace pattern with skulls.

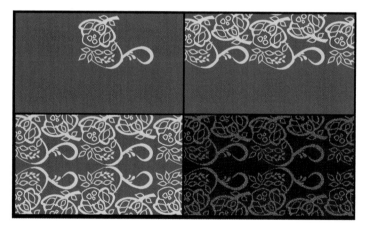

3. Save your lace pattern to back it up, and then save it again as *Lace 1*.

   You will be collapsing this image, but it is important to keep the original lace pattern just in case you need to alter it in some way down the line. Lace is a repeated pattern, so you need only to create one lace element, and then duplicate it.

4. After you fill half of the area, select all the shapes and layers and collapse them. Then duplicate that collapsed layer, flip it vertically, and translate it down to the bottom of the page.

5. Create a new layer under the two layers that you have just created and fill it with a **darker gray** color. Save your file. It should be looking pretty good.

6. To create a proper lace look, collapse the three layers into one layer, and open the Filter gallery. Select the texture called Stained Glass, and set it to a Cell Size of **3**, a Border Thickness of **3**, and a Light Intensity of **0** (**FIGURE 3.32**). This does a good job of mimicking the appearance of a fabric. Click OK, and return to the main window.

FIGURE 3.32 Use the stained glass filter.

7. Select the image, and click Copy.

8. In the main window, duplicate the spinner box layer, and create a new layer below that copy. Merge down the shape layer.

9. With the Magic Wand tool, select the inside of the box. Choose Edit > Paste Special > Paste Into, and scale to fill the space (**FIGURE 3.33**).

10. Adjust the brightness of the lace image until almost no contrast is left in the image.

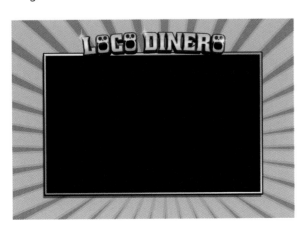

FIGURE 3.33 Use a lace pattern as a subtle background for spinners.

Making a Skull

Now that you have some idea of where you're going, you'll need some assets to get you there. Because the character symbols are the highest-resolution images you will make, you should start with them. In this case, they will not only serve as wheel symbols, but you can also use them as decorations around the game skin.

FIGURE 3.34 Finished skull character.

Sometimes choosing which symbols to make can be a hard decision. You want something that is going to sell the game theme, but it also has to be exciting enough to draw attention. For instance, for this Day of the Dead game, the first thing that comes to mind is the painted skull. It is a very intriguing visual element and has many design possibilities. It is the No. 1 icon of our holiday and an easy choice for the first symbol. Other things are associated with the holiday, such as flowers, cakes, graveyards, bands, and drinks. But the skull head, shown in **FIGURE 3.34**, will be our linchpin symbol.

1. Create a new layer named *skull base*.

2. The next step in making a skull is the same as you performed with the concept drawings: lay down a medium tone—a blue-gray in this case.

3. To get a perfect arch on the top of the skull, use the Elliptical Marquee selection tool and fill the shape. Then erase areas for the mouth and add shapes for the jaw (**FIGURE 3.35**).

4. Make a cut for the mouth because you are going to use a stroke around the outside. Open the blending options and click the Stroke tab. Make the stroke **8 px** and a **darker gray** color, but not black.

5. Use the elliptical tool to create the eyes and nose (**FIGURE 3.36**). Scale the left eye down a bit to give a feeling of volume.

FIGURE 3.35 Base layer for the skull.

FIGURE 3.36 Create the eyes and nose.

6. Next, you will create the telltale markings of the Dias skull. This can be done in several ways. You could find some symbols in the Photoshop library that might work, or you could choose the Freeform Pen tool and create your own. You can create them in a flat plane, and then use the Warp tool to make them look like they are curving around the shape. So many different ways. The skull in **FIGURE 3.37** was created using a mixture of these methods.

The teeth were created using three different layers (**FIGURE 3.38**). The first layer was just a colored plane. It is pretty close to white, so it sticks out as being a separate area from the whitish skull. The next layer is the dark separation lines between the teeth, which were just hand-drawn with a hard brush tool. The third is the shadow layer.

FIGURE 3.37 Create the telltale markings of the Dias skull.

FIGURE 3.38 Add shadows to the teeth.

7. Create a new layer and call it *tooth shadow*. With the Magic Wand tool, select the white of the white layer you created. In the shadow layer, strip a **dark gray** color across the top. Adjust the Opacity value to look like a proper shadow, and you're done with the teeth.

8. Create a new layer and call it *skull shadow* (**FIGURE 3.39**). Use the Magic Wand tool to select the very first layer you created. With that layer selected, return to the new skull shadow layer, and just as you did with the teeth, create a shadow line in a **dark gray** color along the bottom of the skull. Adjust the Opacity value to match the teeth, and save your work.

9. This next step may seem a bit repetitive. Create a new layer and call it *skull highlight* (**FIGURE 3.40**). Once again, use the Magic Wand tool to select the very first layer you created. Return to the new skull highlight layer and again create a highlight in a **light gray** color along the top of the skull.

NOTE The Magic Wand tool may be hiding. The default setting will let you paint selections, but pressing Shift-W will revert it to the old useful version.

FIGURE 3.39 Add a dark-gray shadow.

FIGURE 3.40 Create a light-gray highlight.

10. Finally, create a new layer called *eye right* (**FIGURE 3.41**). Use the elliptical selection tool to create a small, vertically oriented shape the size of a pupil, and fill it in with a **light gray**. With the shape selected, stripe a bit of **darker gray** across the top to give it the impression of sitting inside the eye socket. Duplicate the layer and rename it *eye left*. Now with the eyes on separate layers, you can move them around to suit your needs.

FIGURE 3.41 Add eyes on a separate layer.

11. Combine all the layers into a layer group, and name it *Skull Head*.

Flower Symbol

The second symbol you'll be using is a flower. This may seem like a lame choice, but a flower has many benefits. You need to make only one master flower, and you can produce many variations quickly. A flower adds a lot of color and can be customized to fit any size. If the skull is the linchpin, the flower is the workhorse.

1. Begin with an actual image of a flower. We used a rose from the garden and modified it by simply drawing on top of it (**FIGURE 3.42**). It is available in the Resources folder. Create a new layer, and name it *rose outline* (**FIGURE 3.43**). Using the Shape tool with no stroke, paint over the darker areas of the flower to form a rough graphic approximation of the petals in outline. Make sure you create a closed border around the petals.

FIGURE 3.43 Rose outline.

FIGURE 3.42 Photograph of a rose from the garden with modifications applied to it.

2. Create a new layer named *flower color* and place it below the rose outline layer. With the Eyedropper tool, select a **red** from the photo of the rose. Choose the Paint tool with a hard brush, and paint in the petals.

3. Create another layer called rose shadow above the rose color layer (**FIGURE 3.44**). Select a slightly **darker red** from the image. Paint in the shadow areas along the inside of the outlines. The important part here is to make sure that you have the color portions as separate layers so you can later create multiple flowers in various colors.

FIGURE 3.44 Rose shadows.

4. Find an image on the Internet with multiple flowers to use as reference. Create several color variations of your flower using the colors in the image using the Hue/Saturation adjustment (**FIGURE 3.45**).

   Just a warning, the shadow color layer will need to be adjusted as well and a simple Hue/Saturation adjustment might not give you the effect you want. You may need to repaint it with a better color choice.

FIGURE 3.45 The layers of the rose image in progression.

5. Collect your layers into a single layer, and name it *rose red*.

6. Duplicate the original red rose group four times, and name the groups *Pink Rose*, *Carmine Rose*, *Yellow Rose*, and *Orange Rose*. Change the colors to match the names using the flower image as a guide (**FIGURE 3.46**).

FIGURE 3.46 Create different-colored roses from the reference image.

The Mighty Dollar

The third symbol you will use is a customized dollar image. The dollar sells the "dinero," or money side of a slot machine, and it will act as the color background for your titles.

1. To make the dollar, start with a new layer called *dollar background*. With the Rectangular Marquee tool create a dollar-shaped rectangle, and fill it with a **green color** (FIGURE 3.47). In the Shapes gallery, select one of the frame shapes. Set the fill color and the stroke to a **darker green**, and stretch it across the rectangle using the Transform/Scale function.

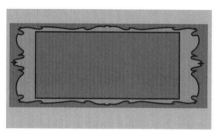

FIGURE 3.47 From the Shapes gallery, select one of the frame shapes.

2. From the Shape gallery, select a shield shape (FIGURE 3.48), and scale it up to form the area for the dollar's face. The shape used here was rotated 180 degrees. Change the colors of the shape to match the dollar's colors, and center it in the middle of the dollar.

FIGURE 3.48 From the Shape gallery, select a shield shape.

3. Open the skull-head file you made previously, and then merge all of the layers. Be careful not to flatten the image, because doing so will give you a white background that you don't want.

4. Choose Image > Adjust > Hue-Saturation, and open the editor. Check the Colorize box. Set the Hue to **138**, the Saturation to **42**, and the Lightness to **–19** to produce a light green color, as shown in FIGURE 3.49.

FIGURE 3.49 Change the skull to a light-green color.

5. Center the skull in the middle of the shield (**FIGURE 3.50**).

FIGURE 3.50 Center the skull in the shield area.

6. Choose the Text tool, and change the color to match the white area of the skull. Then type the number **100**. From the Blending options menu, choose Stroke, and make it a **darker green** color than the dollar's background. Place the 100 text in the upper-right corner of the bill. Duplicate the text layer three times, and place the copies in the three remaining corners (**FIGURE 3.51**).

FIGURE 3.51 Add the numbers to the corners.

7. Save your file once as a PSD or a TIFF image, and then save your file again as a PNG image. Because you may need these dollar files again, you saved a master file, but the master is too memory-intensive to be repeated all over the face of the game. A smaller PNG-format is the answer.

START DECORATING

Now that you have some art to play with, it's time to start laying things out. Make sure that all the decoration files you are working with are in PNG format, including the five flowers, the skulls (green and white), and the dollar. You may also want to create a new folder on your desktop to store just those PNGs.

1. Import the three icons to the spinner area, as shown in **FIGURE 3.52**. You can bring in the rest of the flowers later.

FIGURE 3.52 Bring in all the elements.

2. The first thing to do is snazzy up the border trim. In the chat layer, select the main shape.

3. Open the blending options, and select Bevel & Emboss, Stroke, Gradient Overlay, Drop Shadow, and Inner Shadow.

4. Set the gradient to a **light-green** color at the bottom and a **darker green** at the top.

5. Adjust the stroke to be **8 pts** and **black**.

6. Set the Inner Shadow opacity to **20%** and at a slight angle, then do the same for the Drop Shadow.

7. On the Bevel & Emboss tab, set the Style to **Inner Bevel**, the Technique to **Smooth**, and the Size to **8**. Leave the other values at their defaults. Click OK to exit.

8. Now for more fun. Right-click the layer, and from the Stack options popup menu, choose Copy Layer Style. Paste this style into each of the other boxes—doobers, current jackpot, bonus, round leaders, payline, and advertising. You can do this the same way you copied the style. Right-click the layer, and from the Stack options popup menu, choose Paste Layer Style.

9. Now you will have to go into each box's blending options to adjust the gradient overlay colors to match the ones shown in **FIGURE 3.53**.

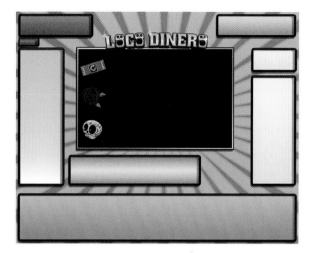

FIGURE 3.53 Paste the layer style to the other areas.

Finishing Skulls

Now that the symbols are in place in the spinner window, you can begin to fill out the rest of the page using duplicate layers (**FIGURE 3.54**).

FIGURE 3.54 Arrange the skulls behind the title text.

1. Hide the two layers, available doobers, and current jackpot. They would just be in the way right now.

2. Select and duplicate the skull layer, and then name the new layer *skull top left*. Move the new layer just behind the N in "Dinero," and ensure that the new layer is behind the text layer. Duplicate the skull layer again, name it *skull top right*, and move the new layer to the right. Flip it horizontally.

3. Duplicate both skull layers again, and name them *skull bottom right* and *skull bottom left*. Translate them down to the bottom of the spinner window, and scale them down to about half size. Arrange them so they are looking away from each other.

Making Money

Now let's spread some cash around.

1. Create a new layer below all the skulls layers, and name it *money background* (**FIGURE 3.55**). Choose the Polygon Lasso tool, and create a shape that looks like a silhouette of a pile of money. Fill it with the same green that is on the dollar. In the Blending options, click the Stroke tab, make it **5 pts**, and set the color to **black**.

FIGURE 3.55 Create a money background.

You want to make it look as if a huge pile of money is behind the skulls. The background you just created will help by filling in any of the color gaps that might occur. However, a few money fans will add some visual interest.

2. Select and duplicate the dollar layer, and name the copy *dollar fan* (**FIGURE 3.56**). Rotate the new layer about 45 degrees counterclockwise. Continue duplicating and rotating layers until a fan is formed (about ten copies). Collapse the dollar fan layers, name it *money fan*, and translate it behind the skull.

FIGURE 3.56 Create a money fan.

3. Copy the money fan layer, and name it *money fan lower*. Translate it behind the skull on the lower portions of the spinner screen, as shown in **FIGURE 3.57**.

FIGURE 3.57 Place the lower money fan.

4. Duplicate the single dollar again and pepper it throughout the image to give the look of a large pile of cash flying around.

5. When you are happy with the results, in a new layer, group all the dollars and the upper dollar fan and call it *money upper* (**FIGURE 3.58**).

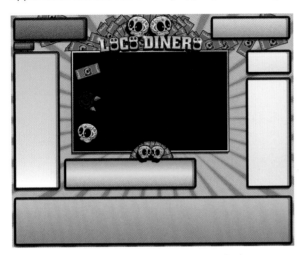

FIGURE 3.58 Collect the money layers into new layer groups.

6. Move the *money fan lower* layer to below the spinner window layer. Make sure you do not group *money fan lower* in with the rest of the money, as it is special and needs to be separate in order to display at the correct level.

Growing Flowers

In a similar fashion, you will duplicate flowers, arranging them into groups and then placing them in strategic locations (**FIGURE 3.59**).

FIGURE 3.59 Add flowers to the spinner window frame.

1. Bring in all the different-colored flowers you made earlier, and put them in the middle of the spinner screen.

2. Reduce them in size by 50%, and arrange them in a row at the bottom of the spinner window. Collect them into a layer when you're happy with the placement, and name it *flowers bottom right*. Make sure the layer is above the skulls and the money layers.

3. Duplicate the layer, and name it *flowers bottom left* (**FIGURE 3.60**). Flip the layer horizontally and translate over to a mirrored position on the right side.

FIGURE 3.60 Duplicate the flowers to other parts of the frame.

4. Duplicate the two layers you just created. Translate them up to the top border of the spinner window. Depending on your layout, you might have to adjust certain flowers, so it's fortunate that they are in layers. Name the two new layers *flowers top right* and *flowers top left*. In the Blending options, apply a drop shadow to each of the flower layers.

Placing PIPs

The pips are where the win or pay lines attach. There are ten of them on each side in this game. Since you already have the flowers out, you will use them as the image portion (**FIGURE 3.61**). A number will be placed over them later to indicate the level of betting. This number placement is often done in code unless the numbers require a special font.

FIGURE 3.61 Use the flowers as pips.

1. Duplicate your flower files again, and arrange them vertically. The order of color does not really matter as long as you don't have two matching flowers next to each other.

2. Scale down the flowers to fit along the side of the spinner window. Try to space them out so that they are an equal distance between centers. Using the guides or grid is very helpful here.

3. When you're happy with the positioning, collect them into a new layer and call it *pip left side*. Duplicate that layer, and call it *pip right side*. Translate it to the right side of the window, and flip it horizontally so that the leaves at the side of the flower point out the other way (always away from the spinner window). Symmetry is better than repetition.

Left and Right Spinner Frame Decoration

So after installing the pips it's obvious that a lot of yellow and orange made the image too busy. To separate the spinner box a little as the main focus of the game, you will create a bit of trim with very little color to act as a visual separator (**FIGURE 3.62**). Sticking with the "Dias" look, you will create a shape that looks similar to a spine.

1. Choose the Pen tool. Create a long shape and make it look like a big bone. The fill color should be the same as the **white** in the skull, and the stroke is **black** at **2 pts**.

2. Now you're going to make a shadow for the bone shape. With the Pen tool still chosen, turn off Stroke, and change the fill to a **medium gray**. Create a long shape inside the bone shape. Make sure you are on a different layer and that this layer is above the bone shape. Name it *bone shadow*.

3. To finish creating the spine, create a new layer above the long shape (**FIGURE 3.63**). Using the same settings we used when creating the bone shape, draw little cross pieces that resemble vertebrae. On top of those, use the Pen tool, no stroke, and place a **darker gray** shape to create a shadow.

FIGURE 3.62 Create a spine-like divider.

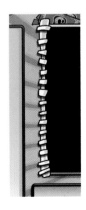

FIGURE 3.63 Finished spine-like divider.

4. The finished look is somewhat spine-like, somewhat cartoon-like, and a decent separation device (**FIGURE 3.64**). Collect the shapes into a single layer, and name it *spine left*. Copy, flip horizontally, and translate the shape to the other side, and name it *spine right*.

FIGURE 3.64 Finished spinner window decoration.

Spin Button

The spin button is the large button that initiates the gameplay. It usually has two states (it is a button after all): active and inactive. Pressing the button in this case will activate a small animation of the button. So you need an image that looks good in its inactive state, and an animation that starts with that inactive state, does stuff, and then loops back to the inactive state.

The image you choose should be button-like, which means a square, rectangle, or circle. You already have a skull ready to go and it is the main symbol of the game, so it's probably a good choice to use here (**FIGURE 3.65**). It also has the potential for some great animation.

FIGURE 3.65 Use the skull as a spin button.

1. Copy one of the skull layers, and name it *skull spin*.

2. Translate it down to where the spin button circle is on the wireframe.

3. Scale it up so it obscures the circle.

   You might add text later, but for now, the image alone is fine.

BACK TO THE SPINNER WINDOW

Now you should fill out some of the icons that appear in the spinner window. The design document calls for three numeric symbols, three alphabetic symbols, and three character symbols. In truth, there would be many more, including some bonus screens, jackpot wins, and the like. But we will not stray from our document (yet). You have the character icons all worked out: the dollar, the rose, and the skull. Put those aside for now and work on the numeric and alphabetic symbols.

Creating Alphabetic Symbols

Creating symbols for the spin area is exactly like making a title. You will use the same techniques that you used to do an entire word to make one letter or number. You are going to be making the J, Q, and K, as a nod to a card deck (**FIGURE 3.66**).

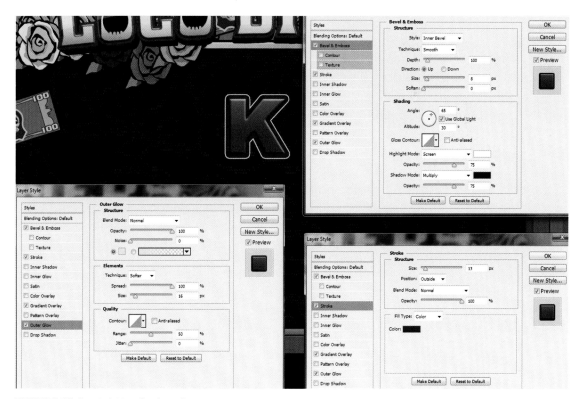

FIGURE 3.66 Create letters for the spinners.

1. Choose the Text tool with an Arial font, and type an uppercase letter **K**. In the Blending options, select Bevel & Emboss, Stroke, Outer Glow, and Gradient Overlay. Make the stroke color the same as the shadow area of the main titles, and in **13 pts**. Set the Gradient Overlay from dark purple to **light purple**.

2. Set the Outer Glow just as we did previously to create a hard line, and make it a **light yellow** color.

3. Duplicate one of the sparkles from the main titles, and add it to the tip of the letter K. Collect the two layers in a group, and name it *K_letter*.

4. Duplicate the group twice. Change one letter group to a **J** and the other to a **Q** (**FIGURE 3.67**). Also change the colors of the gradients to be different from one another, and don't forget to change the folder names. This may seem like a lot of folder renaming, but it's a lot faster than doing it from scratch each time.

   Once you have a template made, it is very easy to generate a lot of these.

FIGURE 3.67 Make other letters from the template you created.

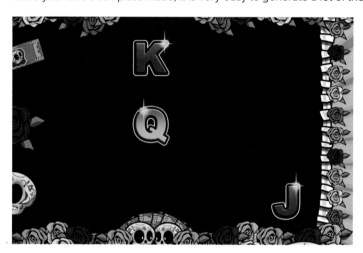

Creating Numeric Symbols

Creating the numerals should be easy now. Just duplicate one of the letter files and type in a number for the letter (**FIGURE 3.68**). The numbers we have chosen are also references to a deck of cards; they are 7, 9, and 10. The one difference is that these have all been made to look like gold. You will also have to move the highlights.

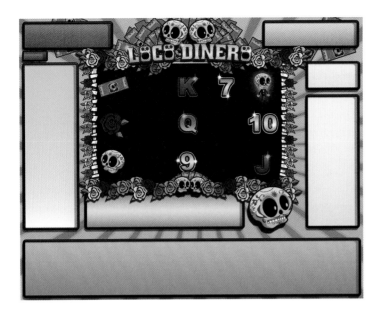

FIGURE 3.68 Create numbers for the spinners.

Filling Out the Window

Remember when we said we weren't going to go beyond what we were asked to do on the design doc? We lied. We liked the little skull guy so much that we gave him a new body (FIGURE 3.69). This kind of ad lib art during a production happens all the time. It is not recommended that you do a lot of it; but if you have a great idea, you should pursue it on your own time and not be afraid to present it to the team. The worst that happens is the art director says no, but the best is that one of your ideas is put into production.

FIGURE 3.69 Add interesting characters to the spinner window.

So we made a full body for the skull head to be used as a bonus win. The skull head will be on one layer and the body on another. The layer group is called *skull full body*. Because the suit is black and the head has a lot of black elements, an outside glow was applied in the blending options.

The addition of the skull guy full body brought up a good point. The skull spinner icon is too similar to the ones you used to decorate the skin and may cause some confusion. You need to change it up a bit, but don't want to change it too much. Not to worry, all you really need to do is change the color a little. The easiest way to do this, and still have the option to change to a different color, is to do it in the blending options (**FIGURE 3.70**).

FIGURE 3.70 Change the skull's color in the blending options.

1. Open blending options and select Color Overlay.
2. Choose a **turquoise-blue** color and set the blend mode to **Multiply**. This will give you the color without diluting any of the detail work.

Lane Dividers

You have copied and moved the icons to fill the board just to show what a screen could look like. Unfortunately, the issue you had with the pips and the main screen is happening again. You need a better visual break between the spinner icons (**FIGURE 3.71**). Let's make some lane dividers.

FIGURE 3.71 Not enough visual break between the spinner icons.

1. Create a tall rectangle that stretches from the top to the bottom of the spinner window. Make sure it is very thin, and about **30x1951 pixels**. Make it a **2-pt.** stroke in **black**.

2. Select the stroke color and change it to a **gray-to-black** gradient.

3. In the blending options, click Bevel & Emboss and Drop Shadow. Change the distance in the drop shadow tab to **25**.

   Because of the offset nature of our spin window and the goofy size due to screen resolution, it's hard to figure out the equal placement of the dividers. If you're good at math, then you can mathematically calculate the placement of each divider using the rulers.

4. If you need another method that doesn't make your head spin, choose View > Show > Grid.

5. With the grid on, you can count the little squares across the screen and figure out the correct distance between four separators to create five slots (**FIGURE 3.72**). It's still math, but it hurts your brain a little less.

FIGURE 3.72 Use the grid to justify the dividers.

6. Once you have a rough idea of the placement, you can move the shapes to whole numbers on the rulers and set the distance using those whole numbers.

7. When you get all four in place, simply slide them all over to where they are supposed to be in the window. Our grid ended up being five squares across with a divider on the sixth.

   The finished dividers should look like those in **FIGURE 3.73**.

FIGURE 3.73 The finished dividers.

Shiny Little Boxes

You will now create a universal shape that you can modify to fit various box needs. You previously made a very similar box for the buttons. This box will act as the background for your advertising, your betting, and most of the individual boxes that will fill your shapes. In a game company, you would most likely create one of these, and the colors would be changed in code when necessary. But to show what a full screen would look like, let's make one for each of the categories you need to flesh out.

1. Create a rectangle using the Rectangle tool. Make the shape **500x160 pixels**, the fill a **blue** color, and the stroke a **black** color **2 pts** wide.

2. Change the fill color to a gradient. Change the stops to a **blue** similar to the one you chose as the fill, and a darker version of the same color. Be careful not to go too dark.

3. In the blending options, select Stroke, Inner Shadow, and Drop Shadow. Make the stroke **2 px** and a **pale yellow** color. Set the Inner Shadow to a distance of **16 px** and a size of **7 pts**. Set the drop shadow to the same numbers. Your shape should look something like **FIGURE 3.74**.

FIGURE 3.74 Make little boxes.

We have duplicated and arranged these elements according to the previous game's layout. This layout would most likely be included in the original wireframe or a supplemental one (**FIGURE 3.75**).

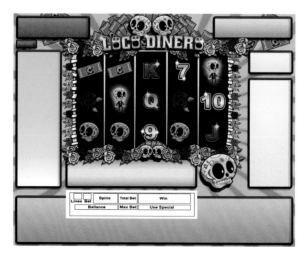

FIGURE 3.75
Supplemental
wireframe.

4. Now make the window where the numbers will appear. Create a new shape using the rounded rectangle tool. Make the fill **charcoal gray** and the stroke a gradient of **2 pts**.

    The numbers will be done in code because they need to change with the gameplay. Make sure you name the blue layer and the window layer similarly, *Bet_Blue* and *Bet_Window,* and also make sure that the window layer is directly above the corresponding blue layer. That's just good housekeeping.

5. Repeat this for all of the blue boxes, naming them appropriately, as shown in **FIGURE 3.76**.

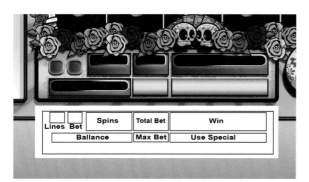

FIGURE 3.76 Wireframe and final boxes.

6. Creating the gold buttons should be old hat for you now. If not, you can refer back to the menu button tutorial in Chapter 2. Just swap the red colors for gold ones.

Notice that the buttons pop out and the boxes with windows recede. In real life this is how information panels are; so as to not frighten you away, we have replicated that here with highlights and shadows.

We will use these boxes and buttons again, so make sure they are named correctly and that they are paired together. Any multilayer buttons you have made should have their layers collected in one layer.

Other Boxes

You're going to be told to do something that you probably would not do if you were working professionally. You're going to create some different-looking boxes so you have a larger variety of tricks in the big bag of tricks that you're filling.

The current jackpot box and doober components

This box has a window similar to the one you made previously, but it doesn't stand out as much because it doesn't include the drop shadow (**FIGURE 3.77**). It's amazing the difference one little effect can make.

FIGURE 3.77 Doober window.

1. The three square buttons and the large rectangle one were made with the Marquee tool, rather than the Rectangle tool. Holding down the shift key and creating a marquee selection gives you a square.

2. Once the shape selection is set, fill it with a color, just as a placeholder. Then in the blending options, select Bevel & Emboss, Stroke, and Drop Shadow.

3. Change the colors in the Gradient Overlay.

4. Fill out the doober box in the same way.

The chat box

Sometimes, as with the chat box, you don't want a large separation between the box you create and the background. You can see this happening with the chat box text-input area. This effect was created by using a color from the lower portion of the background gradient for the fill color of the square shape. Add an inner shadow and an outer glow from the blending options box, and you have what looks like a recessed area in the background (**FIGURE 3.78**).

Round Leaders

You're almost done. The last thing you need to make is a box that will house the round leader information. We have repeated it a bunch of times in yellow. The gray box is where the player's picture will be, and their info will be in text in the space next to it. This box is a mix of the two other boxes you've already made. The yellow part is the button-creation method from the previous chapter, and the gray part is the window method.

FIGURE 3.78 The chat box.

1. With the rectangle tool, create a shape with a width of **635x200 pixels**.

   This size will tile into the current space, with a bit of room left at the end for a scroll arrow. You really need to make only one box in one color and the engineers will propagate it in code. There are multiple boxes displayed here to give a view of what an active game would be like.

2. In the blending options, select Gradient Overlay. This is the hardest part of the process. Select one of the ramps with three colors to give you three stops in your ramp. Change the right stop colors to a **deep orange**, and change the middle stop to a **medium yellow**. Change the far stop to a **light yellow**. You might have to adjust the stop blends to create a ramp like the one shown in **FIGURE 3.79**.

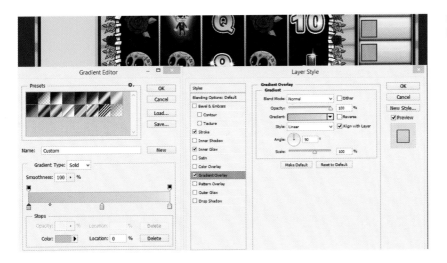

FIGURE 3.79 Round leader board.

3. Click the Stroke tab, and make it **3 px** in a **dark red**.

4. Tic the Inner Glow tab, and make it the same **dark red** at **35 px**.

5. Create a new layer. Using the Marquee selection tool, select an area the same size as the button. Fill it with **white**. Deselect the white fill, and use the Marquee tool to select only the bottom half of the fill. Cut out the selection. In the white fills layer properties, reduce the Opacity to **25%**.

6. Create a new polygon shape that is **195x160 pixels**. Make the fill a **medium gray** and the stroke a few shades **off-black**. Make the stroke width **2 pts**.

   Move the frame to the left side of the box, and center it equally between the top and bottom borders.

7. Collect the three new layers into a group, and name it *leader board yellow*.

   The result should look similar to **FIGURE 3.80**.

ONE LAST PASS

Now that you have most of the pieces in place, you need to perform one final pass just to make sure that everything is working as it should be, and that you are happy with the way all the elements work together.

In a game studio, this would be the time you send a JPG of your work to the whole team to see if anyone has any comments. You don't have to change things just because someone suggests it. It is ultimately up to you and the art director to call it done. That being said, your peers may have opinions or needs that might be helpful to the work and make your piece stronger in the end.

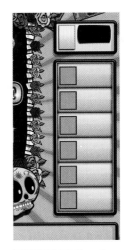

FIGURE 3.80 Round leader boards ready to be populated.

Is Something Bugging You?

While you are awaiting feedback from your peers, it's a good idea to inspect all the elements again one by one. Check for alignment of the boxes, and how they interact with the real estate around them. Check for color and line thickness, and make sure that the blending option elements you wanted to use are turned on. Most of all, look for anything that stands out to you as not right. Chances are, if you feel that way, you are correct and should fix the issue.

CHAPTER 3 WRAP-UP

In this chapter, we covered how to make a game-ready casino skin for a digital slot machine. The techniques you learned aren't just for casino skins but apply to creating any digital social media.

It may have seemed like a lot of work, but in truth, all we were doing here was providing the template for the rest of the work to be done. Our job was to show what the visual design was and to be a guide for the rest of the studio to flesh out respective portions of the game. Your assets will be taken into Adobe Flash and animated into happy little payout wins, and shimmers, and sparkles, and coin waterfalls. The engineers will make sure all of the buttons press, the dials spin, and the leaders of the game are leading. The designers will dial in the metrics, payouts, and monetization.

Finally, when the game is ready for launch, it will go live and players will play. You will go on to your next design challenge, and this process will start all over again (**FIGURE 3.81**).

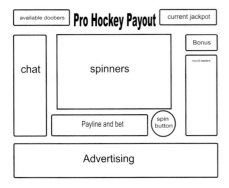

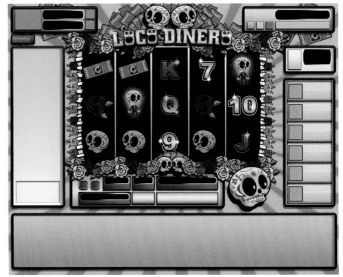

FIGURE 3.81 Wireframe and finished slot machine skin.

4

CREATING A MOBILE GAME

In this chapter, you will examine the process of making a mobile game. Mobile and social games are closely related in content size, and somewhat in style, but they have each evolved into their own separate spaces.

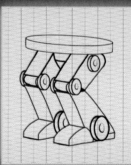

IS THAT A GAME ON MY PHONE?

NOTE To access the resource files and videos, just log in or join peachpit.com, and enter the book's ISBN. After you register the book, links to the files will be listed on your Account page under Registered Products.

All jokes aside, mobile games have by far the most potential of all three of the game types discussed in this book. Console and social games will continue to look better as screen sizes increase and hardware gets faster and smarter; but the largest strides in the future will be on your phone and for just one dominating reason: Everyone has one.

That built-in audience is a prime target for companies that profit by reaching out to as many people as possible. So where do you think all their technology development is going to be aimed? Right at your pocket.

Fortunately for game makers, the returns from game and game-related purchases are high enough to justify continued investment in mobile game companies. The more companies out there, the better chance you have of getting work. So when it is reported that mobile gamers spend over 30 minutes per day playing games, you should smile a little because that is good news for the industry.

THE PIPELINE FOR MAKING MOBILE GAMES

The mobile world as it stands today has been playing catch-up. The computer and console memory specs and computing power are miles ahead of mobile devices. However, it is not an even race. Mobile hardware, spec-wise, is at about the level of a good PC from the year 1994. But considering that the smart mobile phone has not been around as long as the PC, it's doing pretty well.

So when you look at the graphics of mobile games available now and are wondering where the future of mobile gaming is headed, look no further than the current PC/Mac games market for a glimpse of the future (**FIGURE 4.1**).

FIGURE 4.1 Modern mobile games.

Mobile Game Specifics

Knowing the limitations of a mobile device and how to push its performance as far as possible has become a sought-after skill in the game industry. Those who know how to squeeze the most out of every little bit of bandwidth and memory are integral to creating the best-looking games. Right now, console games are at the techno-forefront, followed by social games, with mobile showing up in third place. Obviously, the key to success for the mobile gaming world is being able to replicate the console experience on a phone. Developers are on their way toward that goal, but they are just not there yet.

Levels

The levels in a mobile game are a bit different than you might expect. Take your average games featuring a robot on an alien planet with hostile locals, for example. A normal level in a console game would probably provide about 2 hours of play. That 2 hours x 10 levels costs you 60 bucks, or around 20 hours of average game play.

A mobile game works a little differently. The levels are far shorter, lasting only several minutes at the most. This is because most mobile game players only play while waiting for the bus or standing in line at the bank. Getting involved in a long campaign in which you have to start and stop all the time just does not go over very well. Also, implementing a "save anywhere" feature gets a little memory heavy and is usually not possible in the world of mobile hardware.

Characters

The characters in a mobile game follow this same trend. In a console game, the characters might have millions of polygons. (Polygons are the 3D version of pixels, the basic unit of 3D graphics. They will be further explained in Chapter 5, "Creating Console Game Assets.") Mobile hardware is challenged to animate a character with only thousands of polygons. That makes quite a visual difference. Why is this? Phones just don't have enough computing power yet. Moving the characters, calculating the polygons, and mapping the textures is very memory and processor intensive.

The Bank

You might think of the constraints for making a mobile game as similar to dealing with a bank. You have only so much money in the bank that you can draw on. Although you can take money out, the bank is not going to give you more money than you start with. Mobile games are like that. The phone can only process so much data at a time. If you factor all the things in a game happening at once—the audio, the effects, the playable character, the non-playable characters, the environment, the HUD, all the code, tracking your play history—you can see how you quickly you can become technologically overdrawn in a mobile game.

How do you work with this? You budget your game, processing only those things you need at the moment you need them. Those Level Three aliens do not need to be loaded in Level One so they are stored (probably in a compressed file format) until they are needed. When their time comes, the Level One aliens are dumped from memory so all available storage and computing power can go to running their Level Three companions. Similar resource budgeting and asset swapping is applied to audio and special effects and levels. This way you are always using the most amount of game budget on precisely what you need to be showing at the time.

Your creative choices can also contribute to optimizing your use of hardware resources. If you need more aliens onscreen in Level Four, then Level Four is designed as a graphically simple environment with snow and no trees to calculate. With mobile games, you borrow from here to enhance there. If you find you need trees in the level, then you reduce the aliens' graphic detail. Same fixed techno-budget, you just spend it differently.

NOTE A frame rate is the number of full-screen images per second that a device can display. Higher frame rates require increased processing power. The lower the frame rate, the choppier the onscreen movement. Unfortunately (that budget thing again), increasing graphic detail lowers frame rate.

Digital game makers have worked like this since games began. Working out a realistic technology "budget" is usually done at the beginning of a project, and then revised on the fly as the project progresses. The keepers of this techno-bank are the engineers. They are ultimately responsible for ensuring that the game remains within a certain memory footprint, and able to run at a reasonable frame rate.

Aspect Ratios and Screen Resolutions

Mobile phones, smartphones, cells, and whatever else you want to call them, mobile devices come in a variety of sizes, and as with the social game scene, they represent an ever-moving target to try and find an aspect ratio and resolution to build to (**FIGURE 4.2**). As the mobile device window size remains in constant flux, the resolution gets better and better, and the amount of pixels one can use at a time also shifts. Fortunately, it always seems to lean toward more pixels not less, so that is good news.

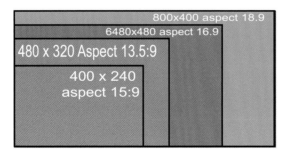

FIGURE 4.2 Mobile pixel ratios.

Generally speaking, before you start a mobile game you do some research to see what the current trend in screen specs is. Just like you did with the social game, you pick one that will allow you to stretch or reduce the screen to fit other screens that might be just a little off your numbers. This allows you to make one game that will be playable on multiple phone types.

EXERCISE 7: CREATING ASSETS FOR A MOBILE ROBOT SHOOTER

With the standard graphic tools you've already used, as well as some new ones, you will create assets for a 3D robot shooter game. You will create characters, several level maps, and some asset textures. You will also animate a 2D explosion effect using a sprite sheet.

The Story

Your game this time is called *Nebula Pirate Robots*. In this game, you don your robot armor, and with two robot friends, land in an alien environment where you fight your way through bloodthirsty aliens who want to steal all the energy pods in the universes. You and your friends are also collecting the pods to power up your super robots and defeat the alien queen, shown in **FIGURE 4.3**.

FIGURE 4.3 Fighting the alien queen.

How to Begin

By now you should be familiar with the art process for starting a game.

▥ Create a theme or a story

▥ Collect images in mood boards

▥ Sketch conceptual drawings

▥ Initiate product development

▥ Build the game

▥ Make loads of money and become famous

For this game, the art director had some mood pieces created by a company that specializes in doing conceptual illustrations (**FIGURE 4.4**). This is a common industry practice when the art director knows what look he is going for and no one on his team can satisfactorily meet those needs. These images will be used for inspiration instead of mood boards. From these images, you will start work on some character variation sketches.

FIGURE 4.4 Conceptual illustrations for a robot game.

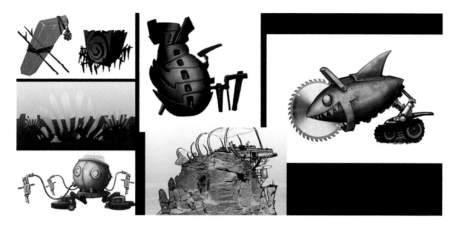

Character Variations

You draw character variation sketches when you have a pretty good idea of what your character is going to look like but want to explore subtle variations in its look, or when you need multiple versions of a single character for a team or a squad. For this exercise, you will create a three-robot squad, all about the same size and built using the same material but with different-looking shells.

In a mobile game—where you need to cut any corner you can to save on memory— you should determine in advance the assets you will need for the game and how to most efficiently implement them. Remember, everything you put into a mobile game has a cost, so the more times you can multipurpose the same assets, the better it is.

Creating the lower half of the robots

To save on memory, all three robotic units will have the same legs. This means you only need to make one set of 3D legs, with one set of animations, which only have to be coded once. Multipurpose. You will then create different chassis for the legs and change their color to match each new chassis. Changing the color is the easiest (and techno-cheapest) way to create a visual difference.

1. Open a new file, 15 inches wide by 5 inches high at 300 dpi.

2. Open the diametric perspective grid provided in your Resources folder (**FIGURE 4.5**). Scale the grid to fit in the window, which should give you the proper perspective depth on the grid.

TIP One function in Photoshop will come in very handy here. First, select the Pen tool and the size and style of brush you would like. Shift-click anywhere on the page. Then while still pressing the Shift key, move your mouse pointer somewhere else and click again. Photoshop will draw a line between the two clicked points. This is not a vector line, as is created with the Shape tool, but it is a good raster facsimile.

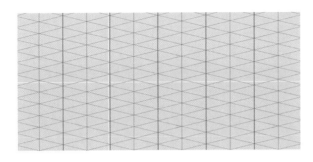

FIGURE 4.5 A diametric perspective grid.

NOTE A diametric perspective grid allows you to view a grid in a *fake* 3D environment. This will be helpful here because you are designing robots to later be constructed in 3D modeling software.

3. Begin sketching the lower half of the robot from about the waist down. Use the grid lines as the outline for the shape of the left leg. The guidelines that you used in drawing this foot are highlighted in red (**FIGURE 4.6**).

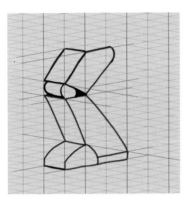

FIGURE 4.6 Use volume boxes to help draw shapes.

4. Duplicate the layer and translate it 1 grid space to the right while remaining on the front line that the toes touch (**FIGURE 4.7**). Use the corners of the toes as a guide. As you use the grid more, it becomes easier to see the lines that should not be there. Erase any lines that would not show on a solid object (**FIGURE 4.8**).

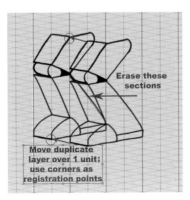

FIGURE 4.7 Erase any lines that would not show on a solid object.

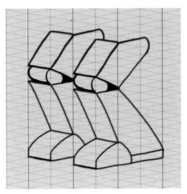

FIGURE 4.8 The robot feet.

5. When the second leg is in place, begin work on the waist disk. This is where the two halves of each robot will connect.

   Because a disk is a hard shape to draw in perspective, you will need to create a volume box using the Line tool (shown in **FIGURE 4.9** in red). You then create an oval shape using the Shape tool with no fill and a 1-pt. stroke. The oval shape is then fitted into the bottom square of the red volume box by choosing the Edit > Transform > Distort tool.

6. Duplicate the oval layer and translate it up to the top section of the red volume box. You now have a top and a bottom oval. Connect the two with a line drawn from one to the other at the far edges of the ovals, creating a volume (**FIGURE 4.10**). Readjust the height of the hip disk, if necessary, and then erase any lines that may have strayed from the design or bled over.

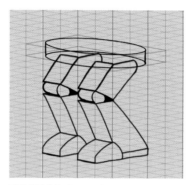

FIGURE 4.9 Create the torso base using an oval shape for the hip disk.

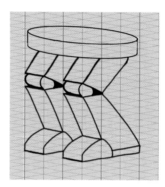

FIGURE 4.10 Fine-tune the torso base.

Now you will create the leg joints, using the same technique to create a cylinder shape on the left ankle.

7. Using the Shape or Brush tool, create a center bolt.

8. Copy this shape to the right ankle, the right knee, the left knee, and the left hip. Then erase any extra lines that need to be removed to make this look like a solid volume (**FIGURE 4.11**).

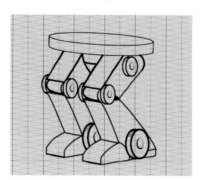

FIGURE 4.11 The completed lower portion of the robot.

Collect all the lower-half layers into a group, and name it *legs*. Scale down the group 30 percent, and move it toward the bottom of the page. Make sure you realign it with the background grid.

Creating a robot torso

Now, let's move on to the body (**FIGURE 4.12**).

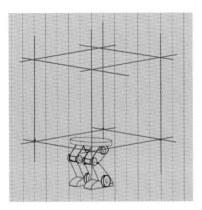

FIGURE 4.12 Volume box for the robot torso.

1. Start as you did when drawing the hip disk. Define a volume of a size appropriate for the torso. Use the Line tool with a **red** color so it is easy to see. If you're having trouble, try counting the spaces on the background grid. Start at the hip disk and find the line to the right that is one big square away. Stripe a big line. Now do the same on the left, followed by the front. In the back, go two spaces. Your robot is going to have stuff back there and you need a bit of extra room.

2. Using the volume (or bounding box, as it is called in 3D), create your robot shape (**FIGURE 4.13**). You will find that the first line is the hardest. Once it is set, the rest of the shape flows much more easily.

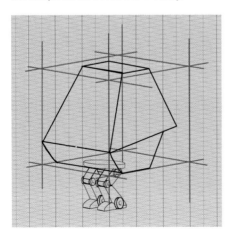

FIGURE 4.13 Begin sketching the torso.

3. When your shape is defined, select the red volume and the black outline layers, and collect them into a new layer group, and name it *Torso*. You can hide the red line for now by turning off its visibility.

4. Now create the head in a skull shape (**FIGURE 4.14**).

5. To build a volume box for the left arm, use a red Line tool, and guided by the grid, lay out a rough arm shape off to the side of the robot (**FIGURE 4.15**). Don't worry about the detail right now, just make sure it is roughly arm shaped. The appropriate volume is what you are after.

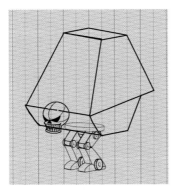
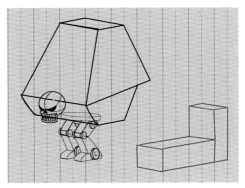

FIGURE 4.14 Position the skull within the main shape of the torso.

FIGURE 4.15 Create the volume box for the arm.

6. Once the volume box is completed, start creating your arm (**FIGURE 4.16**). Keep in mind that this will be pretty small onscreen and a lot of detail might not show up. It is better to try and make the larger shapes work for you. Also, remember that the fewer pieces you have to build in 3D, the better.

At this point things will start to get confusing, with lines intersecting all over the place. It is helpful to create a backfill layer for all of the elements. This will give you the option to eliminate the transparency if you need to, and aid in the final render (**FIGURE 4.17**).

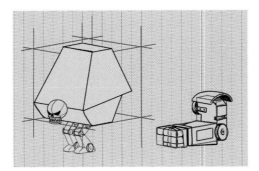

FIGURE 4.16 Create the arm.

FIGURE 4.17 Create a background shape to control opacity.

7. Select and duplicate a layer group such as "legs." Flatten the new layers, (not the originals) and with the Magic Wand tool, select the flattened shape. From the grid, select the **lighter gray** color, and choose Edit > Fill. Fill the shape with the foreground color you just selected. Rename this layer *backfill*, and place it on the bottom of the original stack in the "legs" group. Repeat this process for all the groups.

8. Move the arm group into place. You will also need to draw the small bit of hand that is showing on the right side. Make sure that layer is below the torso layer.

    Now it's time to decorate. You might have design requests from the designer or feel inspired by a favorite missile launcher, but now it's time to design some attached weapons.

9. Create a new layer at the top of the layer stack, and draw some weapons in place (**FIGURE 4.18**). You might need to erase some of the torso or some of the other sets, and that is fine. Draw your attachments first, and later you can go back into the black line sections and erase all you want.

    If you find that you are still having a hard time seeing what is going on, you can add tone to the shape (Figure 4.18).

TIP A good way to create a non-raster oval is to use the Ellipse selection tool and choose Stroke from the Edit > Stroke menu. Make it black at 4 pts. Make sure it is on its own layer. (You can add a stroke to any selection shape, by the way.) Keeping the shape on its own layer allows you to move it around and erase it if you need to.

FIGURE 4.18 Add shadow to enhance the image.

10. Select and duplicate all the layers and layer groups. Merge all the duplicate layers, and use the Fill tool to select a darker or lighter **gray**. Do not add color yet.

11. Next, duplicate the "legs" group, and name the new layer group *M2_legs*. Move the volume boxes for the torso and the arm into place, and you are ready to make the next robot in the series (**FIGURE 4.19**).

FIGURE 4.19 Begin creating the second robot.

To create a second robot, continue your robot assembly line by designing a new model to establish some visual contrast.

1. Begin as you did previously by defining the torso above the leg group.

    Try to make this design unlike the silhouette of your previous robot to create a solid visual difference between the two. If it helps, you can give them classifications like "water robot" and "air robot." Knowing what a robot will be used for may help you think about what attributes to use in your design.

2. When you've finished your torso, and repeated the backfill layer creation and the layer grouping, you can move on to creating the head. As before, when making a new torso, your emphasis should be on designing a very different-looking head. If you created a round head previously, then create a square one this time. When you are happy with the design, create the backfill layer, and collect the layers in a layer group called *m2_head*.

3. You have the torso and the head, now let's finish the arm. Using the arm volume box again, begin to create the arm. As with the head and the torso, strive to make this arm a bit different from the previous robot's arms. Sometimes finding an interesting way to bend the elbow or an unusual hand shape will dictate the look of the arm. Those are both great places to start. Think also how this arm will attach to the robot body and what its range of movement might be. When you get something you like, create the backfill layer, and collect the arm and the backfill into a layer group named *m3_leftarm*. You will also need to create the right arm and do the whole backfill/layer group thing.

4. Following the same process, create any weapons or torso details you might want, if you have not done so in the torso layer. You will need to do the whole backfill/layer group procedure here as well.

    Everything is good to go. So, collect all of the m2_ layers in a layer group called *Robot_02* and move them into the layer stack just above the Robot_01 layer.

Creating robot number 3

Because you've already done this twice, you should be able to create the third robot on your own. If you get lost, just refer to the previous sections for help.

When your three robots are finished, you can add color to them. Either add the same color to all three to show the variation on one robot, or make them three different colors to show one robot as three different characters.

The same process you used to make a drawing of a robot could eventually be used to make the 3D version. The legs would be modeled separately from the torso. The arms would get the same treatment. Each would get its own animations to match the timing of the others.

This 3D modeling process can get quite complicated, but in the end, it is the way to go. Why is this the way to go? It will buy you loads of different robots if you want them. In the engine, any arm can be combined with any torso, as long as they are rigged correctly and use the same animations. So with just one set of legs, three torsos, and three arms, you get tons of variations, and more importantly, upgrade items that can be sold to the user (**FIGURE 4.20**).

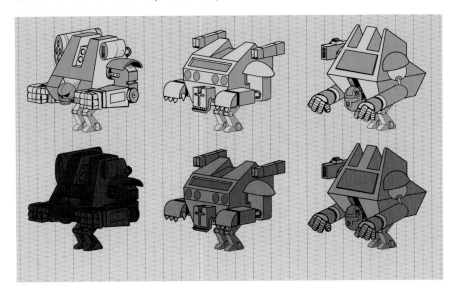

FIGURE 4.20 Robot variations.

A single arm can be mirrored in the engine along with its animation, so you really only need to make either a left or a right arm.

CREATING LEVELS

In the beginning, there were robots, and the designer saw these robots and said, "Now where can they fight swarms of aliens for somewhere between one to two minutes?"

Creating levels is a job that takes a village. Many things have to come together to make a level work correctly, and if you plan on churning out hundreds of levels that only last a minute or two each, you'd better make sure that everyone knows what they are doing from the start. If not, you will be redoing a lot of stuff in your future.

What is this stuff, you ask? Well, it all starts with—guess what—an idea that is usually handed down from the designer, or in a larger studio, a writer who hands it off to the designer. In your sample game world, the designer and the art director hired a concept company to flesh out some images to be used as examples or inspiration for levels. The look of the level you need to create is shown in **FIGURE 4.21**.

FIGURE 4.21 Spaceport city.

The designer's instruction to the concept house for this image was:

Create a spaceport with ships coming and going, and cargo stacked around. It should be industrial, and have a dirty modern feel to it. This is the first level of the game.

The concept house did its job, and it is enough for you to start laying out some of the groundwork that will turn into this level.

The first thing you need to do is identify all of the elements that need to be in the level to make it work. These might be a road, or a special rock, or a bridge the player has to cross. Your level design must include anything that is a critical part of the gameplay.

You can get this list from the designer, who has thought this through. Even so, it is also a good idea to sit down with the designer and have her walk you through her design process (**FIGURE 4.22**). This is the kind of meeting that dry erase boards were invented for.

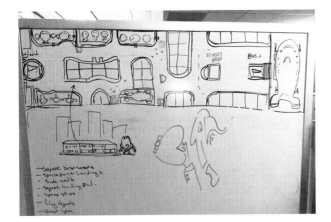

FIGURE 4.22 Doodles on the whiteboard.

Here are the mission-critical items that the designer wanted addressed. Keep in mind these might change, but you need to start somewhere.

- Square buildings
- Spaceport landing pads
- Sidewalks
- Square landing pad
- Spaceships
- Flag objects
- Streetlights
- A floor is implied
- A height elevation drawing showing how tall the robots can be

At this point, you should be able to draw a rough layout. It has a beginning, an end, and a variety of stuff in the middle.

Creating a Basic Level Map

The level map is created in multiple sections that can be recolored and moved around as the level is dialed in. The sections are the ground plane, the road, the buildings, and all the movable objects such as crates and trees. When you are done, you will have a pretty good idea of what the level will look like from a top-down view. By conceiving the level in this way, you can make changes before time is spent in 3D modeling.

A good way to start is to take a picture of the whiteboard and the work you did with the designer. You can then bring that right into Photoshop and draw on top of it, after some careful cropping and stretching. Keep in mind that this is just the rough sketch, not the final. The map could change quite a bit before you are done.

Creating the Navmesh

The first step is creating the ground that your characters will walk upon.

1. Once you have your image ready to go, create a new file in Photoshop. Name it *LV1_Spaceport*, and make it 20 inches wide by 5 inches high at 300 dpi. In the filename, LV stands for level, and you add "1" to indicate the first level, followed by a description of what is in that level.

2. From the rough map file, which you should have open, select the layer that has the rough map on it, and drag it into your new LV1_Spaceport file. Save the file.

3. Create a new layer and call it *Navmesh* (**FIGURE 4.23**). This word is an abbreviation of *navigation mesh*, and it will be the ground on which the hero and the bad guys will travel. By constraining the characters' movements to a particular piece of geometry, you ensure that they will not clip (penetrate) through larger pieces of the world. You also only have to create the physics code once, and then just apply it to the path. That way any new characters you add will follow the rules of the code you set as long as they are walking on the path. Also, physics code is expensive to run so you do not want it applied to the whole world, especially to the places you can't go.

FIGURE 4.23 Navmesh sketch.

4. Set the navmesh layer Opacity to **60%**. Using the Pen tool, choose a **red** color (**FIGURE 4.24**). Trace the outline of the floor area as best you can. Do not worry about the details too much, you will clean it up later. In fact, the fewer points you can use, the better.

FIGURE 4.24 Highlight areas of possible travel.

5. Now choose View > Show > Grid to turn on the grid. This will help you clean up your lines.

6. Choose the Direct Selection tool, a few tools down from the Pen tool. Try to align the points with the nearest grid point, so when your 3D modeling begins, the shapes can be built with a minimal number of polygons (**FIGURE 4.25**). Everything you do at this point should be geared to saving polys.

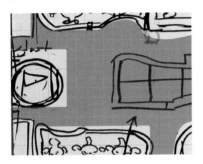

FIGURE 4.25 Create a vector image to get right angles in your mesh.

7. When you get your shape to a respectable state, you can create a new layer just below the navmesh layer, and merge the shape down. Make sure that you raise the layer opacity before you do so. This merge will convert the navmesh from a vector shape to a raster image. You did not ultimately want this shape as a vector shape, but it is easier to align it in that state. You could do this whole part with the Brush tool, if you wanted, but you would need a very steady hand.

TIP Press the number keys to quickly set visibility (1 is 10% and so on).

8. With the shape now editable in raster mode, you can clean up any stray lines and make any cutout corrections you might require. This navmesh will be used as a template to make the polygon mesh (**FIGURE 4.26**). For now, you will not apply any colors.

FIGURE 4.26 Vectored navmesh.

Creating the ground plane

Creating the ground plane is very easy because it is, very simply, the size of the whole file. In this case, it's 6000x1500 pixels at 300 dpi. The ground plane is the very bottom of the stack, which means it is the most obscured of the elements. This is great because in 3D, the ground plane usually receives a tiled texture, which is a 2D image that is applied to the polygon multiple times to make the ground plane look like a single image. It is usually a lot smaller than 6000x1500, more like 512x512. The repeating texture then fills in the 6000x1500 area. 512? Why this odd number? It's all about the Power of Two rule.

THE POWER OF TWO RULE

The Power of Two refers mostly to a system that is used in making textures for 3D models. Computers process data in chunks that must be in a certain format and size or the computer that is processing them will have to work harder, which can limit game performance. Textures in sizes that conform to a power of two—such as 8, 16, 32, 64, 128, 256, 512, 1024, and 2048—get through the processing pipe faster. It becomes a bit of a limitation on the art side to work this way, but if it means getting more textures into the game, it's worth it. Also, it has been the established method for years, so everyone works this way.

You are going to create a 512x512 texture tile that will be applied to the ground plane. It will be a tiling texture that looks like it is not repeating, especially when you are suggesting grass or dirt (**FIGURE 4.27**). For this reason, natural tiles are generally harder to make. Second, a tiling texture must be able to be located next to another tile on any of the four sides of the square, without the seam showing.

FIGURE 4.27 Ground textures.

Because this level is a spaceport, you will be making a metal grid tile.

FIGURE 4.28 Create a metal tile for the outer frame.

1. Begin by creating a file that is 1024x1024 at 72 dpi. (Most final images going into an engine are at 72 dpi.) You will reduce this to 512x512 later, but if you need a higher-resolution version in the future, you will have it. Fill it with a **dark gray** color (**FIGURE 4.28**).

2. Choose Image > Canvas Size, and set it to 1050x1050, which will create a perfect stroke space around the outside edge. Fill the new empty space with a **lighter gray**. Choose Image > Size, and change the size back to 1024x1024.

3. Using the Magic Wand tool, select the inner square and cut it from the file. Then choose Edit > Paste Special > Past in Place. Name the lower layer *trim*, and the upper layer *base*.

4. Select the trim layer, and in the blending options, select Bevel & Emboss and Gradient Overlay (**FIGURE 4.29**). Set the Depth to **113** and the Size to **8**.

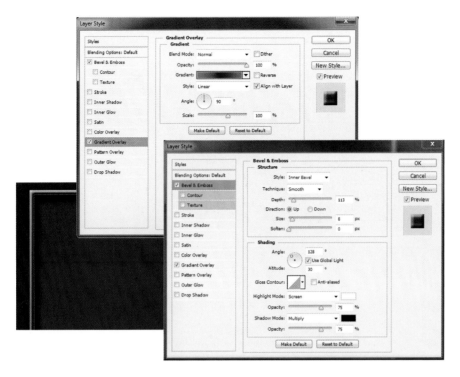

FIGURE 4.29 Blending options.

5. Using the Shape tool, pick an industrial-looking pattern from the shape gallery. In this example, the multiple diagonal line shape was used (**FIGURE 4.30**). Position the pattern in the middle of the square so there is a small border. In the blending options, select Bevel & Emboss and Drop Shadow. Make sure Bevel & Emboss is set to **Pillow Emboss**, and that the Depth is set to **164** (**FIGURE 4.31**).

FIGURE 4.30 Place the shape from the gallery.

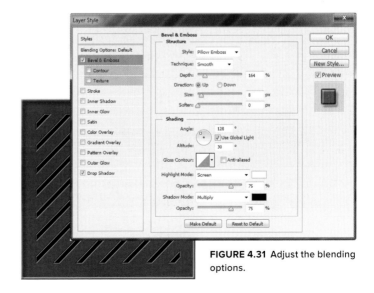

FIGURE 4.31 Adjust the blending options.

6. Create a new layer called *emblem*. Using the Ellipse tool, create a circle in the middle of the page (**FIGURE 4.32**). Fill it with the base color, and once again select Bevel & Emboss and Drop Shadow.

7. From the Custom Shape tool library, select a shape that will work as an emblem, such as the atomic shape. Center it in the circle, and open the blending options. Select Bevel & Emboss and Drop Shadow. Make sure the Style is set to **Emboss** and the Direction is set to **Down** (**FIGURE 4.33**). Save your file.

FIGURE 4.32 Add a circle shape.

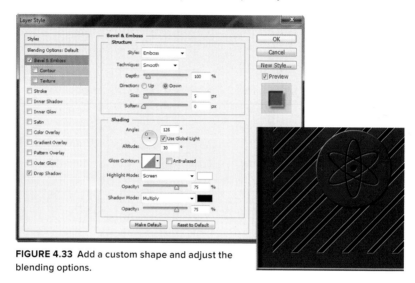

FIGURE 4.33 Add a custom shape and adjust the blending options.

8. Create another layer called *dirt*. Select one of the scatter brushes, such as number 24, and then select **black** as your fill color. Dot the pattern around the layer, changing the size and position (**FIGURE 4.34**).

9. Create a new layer and call it *dirt2*. Select an **orange** color, and switch to a different scatter brush (**FIGURE 4.35**). Repeat the painting process, but do not paint as much of the area as you did previously.

10. Create a new layer, and call it *dirt3*. Using a **blue** color and a new scatter brush, once again apply small doses of paint, and add more shapes to the mix (**FIGURE 4.36**).

FIGURE 4.34 Begin creating a "dirt" layer.

FIGURE 4.35 Add color to the dirt layer.

FIGURE 4.36 Add more color and shapes to the dirt layer.

11. Adjust the opacity of the three layers until you are satisfied with the look. When you are satisfied, merge the three layers together, return to the diagonal shape layer, and select the inside of the grooves using the Magic Wand. Then on the dirt layer, erase the dirt in the grooves but not the dirt on the emblem section.

12. If you feel the need, you can add another dirt map. In the example, the shadows were accentuated a bit with a layer inserted under the emblem layer.

13. Now it is time to test your tile. Save the file as a TIFF or PSD. Collapse all the layers and save it as a PNG. Choose Image > Canvas Size, and change the file size to 2048x2048. Locate your image in the upper-left corner. Duplicate the layer three times and move each layer to a corner of the square (**FIGURE 4.37**). Check for obvious mistakes and verify the tile blends with other tiles.

FIGURE 4.37 Duplicate the tile and position one in each corner.

When a tile like this is used in a game, a shader and lighting are often applied. So even if the lighting in the drawing is not perfect, the engine will bring it together. That being said, it is a good idea to do the best you can with the illustration because the game engine can do only so much to make a tile work.

FIGURE 4.38 shows what the tile looks like rendered in 3ds Max with simple lighting and an object added to show what a shadow looks like on the tile. The tile in the image is set to repeat five times over the surface of the ground plane. A simple shader has also been added.

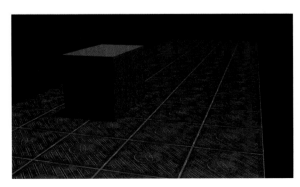

FIGURE 4.38 The tiles applied to a ground plane.

14. Now that you know the ground plane will work, you can apply it to your level map. Save a PNG version of your tile that has only one tile. You may need to crop it to fit. Make sure it is 1024x1024.

15. Open your level map file again and import the tile image. Tile the image across the entire ground plane without going beyond the borders (**FIGURE 4.39**). This is best done by placing the tile down, and then selecting and duplicating the two tiles. Then select the four new tile layers and duplicate them.

16. When you have the area filled, collapse all the layers together into one layer called *ground tile*, and scale it the little extra bit to fit the area. You just need an idea of how it works; you have the tile for the actual game asset.

FIGURE 4.39 The navmesh on top of the ground plane.

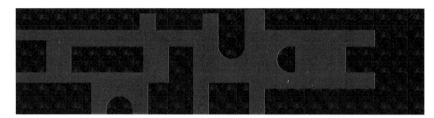

Creating Stand-in Buildings

Designing a building is a bit of a trip down architecture lane. Just as in real architecture, the design must fit into your environment. You can't have a Victorian house at your spaceport; it just won't do. So you need to design a building that will look right for the location. It should have all the trappings of a spaceport café, or storage unit, or customs office. Think space station meets shipping yard. Actually, any of those would be fine, but because the concept illustration had a café in it, that is where you will start.

Because you are only making a level map, you have no real need to flesh out a fully realized building design. Players will see it only from the top. But in the interest of learning, you will flesh out an isometric view of the café, and then generate a top-down view based on that design.

You can go about designing a structure for a 3D environment in two ways. One is to just design the building as best you can, and then let the 3D modeler figure out how to bring it in within the polygon budget. The other is to design the building with the poly budget in mind, making sure that everything you place on the page has been considered from a modeling point of view. You are going to use the second method.

1. Begin by opening up the diametric grid file you used on the robots. Scale the grid down in height by 50% to get a more front-on perspective. Make sure your file is 6 inches high by 10 inches wide at 300 dpi (**FIGURE 4.40**).

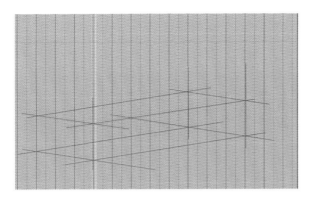

FIGURE 4.40 Create the volume box for the first part of the building.

2. Using the Line tool with a **red** color at **4 pts**, begin to lay out the foundation of your space café. It will be three polygonal shapes: the main floor, the smaller second story, and the roof sign. It has purposefully been kept simple to keep the poly count low. But this means that you'll have to do quite a bit with texture.

3. Once you have the main floor in place, create a new layer called *2ndstory*, and repeat what you did with the first layer, except leave a bit of a border. When you are dealing with low poly models, any surface area that you can create to reflect light is a good one.

4. When you have finished the 2ndstory layer, create a new layer called *roof sign*. Using the Line tool, finish creating the layout for the shape (**FIGURE 4.41**). It will look a little like a bunch of crazy toothpicks. Do not worry.

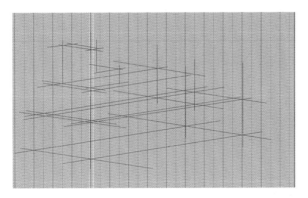

FIGURE 4.41 Create the volume box for the second part of the building.

5. Select the Line tool and choose a **black** color, and keep the size at **4 pts**. Create a new layer called *blackline*, and begin to outline your shape (**FIGURE 4.42**). If it helps, you can reduce the opacity of the red line layers just a bit.

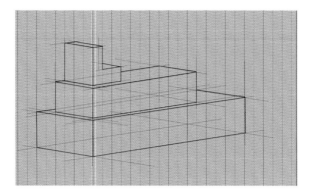

FIGURE 4.42 Begin creating the building.

With the main structure in place, you can start working on the decorations, which include windows, doors, vents, signs, and pipes. In 3D, most of these will just become part of the texture, but that would depend on how many polys you've spent in other places. However, these elements always look better in 3D if you actually build them.

Begin with the doors (**FIGURE 4.43**). They are good to nail down because they give the structure a sense of scale. Your average industrial external door is about 7 feet high by 34 inches wide. Space café doors are just a little bit larger than that. Don't worry too much about fully fleshing out the doors right now. Just use the grid to indicate where they are. If you really can't help yourself, you can indicate a door jamb.

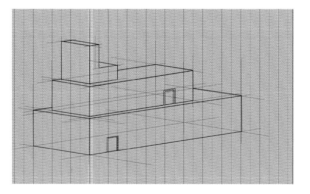

FIGURE 4.43 Flesh out the doors.

6. With the doors in place, the next logical element is the windows (**FIGURE 4.44**). Windows in a space café differ from those in a real diner. Instead of being big and open, they are small, more akin to what you would see on a boat or an airplane. Smaller windows will help sell the idea that the environment is in space. Notice that the windows were also given a bit of dimension.

    Now you will add some things that look terribly important, but are really there just to fill some of the empty space. Repetition on a building is very common. In fact, you almost expect it. So let's not disappoint.

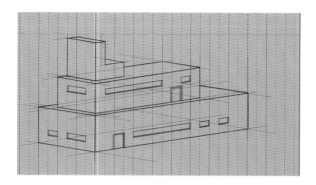

FIGURE 4.44 Create the windows.

Just above the lower door, use the Pen tool to create a trapezoidal shape similar in size to the door (**FIGURE 4.45**). Make sure the bottom line is on a horizontal grid line and that the outer edges also line up with vertical grid lines. You will need these markers in the next step. The look you are going for is a protruding piece of geometry.

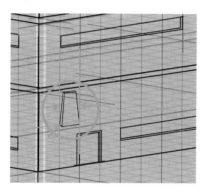

FIGURE 4.45 Create the first part of the wall decoration.

7. Now collapse any shapes to a single layer, and call it *decoration*. Duplicate the decoration layer and slide it 2 grid spaces over to the right. Repeat this until you run out of building (**FIGURE 4.46**). Collect all the layers into a layer group, and name it *decorations lower*.

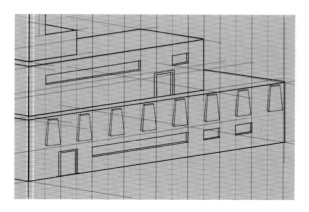

FIGURE 4.46 Duplicate the decoration layer.

8. In the remaining empty spaces on the café, continue to create visual distraction or interest, depending on your view of life. In **FIGURE 4.47**, you can see the space for signage, a large tank of some sort, and a ventilation unit. All of the things a space café cannot do without.

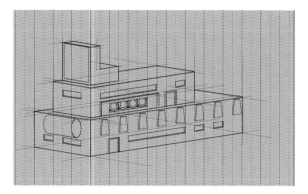

FIGURE 4.47 Continue to create visual interest by adding details.

9. Create a new layer and call it *sidewalk*. Choose the Line tool and create a **1-unit** sidewalk around the base of the building (**FIGURE 4.48**). This will help sell the scale of the building and give you a place later on to put things such as lights and space café vending machines.

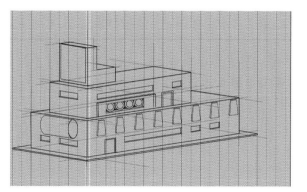

FIGURE 4.48 Create a 1-unit sidewalk.

10. Collect all of the layers and duplicate them. Collapse the new layers into a single layer, and name it *color*. Fill in the shapes you have created using **gray** tones. You can also use tonal ramps if you want. Color the windows in **green** (**FIGURE 4.49**).

    You should have produced more than enough for the 3D artist to start work, and far more than you need for your level map. If you were concepting this, you would also apply colors and finished details such as the signage and perhaps stuff in the windows. You would also do a reverse angle if it were needed.

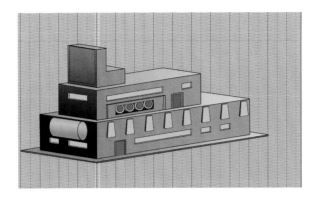

FIGURE 4.49 The finished space café with colors applied.

Creating real stand-in buildings

Creating the building markers for a real level map is far easier than what you just did. The kind of building you actually need to make has the footprint of the building and callouts for any doors, windows, or turrets that might be important. No grids, no shading, very simple. The building images are generally done as in an architectural drawing: a large whitish area with a few hash marks and an indication of which way the door swings (**FIGURE 4.50**). If the building is accessible, you might need some indication of the inside layout, but usually that is a separate map with more detail.

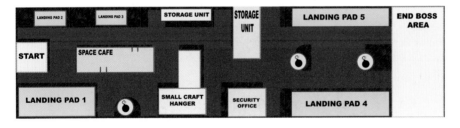

FIGURE 4.50 Create the level layout tags.

1. Open the level map file you were using. With the Shape tool, create a rectangle that fits the area in the middle. Fill the shape with a **white-gray** color and make the Stroke **blue**. With the Text tool, write *SPACE CAFÉ*. Collapse the layers into a single layer called *space café*.

2. Repeat this for all the sections, giving each a name based on what you and the designer discussed. Because these items may change at any time, make sure that they are all on their own layers.

   Most studios have a visual shorthand for calling out repeated items without spelling out the actual name again and again. This accounts for the yellow dots with the red borders and the little pictures of bombs. They stand for a destructible object in this case; that is, an object that can be shot and has the potential for causing damage to bad guys or other players. You might also see shorthand symbols for things like lights, spawning points, save points, and various other common game objects.

3. To make the destructible object icon, choose the Ellipse tool and draw a small **circle**. Make the fill **yellow** and the border **red**. Create a new layer above that layer, and with the Brush tool, create a little image of a bomb. Merge the two layers together, and name the new layer *destructible object*.

   This map is now more or less ready to take to the designer. She will place notations on a new layer to indicate where spawn points may be and what special purposes the various buildings might have, if any. After that, the map is distributed to the team as a guide for what is needed to flesh out the level. A list of assets will be created, and engineering will document the tasks that might be needed for this particular scenario to explain the functionality. The main point of a map like this is to get everyone synchronized on the objectives rather than waste time and energy spinning in the wrong direction.

Creating a Texture Atlas for the Navmesh

Remember that tile you made for the ground plane? You're going to take it a step further. A texture atlas is a group of textures that are all on one sheet, and then applied to one or more objects repeatedly in a game engine to give a more diverse, less tiled look. The reason for putting them on one sheet is that they load faster as a slightly larger file than they would as five little files. You're going to make a series of tiles, collect them on an atlas, and then apply them to the navmesh.

First, you need to identify the types of tiles you will need for the navmesh object. You do this by looking at the layer in Photoshop and seeing how it turns and bends, while trying to come up with some options that will work in multiple locations.

1. Open the level map file. Hide everything but the red navmesh layer.

2. Create a new layer. Identify similar shapes in the path that could use a single tile once or multiple times. With the Brush tool, mark these in rough outline using a black color. Identify as many sections as you need.

3. Number each similarly shaped area.

   As you can see in **FIGURE 4.51**, you have identified four map types. Each of these tiles will need to look as if they are made from the same material, but they do not all need to tile from every direction as did the previous tile.

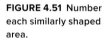

FIGURE 4.51 Number each similarly shaped area.

Now you will break each of the numbered areas out into individual maps. Remember that each map needs to fit into a power of two square, which is 512x512.

4. Open a new file in Photoshop that is 1024x1024 at 72 dpi. Name it *navmesh_t1*. As you can see, this is a larger area tile, which means that the detail will have to be smaller.

   "Why is that?" you ask. Let me explain. The tiles you make will start out the same on the tile atlas, but when applied to the sections of the object in a 3D software package, they may end up displaying at different sizes (**FIGURE 4.52**). So, if you have details like the black border and the 33 in this image, they must start out at different sizes in the 512 maps so that when reduced they are the same scale.

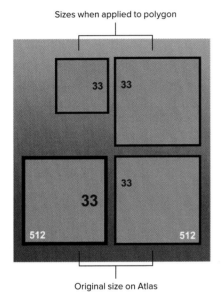

FIGURE 4.52 Tiles may end up displaying at different sizes.

   Notice how large the black trim and the 33 have to be in the original tile to appear to be the same size in the model. It is important that you identify these situations in advance, or you will get way down the road with your project and then have to redo your work.

5. Create a new file that is 1024 inches in height and 4540 inches in width at 72 dpi. Select an example of each of the tile shapes, and import them into the new file, placed next to each other. You do not need to add the numbers here.

   Once you have the pieces, you can begin work on filling them in with space station road-looking art. A good way to start is to create a stroke around each of the shapes (**FIGURE 4.53**). Because these will look like metal floor tiles in the game, a border is a great natural break. It will look like the edge of the tile. If you were drawing dirt, it would be much harder to hide the seams of the tile.

FIGURE 4.53 Lay out your shapes next to each other.

6. Fill the shapes with a **gray-green** color (**FIGURE 4.54**). This is a popular space-station floor color. In the blending options, turn on Bevel & Emboss, and set the Depth to **360**. Then create a new layer and call it *background*. Move it to the bottom of the stack, and fill it with a **gray** color. Once again, this is done so you can see what you are doing.

FIGURE 4.54 Fill the shapes with a gray-green color.

7. Select all the green areas, and copy and paste them. This will create a new layer that you can name *lid*. Name the original layer *base*. In the blending option of the lid layer, turn on Drop Shadow and Bevel & Emboss. Marquee select the first shape in the lid layer, and center it over its base layer counterpart (**FIGURE 4.55**). Repeat this for all the shapes. Note that the third arch shape will also need to be scaled a bit to fit.

FIGURE 4.55 In the blending option of the lid layer, turn on Drop Shadow and Bevel & Emboss.

8. From here you can add a central theme to each tile (**FIGURE 4.56**). You have gone with a grate theme because this spaceport has a lot of rain, and drainage is important. Oh, and you added one tile one for visual variety.

FIGURE 4.56 Add a central theme to each tile.

9. After your central theme is in place, you can create a new layer above the others and call it *dirt map1*. You're going to be adding some years to your tiles, just as you did with the ground plane tiles (**FIGURE 4.57**).

FIGURE 4.57 Add some colored dirt to the tiles.

10. Select a black color and a scatter brush, just as you did before, to create some interesting shapes. If you go too heavy with the paint, you can lower the opacity, or select the Eraser tool and a different brush and work back the other way. When you are happy with the mess you have made, create another map, and using a color (such as blue), add some colored dirt.

11. Duplicate all the layers and, with the exception of the gray background, merge the new ones together. Hide the old layers.

12. Create a new file that is 1024x1024 at 72 dpi, and name it *texture atlas*. This will be your texture atlas, as the name suggests. You will stack your files in a square so they will be made easier to read by the game engine.

13. Create a red, square shape that is 512x512. Place it in the upper-left corner, and duplicate it to the lower-right corner (**FIGURE 4.58**). Collapse the layers. These squares will be used to size your texture maps to 512x512.

FIGURE 4.58 Create a red, square shape that is 512x512.

14. Marquee select tile number 1, and paste it within the upper-left red square. Scale the image until it covers most, if not all, of the red square. As you can see in **FIGURE 4.59**, you have now made your texture 512x512.

15. Repeat this process for the remaining tiles, stretching them to fit the entire space (**FIGURE 4.60**). Don't worry; you will squish them back to their normal sizes later.

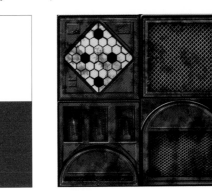

FIGURE 4.59 Marquee select tile number 1.

FIGURE 4.60 Repeat the selection/paste tile process for the remaining tiles.

16. Create a layer above the red-checkered level and fill it with a black color. Save the file as a TIFF and a PNG. Obviously, some space on this atlas has not been utilized. Space on a texture atlas is never wasted, and usually you would put a texture for something else into these areas. For now, you will leave it blank, but you should make a mental note that you have some space for a small texture if you need it.

With your texture atlas, you will now simulate how it would be applied to a mesh object in a 3D software package such as Autodesk Maya or 3ds Max.

Applying the Texture Atlas to the Navmesh

Without the aid of 3D software, applying a texture to a mesh is a bit difficult, to say the least, but you can simulate the process using Photoshop layers and some creative pasting.

In a 3D world, a 2D image is projected onto the surface of a 3D object. The projection can be cut into small sections based on the 3D topology. Each polygon can have its own 2D map, but most of the time the process goes more like this: One 2D image is carefully positioned over multiple polys on an object to give the illusion of it having color, being painted, or wearing pants or dragon scales, or whatever (**FIGURE 4.61**). That is exactly what you're going to do with your navmesh.

FIGURE 4.61 Apply 2D maps to each polygon.

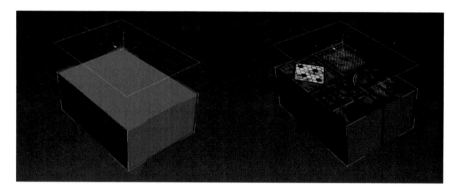

1. Open the navmesh file you've been using with Level map master.tiff, and hide all the layers except for the red navmesh layer.

2. Also open the texture atlas.png file, and copy the whole file.

3. Return to the navmesh layer, and use the marquee tool to select the red area.

4. Choose Edit > Paste Special > Paste Into. You should now have a version of the texture atlas floating around in the red area. Move the texture atlas layer to the area you identified as a number 1 zone. Move and scale the atlas in area 1 to fit the space (**FIGURE 4.62**). Don't worry about spillover from the rest of the atlas because you will cover it up soon.

FIGURE 4.62 Move and scale the atlas in area 1 to fit the space.

What you're trying to do here is use the four images on the atlas to fill out portions of the red area. Generally, you would do this without any nonlinear scaling because the stretching is an obvious tell that a texture is being applied.

5. Repeat this technique until the entire red area is filled (**FIGURE 4.63**). Refer to the number map you created earlier, if you need to. Do not worry about strictly adhering to the number map, as it was more of a guide than anything else. Try to introduce variation into the pattern if you can.

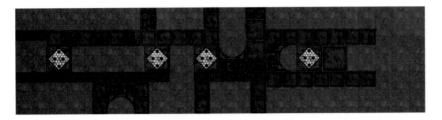

FIGURE 4.63 Fill the entire red area.

A top-down view of the ground map never looks as good as a perspective view. If you were working in 3D software, you would just apply the tile to the meshes and look through the virtual camera to check your work. However, in Photoshop, while it isn't that easy, it isn't impossible. You just need to work some Photoshop magic to see what your ground maps will look like in game view.

6. Collapse your many, many, layers to a single layer.

7. Create a new layer, and fill it with a black color. Move this layer below the ground map layer.

8. Choose Edit > Transform > Distort. Drag the upper-right control handle to the lower-left corner. Move the controller from the lower-right side to the lower-left side. Move the two left-hand side controllers to the upper middle of the screen. This should give you a nice, perspective-style view, as shown in **FIGURE 4.64**. Basically, you are flipping it upside down.

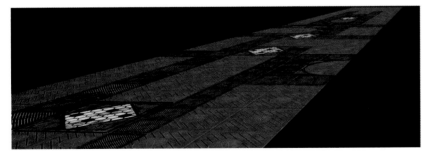

FIGURE 4.64 Games-eye view of the ground map.

You can use this technique to test your building sketches as well. Just adjust the ground plane image with the Distort tool to match the direction of the diametric grid (**FIGURE 4.65**).

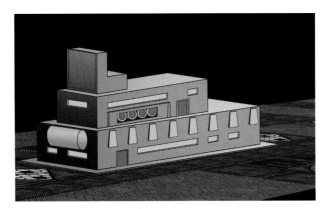

FIGURE 4.65 Building and grid in game view.

MAKING PROPS, PICKUPS, AND OTHER STUFF LYING AROUND

Prop creation is often a misunderstood task at a game company. Because it is not part of the main character set or the main-level layout, the task of creating the props is often given a lower priority. But just like the main characters and the main level, props play a huge part in the game.

A prop in the game world can refer to many kinds of objects. A crate in a warehouse is a very obvious example of a prop, but so is that burning train right behind the crate, and that crowbar on the ground, and that dead guy those zombies are eating. A good definition for a prop is anything that supports the scene but is not part of the level layout or character set. This is not to say that characters can't use props, but they are not generally part of the actual character mesh.

To further understand props, you will organize them into categories. These are Common, Dynamic, Supportive, and Interactive.

- **Common props** are all the stuff you see lying around a level. They generally do not move and you cannot pick them up. They are the pipes, vents, desks, shelves, fallen columns, and skeletons that you pass while playing your game. They are sometimes called static props, and in more than a few engines, they have their own classification.

- **Dynamic props** are props that you can interact with. This includes items such as exploding barrels, levers, switches, buckets, and bowling balls. Dynamic props generally have attributes that cause them to move or react in some way. Sometimes this means that a physics modifier is attached to the prop, which causes said prop to react with a gravity-like behavior when you hit or shoot it. Other times, as with a dynamite barrel, an explosion is triggered that inflicts damage across a particular radius. Dynamic props can also simply change states, such as a light coming on or a switch going from up to down. Any prop that moves or does something is a dynamic prop.

■ **Supportive props** are also known in the game world as *pickups*. These are items to watch for while playing a game. They can change the way your characters perform. They can add or take away health, give ammunition, change your weapon, and do any number of other things. The physical properties of a pickup can vary a great deal. They tend to look like suitcases or magic vials. The pickup is very akin to the doobers we spoke about previously in the book. It is more a quickly recognized icon than a fully rendered version of an object. Bullets, for instance, are pickups. In a game, you do not pick up individual bullets, but you often find a clip or a case of bullets, or find health icons. How would you pick up health, and what would it even look like? In most games, it looks like a first aid kit, of course, or a beaker, or some liquid that glows. When you create a pickup, keep in mind that the player is looking for something that symbolizes their idea of an item or concept.

■ **Interactive props** are items that the in-game character can interact with, such as guns, cars, jet bikes, elevators, and zip lines. These props often aid the player in completing a task in the level. They are generally complex and animated, and rival the main character in poly count. For this reason, few interactive props are scattered around, or if they are, they use the same 3D model with different textures.

And Then There Were Crates

One prop reigns supreme as the king of all props. The first and most often thought-of prop in the game world is the crate. Crates are very popular for one good reason: they have, by the very nature of their shape, an extremely low poly count. Mix that with a little visual identification memory for most players, and you get a low-poly object that is easily recognized and extremely believable, and one that you can build with minimal effort. "Ah," you say, "that is why they are in every game ever made." Yes, but there are other reasons as well.

Think of crates as the spackle of the game world. They can be used to hide seams in the level layout. They can be used to direct your eye in a certain direction; they can be used to hide ancient hog demons until they are ready to attack. Suffice it to say, they get used a lot.

Crates can also be used to set the mood of a level. A room full of pink crates with a cute bunny on the side will feel much different than a room full of black crates with a toxic waste symbol. All it takes to change that "crate mood" is a new decal on the side or a different color. The best part is that you only have to make one model, and you can just change it as often as you'd like.

EXERCISE 8: CREATING PROP DESIGNS AND TEXTURES

You are going to design four crates, each with its own special feel, but all using the same geometry. Essentially, you are making four textures for one crate object.

Creating the Roughs of Four Crates

The game designer has identified the four crates he wants. He needs a wood crate with the word MUNITIONS on it; a space-aged crate with a window to some glowing matter inside; an old, rusted metal crate with rivets; and for some reason, the afore-mentioned pink crate with a cute bunny emblem. He would like to see roughs before you go to final, so you should start with those.

1. Open the diametric grid file. This may seem like overkill for a few crates, but it will easily give you perfect perspective, and if you can get that for free, you should take it.

2. Create a new layer above your grid layer, and then create a bounding box using the Line tool with a **red** color and no stroke (**FIGURE 4.66**).

3. Place a new layer above the red layer, and name it *crate*. Change your line color to **black**, and create a shape from the bounding volume (red lines). Collect your shapes into a single shape layer by choosing Merge Shapes (**FIGURE 4.67**).

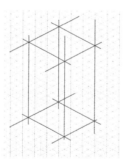

FIGURE 4.66 Create the bounding volume for constructing a crate.

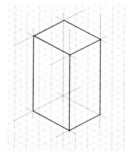

FIGURE 4.67 Create a main shape for the crate.

4. Now you are going to create a relief in the crate shape to give it a bit more depth (**FIGURE 4.68**). Using the grid, go 1 unit in and create a rectangle on both sides and on the top of the crate.

5. Add a bit of thickness to those shapes by creating an internal lip (**FIGURE 4.69**).

6. Finally, collapse all the layers to a single layer. Create a new layer, and merge the shape layer down. Rename it *crate*, if you wish to. Then use the Fill tool to add some shading, lighter on top and darker on the side with the largest face being the neutral tone (**FIGURE 4.70**).

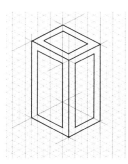

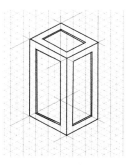

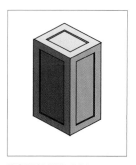

FIGURE 4.68 Create a rectangle on both sides.

FIGURE 4.69 Add volume by adding an internal lip to the crate.

FIGURE 4.70 Add some shading to the crate.

7. Duplicate the new crate layer four times and spread them out. These will be four roughs once you add colors and detail.

8. Using the marquee selection tool, select the first crate interior by selecting the space around the crate, and from the Selection down-down menu, choose Select > Inverse.

9. Create a new layer and fill the marquee selection with a **brownish** ramp. Change the layer style from Normal to **Multiply**. Repeat this technique for the rest of the crates, giving each one its own individual color (**FIGURE 4.71**).

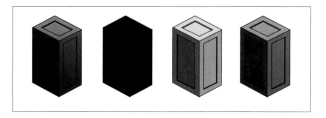

FIGURE 4.71 Give each crate its own individual color.

10. When you have the main colors sorted out, return to the first crate, and create a new layer called *crate_wood*.

Building a Wooden Crate

Put aside the hammer and nails. The only shop you'll be using to hammer out this wooden crate is Photoshop.

1. Choose the brush tool with a **black** color and begin to draw the planks of the crate. Vary the width of the line to simulate uneven placement of the planks. Also draw diagonal lines across the corners to simulate the miter cut of the frame.

2. Create a new layer, and call it *nails*. Turn on Bevel & Emboss and Drop Shadow, then select the brush tool with a hard brush and a **gray** color. In the corners of the crate, draw two circles on either side of the miter cut (**FIGURE 4.72**). Repeat for all corners.

3. Create a new layer under the crate_wood layer, and call it *rings*. Choose a brush tool with a **brown** color just a bit darker than the brown on the crate. Using a small brush, draw the natural lines that occur in woodgrain (**FIGURE 4.73**). Make sure they run lengthwise with the board because most wood is cut that way.

4. Using the Text tool, add the MUNITIONS label, and then rotate and scale it to fit. Create a new layer below the text layer and merge it down to make it editable. Using the Erase tool at **30%** opacity and a Scatter brush, distress the text a bit.

5. Create a new layer at the top of the stack, and name it *shadow*. Choose the brush tool with a soft brush. Change the brush color to **black** and set Opacity to **20%**. Open the shadows around the inner parts of the crate to help sell the 3D dimensionality (**FIGURE 4.74**).

FIGURE 4.72 Turn on Bevel & Emboss and Drop Shadow.

FIGURE 4.73 Draw the natural lines that occur in woodgrain.

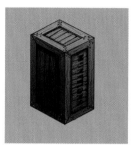

FIGURE 4.74 Add shadow and color to finish the wooden crate.

Building a Space Crate

In space, no one can hear you build a crate.

FIGURE 4.75 Create another pill shape.

NOTE The blue color is turned off here so you can better see the shapes.

1. Move over to the second crate, colored blue. Use the Rounded Rectangle tool to create a pill shape (**FIGURE 4.75**).

2. Using the Distort tool, adjust the perspective to match that of the crate's left front panel. Duplicate that layer, and choose Edit > Transform > Flip Horizontal. Move the layer into place on the crate's right side.

3. Create another pill shape, and use the same techniques to place it on the top panel.

4. Create a new layer, and merge all three pill shapes and the blank layer to make the pill shapes editable. Using the Magic Wand, select the inside of the three shapes.

5. Create a new layer named *space matter*. Choose the brush tool with a soft brush and set Opacity to **60%**. Select a **bright green** color and paint in the selected area.

6. Choose a scatter brush in a **darker green** color, and stipple that around to create particle-looking matter. Continue doing this until you have found a space matter that works for you. Then, in blending options, turn on Bevel & Emboss and Outer Glow (**FIGURE 4.76**). Set Bevel & Emboss to go **Down** instead of Up, and change the glow color to match the **lighter green** color.

7. Choose the Line tool, change its color to **bright green** with a **5-pt.** size and no stroke. Draw a geometric pattern on the case that looks like a circuit board. Work your way around the crate until you are happy with the look. Create a new layer and merge all the line layers with the new layer. Name the layer *lines*, and change the layer mode from Normal to **Color Dodge**.

   What would a space crate be without some control buttons?

8. Using the rectangular shape tool, create four or five different-colored squares. Line them up vertically. Collapse them into one layer, and with the Distort tool, fit them into the space at the top of the crate (**FIGURE 4.77**). Make sure the perspective works. Now select Bevel & Emboss and Drop Shadow.

FIGURE 4.76 In blending options, turn on Bevel & Emboss.

FIGURE 4.77 Add control buttons to finish the crate.

Restoring a Rusted Metal Crate

The rusted crate is a bit of a different story because its gray texture is just the beginning. To make a rust texture, you need to incorporate a lot of transparent layers all working together (**FIGURE 4.78**). You are trying to replicate years of neglect.

1. With the Magic Wand select around the crate, and then choose Select Invert to select the crate.

2. Create a new layer (you will do this a lot with this crate.) Choose the brush tool with a scatter pattern and a **reddish-brown** color. On the same layer, repeat the technique with a **black** color, and then with a **gray** color. Keep choosing different brushes and sizes. The goal is to produce as much visual noise as possible. When you are done, set Opacity to **50%**.

FIGURE 4.78 Produce as much visual noise as possible using a reddish-brown color and a scatter pattern.

3. Create a new layer and repeat the process. This time start with a **dark orange** color and work in a **red** color. Choose Filter > Noise, and adjust the noise level to resemble rust particles.

4. Create a new layer, and in the blending options, turn on Bevel & Emboss and Drop Shadow. Choose the brush tool with a scatter brush and a **gray** color. Paint in some sections to create the look of chipped paint.

5. Create another layer, and using the brush tool with a scatter, paint some dirt on top of the painting you just did. You may need to place several layers of paint and dirt to get the look right. Don't worry about the number of layers you have to use; they are free.

6. Create a new layer, turn on Bevel & Emboss and Drop Shadow; then repeat the process you used to create nails for the wooden crate, except call this layer *rivets*, as you are now working with a metal object. Pepper them around in patterns (**FIGURE 4.79**).

7. Choose the Custom Shape tool, and select a foreboding emblem. As you can see in **FIGURE 4.80**, we used the classic radioactive symbol. Create a new layer, merge the symbol down, and use the Eraser tool to distress it a bit.

FIGURE 4.79 Create nails.

FIGURE 4.80 Create erosion on the crate.

8. One more thing: Create a new layer and turn on Bevel & Emboss. Make the bevel go down. Select a scatter brush with a **black** color. Use this brush to poke holes in the crate. That's just what you want to see when running across a crate with a nuke symbol: a few holes in the side.

Prepping the Fluffy Pink Bunny Crate

The pink crate is the easiest of all your crates (**FIGURE 4.81**), and that's because you only need to do a few things to it. The pink color is enough to sell the image.

1. Create a new layer called *dirt*. Choose the brush tool with a scatter brush. Select a **pink** color that is a bit darker than the pink on the crate. Pepper the darker color around to add some visual interest.

2. Create a new layer, and call it *bunny logo*. Create the cutest bunny logo you can, and then duplicate the layer. You always want to keep the unaltered original in case you need to change it in the future.

3. Use the Distort tool or the Perspective tool to place the bunny logo on the left side of the crate.

4. Duplicate the original logo, and using the same technique, place it on the top panel of the crate (**FIGURE 4.82**).

5. Create a new layer, and just as you did before, use a soft brush with a **black** color and an opacity of **30%** to darken the shadows around the inside edges (**FIGURE 4.83**).

FIGURE 4.81 Create the cutest bunny logo you can.

FIGURE 4.82 Duplicate the original logo.

FIGURE 4.83 Use a soft brush to darken the shadows.

6. Save your file and you are done.

   As you can see in **FIGURE 4.84**, all of the crates match the specs from the designer. You have wood for the wooden crate, space matter for the space crate, rust for the metal crate, and adorable bunnies for the pink crate.

FIGURE 4.84 The four crates with the final touches.

These crates may seem a bit cartoony, but they get the point across. A modeler could take any one of these and create a 3D object with very little effort. Even if these crates were meant to be rendered realistically, your modeler would have a pretty good idea of what to include in the mesh and the texture.

CREATING A CRATE TEXTURE MAP

You will now create a texture map for one of these crates. This will bring together all the techniques you have covered in this chapter and give you a sneak preview into the next chapter.

Making Side Pieces

Just in case you didn't know, a texture is an image that is applied to a 3D object to give it color or tone. It can also be used as a vehicle to deliver lighting or displacement information. The texture you're making for this crate is set up just like the layout you did for the texture atlas with a bunch of information squeezed into a square. However, when the image is applied to only one object, it is just called a texture. You will make your texture in three parts. You could have gotten away just using two parts, but the game engine is going to calculate the area for that third part no matter what you do, so you might as well use it.

1. Open a new file that is 1024x1024, and name it *crate_wood1*.

2. Create two 512x512 squares, and stack them on top of each other on the right (**FIGURE 4.85**). Be very careful with your positioning. In a texture, every pixel counts, so you want to make it nice and tidy from the beginning.

   The larger part will be used for the four longer areas, and the two squares will be used for the end caps. In previous exercises, you illustrated your images to get the look you needed; but this prop requires a little more realism, so you will use a photo as the base and work from there (**FIGURE 4.86**). Actually, most 3D programs have premade wood textures that work really well, but in the interest of advancing your skills, you will make your own.

3. Find a picture of a piece of wood that looks like it's from an old crate. You are looking for an image of a board around 3 feet in length.

4. Import the image into your main file, and just like a carpenter, build a frame. Scale your wood picture thinner, if necessary, and slide it against the right wall. Duplicate the layer, and slide that up against the left wall. Duplicate that layer, and rotate it 90 degrees, and move it to the bottom. Duplicate that layer one more time, and move it to the top. You should now have a wood frame with a blue center (**FIGURE 4.87**).

FIGURE 4.85 Create two 512x512 squares.

FIGURE 4.86 Use a photo as the base and work from there.

FIGURE 4.87 You should now have a wood frame with a blue center.

5. Because you are a good carpenter, you're going to give your frame a miter cut, which means that you cut the top and the bottom pieces at an angle (**FIGURE 4.88**). (You needn't cut the side pieces because it's just an image.) Select the bottom piece layer, and with the Polygonal Lasso tool, select an area from the bottom corner to the inside joint where the two pieces come together; then select around the outside edge of the board image. Close your loop, and cut out the selection. Repeat this on the other side, and with both pieces of the top.

6. This looks great, but it's not as realistic as it might be. Merge all three layers, and in blending options, select Bevel & Emboss and Drop Shadow.

7. Create a new layer called *nails*. In the blending options of this layer, turn on Bevel & Emboss and Drop Shadow. Now select a neutral gray color and hammer some nails into the corners of the wood frame (**FIGURE 4.89**). Or, as you say in Photoshop, select a brush tool with a hard edge and 100% opacity and flow, and put two dots on either side of the seams of the top and side pieces.

8. Create another new layer and call it *wood edges*. Select a brush tool with a sharp brush and set Opacity to **85** and Flow to **60**. Using a **black** color, work a deeper line into the section where the two pieces of board meet. You may also want to add some subtle highlights. While you are there, dirty up the nails a bit by scribbling on top of them with the black and the highlight color (**FIGURE 4.90**). Don't worry about accurately rendering your nails. The lighting in the engine and the resolution constraints will fill in the rest.

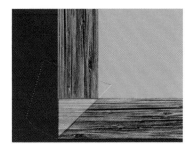

FIGURE 4.88 Give your frame a miter cut.

FIGURE 4.89 Hammer some nails into the corners of the wood frame.

FIGURE 4.90 Dirty up the nails a bit by scribbling on top of them.

9. Import your wood image and rotate it 90 degrees. Move the new layer under the wood-frame layer. Duplicate it four or five times. If you need to scale it a bit to fit, that is fine. It is important to maintain the spaces between the boards. You need to see blue between each one. In the blending options, select Bevel & Emboss.

10. Now return to the blending properties and adjust the drop shadow to appear a little stronger (**FIGURE 4.91**). Set Distance to **28**, Spread to **3**, and Size to **8**.

11. Now for some detail. Select the Text tool, and type **MUNITIONS** as you did previously. Rotate the text 90 degrees clockwise, and place it in the middle of the wood frame. Make sure that the text layer is the top layer.

12. Create a new layer, and merge the text layer down to make it a raster image and, therefore, editable. Using the Eraser tool with a hard-edged brush, erase the portions of text that are between the boards. Now choose a scatter brush. Set Opacity to **33** and erase portions of the text to give it a worn look that matches the wood (**FIGURE 4.92**).

13. Save your file.

FIGURE 4.91 Maintain the spaces between the boards.

FIGURE 4.92 Give the boards a worn look.

Texturing Cap Pieces

Now that you have created the sides of the crate, the cap sections should be easy. You have all the assets that you need. You just have to do a little creative cutting and pasting.

1. Select and duplicate the wood frame, nails, and wood edges layers. Merge the layers, and then slide them to the other side of the screen (**FIGURE 4.93**).

2. Select and copy the lower half of the new wood frame layer, and then paste it in place. Translate it up until the bottom of the frame covers the orange background area.

3. Choose the Eraser tool at **33%** opacity with a soft-edge brush, and blend in the two pieces (**FIGURE 4.94**).

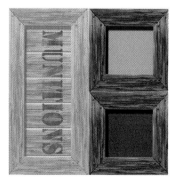

FIGURE 4.94 Blend in the two pieces.

FIGURE 4.93 Slide the merged layers to the other side of the screen.

4. Merge the two layers, and using a marquee selection tool, select the entire square frame, and then duplicate and paste it. Move it down to the lower position, covering the red area (**FIGURE 4.95**).

5. Bring in your wood again and rotate it 90 degrees. Move it into place, and cut off or erase the extra portions. Duplicate the layer three or four times, and fill the two frames just as you did previously.

   You have added a decal of some bullets and a break in the wood with some bullets showing through. The break was made by erasing the wood layer a little bit, and then adding an image of bullets under the wood layer (**FIGURE 4.96**).

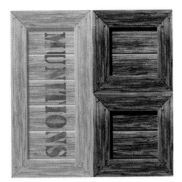

FIGURE 4.95 Move the square frame down to the lower position, covering the red area.

FIGURE 4.96 Add a decal of some bullets to the crate.

Because you started from a real-life object, the texture has a far greater chance of looking like a real object in the game world (**FIGURE 4.97**). Other factors will need to be addressed to fully sell it as a realistic object, but you will learn about those techniques in Chapter 5.

FIGURE 4.97 Using an image of an actual object results in a more realistic-looking crate.

CREATING FX FOR THE MOBILE SPACE

Creating *fx*, or effects, for use in the mobile space is a bit different than in the social or the console worlds. As you've done throughout this chapter, you will need to make effects that will work within a mobile game engine, but aren't so memory heavy that they stop the game. This is where art and tech meet. Most of these methods require a mixture of 2D and 3D work from the artist, followed by implementation by an engineer.

Using 3D Effects

NOTE A particle system in a 3D package replicates the generation of multiple (usually small) items.

3D effects replicate an event using the tools that exist in a 3D program or engine. They may consist of any number of 3D functions played together. For instance, an explosion effect might have a particle system running for the debris, another particle system running for the expanding light particles, and another for the smoke. All three of these particle systems coming together make what looks just like something blew up.

Particle systems tend to consist of an emitter, which acts as a nozzle that distributes the particles in a certain direction. In most 3D packages, it is represented by a square with a pointy bit in the middle.

The second piece of the particle system is a small bit of geometry that is replicated and given physical properties such as weight. It can also be textured and have lighting applied to it. 3D software packages usually include several premade shapes to choose from that have been proven to be low-poly-count friendly. But you can also substitute your own if you like.

The last element is the force applied to the particle, which includes parameters such as speed, strength, and turbulence.

Most 3D software and game engines have premade effects to replicate smoke, fire, explosions, and water. These effects are open, so if you wanted to alter the color of the fire or produce a bigger explosion, you could drag some sliders to make those changes.

Starting off with a premade particle effect is always easier than creating one from scratch. You can purchase a ton of very inexpensive effects libraries for this purpose. If you consider how long it could take you to make an effect on your own, premade effects are often cheaper.

Using 2D Effects

2D effects, often called *sprites*, are simply an animated sequence of images that are played when an effect event is triggered. This means you can illustrate them, or use a photo, or even create them in 3D and then render them as a movie sequence.

How does a 2D projected image sequence hold up in a 3D world? Not too bad. It is possible to always align the effect to the camera view so that no matter how you rotate around the object in the game, the effect is always seen from the perspective you intended. Do 2D effects look as good as a 3D-rendered particle system? No, they do not always look so great, but if your choice is a 2D effect or nothing (as is often the case in the memory-stingy mobile world), you take the 2D effect.

The problem is that 3D effects are just too memory expensive to use all over the place, so they are generally saved for the more important moments such as killing the end boss. The hundreds of disposable bad guys you shoot on your way through the level just get the 2D treatment.

EXERCISE 9: CREATING A 2D SPRITE-BASED EFFECT

You're going to create a 2D explosion effect to show your robot's gunfire hitting an enemy. It will be a 16-frame sequence ready to bring into Adobe After Effects, Flash, or straight into the game engine.

A sprite sheet is a single image containing multiple frames of an animation sequence that a game uses to display as an effect. It usually has a lower memory cost and is a bit old school but is still very commonly used.

Setting Up Your Page

Setting up a page for a *sprite sheet* is easiest if you know ahead of time how many frames you would like to make your animation. Because the images are read by an engine, registration is very important. If you are even a few pixels off with some effects, you can get a jitter. So, if you know you need 16 frames of animation, that should also tell you to create a file with a size divisible by 16. It really doesn't have to be of that, but it makes the entire process much easier for you.

1. Create a new file in Photoshop, and make it 8 inches x 8 inches at 72 dpi.

2. Turn on the rulers. Select the Line tool with a **black** color, and mark off every 2 inches vertically and horizontally. This will produce a grid with perfect 2x2 boxes.

3. Select the little blue guides and position them on the 1-inch marks, both vertically and horizontally (**FIGURE 4.98**). This identifies the exact centers of those boxes.

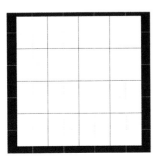

FIGURE 4.98 Mark off every 2 inches vertically and horizontally.

4. Using the Magic Wand tool, select the first box. Create a layer, and using the Fill tool, add a radial gradation. Make sure it is white in the middle and black on the outside edges (**FIGURE 4.99**). Do not let the white area travel outside the square area.

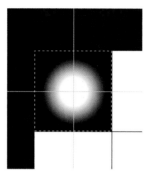

FIGURE 4.99 Make sure radial gradation is white in the middle and black on the outside edges.

5. In the grid layer, use the Magic Wand to select the square just below the one you were just in. Create a new layer, and use the same technique to create a radial gradation, but make it a bit smaller.

6. Repeat this technique for the other two vertical grid spaces (**FIGURE 4.100**). You should have a small radial gradation (fuzzy circle) at the bottom and three more, each a bit larger going up the line.

7. Now duplicate all four layers, and move the new layers 1 grid space over. Repeat this two more times until the grid is filled (**FIGURE 4.101**).

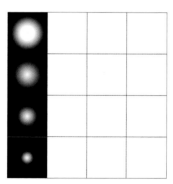

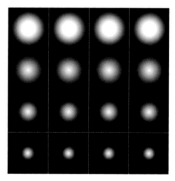

FIGURE 4.100 Repeat this technique for the other two vertical grid spaces.

FIGURE 4.101 Duplicate the layers and move them 1 grid space over.

This will be your animation sequence. As you can see, every four frames the explosion gets smaller. You will also help it along in a second, but first let's add a little cloud texture and some color (**FIGURE 4.102**).

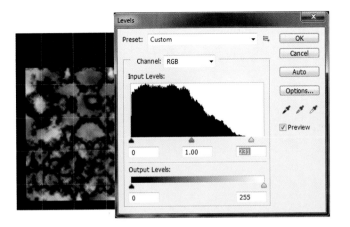

FIGURE 4.102 Add a little cloud texture.

8. Choose Filter > Render > Cloud to add a smoky texture in the box. This looks great, but it is gray and square, which will not read well in the game. Choose Image > Adjust > Levels and increase the contrast a little.

9. Call this layer *cloud*, and change the layer style from Normal to **Multiply**.

10. At the bottom of the layer window, click the "Create new fill or adjustment layer" button, a little circle icon that is half white and half black. From the popup menu, choose Gradient Map. Move the layer to the top of the stack. Change the layer style from Normal to **Color**.

11. Click the gradient bar. Change the first stop to **black** and the stop on the other side to a **pale yellow**. Slide the pale yellow stop to the midway point on the line. Click just under the bar to add a new stop between the black and the pale yellow stops. Change the new stop to a **bright red** and slide it a little toward the black stop (**FIGURE 4.103**). Feel free to experiment with the color until you have something you like.

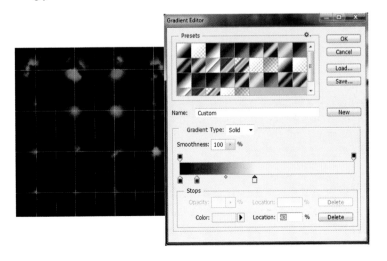

FIGURE 4.103 Add color to the cloud texture.

12. Create a new layer at the top of the stack. Choose a brush tool with a scatter brush. Select a **black** color and paint out some of the explosion in the far-left frames (**FIGURE 4.104**). You do this because the explosion should dissipate as it is being read by the engine from left to right. You can also use this layer to add more color, or lightning, or whatever else you might need.

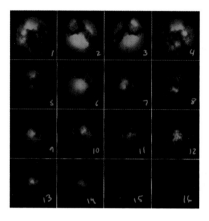

FIGURE 4.104 The final sprite sheet.

13. Save your file.

    You have numbered the frames so that you can see the sequence they will play in. Most sprite sheets are read left to right, top to bottom. On a game production, this sheet would be given to the engineer, who would apply code to it to play the frames at a determined rate, or backwards, or however you wanted them to play.

As you can see, a 2D effect may lack a bit of the 3D finesse, but for something that is on the screen for only 16 frames, or 0.5 seconds, it will look pretty good and be far less greedy with the memory.

CHAPTER 4 WRAP-UP

In this chapter, you covered a great deal of the specific pipelines when creating assets for a mobile 3D robot shooter game. You learned why specific assets are made the way they are, and how to build art with an eye toward saving memory.

As the mobile world progresses, the quality of the art assets you can make for the space will also increase. It is fortunate that the need for faster, better-looking graphics drives the mobile market because with each new advance in mobile technology, you'll get a few more pixels to play with.

5

CREATING CONSOLE GAME ASSETS

Console games are the big brother to mobile and social games. Because of their locked formats and (for now) disc-based delivery systems, console developers can concentrate on cramming as much material into the game as possible without worrying if it will download fast enough or work on an iOS or Android format. But with great power comes great team size.

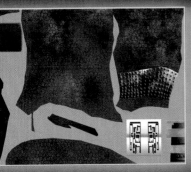

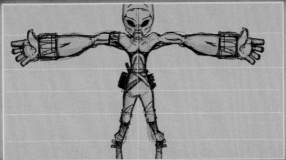

THE CONSOLE GAME TEAM

NOTE To access the resource files and videos, just log in or join peachpit.com, and enter the book's ISBN. After you register the book, links to the files will be listed on your Account page under Registered Products.

A mobile team may have up to 25 people on staff at any given time. That may seem like a lot until you walk into a console studio where 25 is the number of testers on a game. Console development teams currently and commonly number in the hundreds.

The console market consists of three main hardware vendors: Microsoft, Sony, and Nintendo. Since the '90s, these titans have been fighting for their chunk of the game market. Mobile and social games would not be what they are if not for the console market developing the technicians, building the studios, and providing the returns on investment costs. Suffice it to say you would be hard-pressed to find a studio that did not have at least one person who first worked on console games.

Who Is on a Console Team?

The scale of front-line console game development has grown to sizeable proportions. It almost always includes upwards of 250 people and involves multiple studios around the world all working on the same project.

Whereas we discussed social and mobile development in terms of people on the team, console development must be described in terms of departments. The general team breakdown for most departments goes something like this: You have a *lead director* who is the point man for the whole team. On the art side this might be a *studio art director*. Under that supervisor is the *project art director* who is responsible for only that project, followed by *lead artists* who are responsible for leading their teams in whichever portion of the game art they are assigned. Then come the "three flavors" of team artists who do the work: *senior, regular,* and *junior*.

This art team could employ as many as 20 people. A large studio creating a high-profile game could have six or more of these teams all working on different projects. Now multiply those numbers by the engineering team, the design team, the marketing team, and you now find you need a new team: the *management team*.

The management team is structured like the other teams. A studio head has directors under him who manage the various departments and track workflow and budgets. Under those directors, producers work in the trenches with the game makers tracking, planning, recording, and reporting the progress of development. Producers are most often department specific. They are also the glue that holds the game production together. Working with them is a bit like having a babysitter, but in a good way.

A large studio will also have a *human resources* team, a *recruiting* team, an *operations* team, an *outsourcing* team, and even a *food* team since many studios provide meals to their employees.

The main point is that a console team is huge, and it is surprising that anything gets done; but just like a city, their work eventually comes together and we all get to enjoy that work in the form of a game.

A BIT OF HISTORY

Now, not to go back in history too much, but the Big Three were not the first ones to the game space. Atari, Sega, and many others were there throughout the '80s, but most of these studios are no longer with us in a game development way.

The timeline of console development looks something like this: In the '80s there were Atari and Sega, and then Nintendo, which pretty much dominated the home console market. But then toward the late '80s, home computers started to emerge as the dominant gaming space, and console games slumped a bit. Home computers were faster and had better graphics cards and could be customized. Eventually, it was this customization that would kill the home computer market. In the early '90s, it was very hard to make a PC game, as it had to be built to run on too many different cards. Developers were cutting exclusive deals, and because of that idea, Microsoft got into the game world. Microsoft thought: "What if we made a PC just for gaming? If you wanted to make a game for a PC, you would only have to make it work on this one system." It was a big hit with the developers. Sony had this same idea, and it was also a hit. Nintendo as well. Thus was ushered in the current age of console games. It's a locked system, with specific specifications that allow the developer to focus on content and not have to worry as much about the technology.

THE CONSOLE PRODUCTION GAME PIPELINE

Art production on a console game is a monstrous beast that is always moving around and eating people. That description may be a bit dramatic, but it's accurate. Usually, so much work must be done that everyone on the production is going full tilt for the duration of the project. The main reasons for this are design changes, the dreaded feature creep, or things that just don't work.

In the beginning, the initial design documents try to anticipate as many of the game's art assets as possible. From this specification, the art director creates a budget and assembles a team necessary for creating those assets. As the game progresses and the assets are implemented, the needs typically change a bit. This is to be expected, and a good art director will plan for those changes in the budget and schedule.

The art assets are created in a variety of ways. Most of the time, the artists in the studio create the bulk of the assets, but oftentimes due to time and budget constraints, asset creation is farmed out to an *outsourcing house*.

An outsourcing house is a studio that specializes in creating 3D models, or rigs, or cut scenes, or concept drawings. They function like another department, but one that doesn't add to corporate overhead, so they are obviously very popular with studio heads. The problem is that unless your studio has a longstanding relationship with the outsource studio, the work can come back in a form that then needs to be massaged by an in-studio artist, which reduces the time and money savings of outsourcing. This unfortunately happens a lot, so a full-time artist must often be assigned to deal with outsourcing continuity issues.

The Journey of a Console Asset

The art asset begins in the mind of the designer. He writes a brief description of the asset and how it relates to the game. In our example, the asset is an alien enemy drone bent on the annihilation of the human race.

The idea is sent to the concept artist, who illustrates what the character could look like. After the visual concept is approved, that asset design and many others are sent to an outsourcing house to be modeled. After a few weeks, the modeled alien drone returns to the studio in a large batch of assets, and after some minor adjustments, is sent to the texturing department, which adds color, normal, and lighting maps (which you'll learn about shortly).

The model is then sent to the technical artist, who rigs and skins the character and prepares it for animation. Once fully rigged and tested, the model is sent to the animation department, where it receives a series of motion-capture files that create the character's movement in the game.

The model and the animations are then exported into the game engine. Here an engineering team member programs however the character will participate in the game. This includes animation blend trees, artificial intelligence, physics information, and any other metric (dictated by the design team) that the character may need, such as hit points, destruction capabilities, and weapons.

Eventually, a *build* of the game, including our character, is sent to the testing, or QA (quality assurance) department, which runs it through a series of tests to ensure that there are no flaws in the character or in how it interacts with the rest of the game. Game builds usually include just a portion of the game, and they are typically numbered. Any flaws, or *bugs*, will be documented and reported back to the appropriate team for fixing, and also to the producers who watch bug reports to track game progress. The latter part of a game's development is mostly spent fixing bugs. Once everything is corrected, the game can ship and you can play it and post in the user forums about how cool the alien enemy drone bent on the annihilation of the human race is.

EXERCISE 10: CREATING A 3D TURNAROUND MODELING TEMPLATE SKETCH

A template sketch is actually a series of sketches brought together in a 3D environment. In the 2D world, it is called a *turnaround sketch*. It is what has been used for the last 90 years in the creation of animated cartoons to give animators a sense of character volume and proportions.

In a 3D software space, the images are applied to plane objects, set up much like you would stack cards with a view of the character facing front, to the side, and so on. These sketches are then used by the modeler as a guide to creating the 3D model. When the model is done, the sketches are removed, but they ensure that the designs of the concept artist are followed.

We will start by using a concept drawing as a basis for the other drawings, creating a front, back, and side view. These will then be imported into the 3D engine and used as a guide for creating the model (**FIGURE 5.1**).

FIGURE 5.1 Concept art for an alien drone.

1. Open the existing concept drawing, CH5_Alien Drone (provided in the Resources folder), and expand the canvas. Do so by increasing the Image Canvas Size to three times larger in the width. Make sure you anchor the image to the left side of the page. This image was originally 12 inches and we increased it to 36 inches. The new frame will be the front, and the guide on the 24-inch mark will be the center of the new character (**FIGURE 5.2**).

FIGURE 5.2 The original image and the newly created area.

2. Create a horizontal guide that touches the top of the character's head. This will be used to track the character's breakdown across the various views. Repeat this for the bottom of the head, the waist, and the knees.

   Stay with a zoomed-out view to avoid getting bogged down in the details because you want to create a sketch of the character from a front view in a *t-pose*, which means his arms extend out to the side. T-poses are used in the world of 3D to ease the modeling and the rigging process.

   Using your strategically placed guides, you are going to make sure that the character's proportions remain somewhat in line with the original. Truthfully, you will have to guess at how some of it will line up. But that is fine, because this is just a reference drawing.

3. Start with the head. Draw an oval teardrop shape. Do not worry about the eyes or mouth. Align the teardrop shape with the guideline that touches the chin and the guide that touches the top of the head (**FIGURE 5.3**).

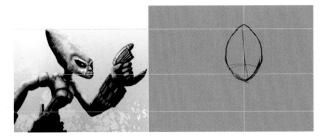

FIGURE 5.3 Rough in the shape of the head.

4. Next, sketch the chest area using the same guideline technique, and then move on to the legs, and so on (**FIGURE 5.4**).

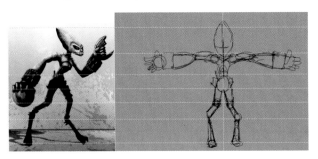

FIGURE 5.4 Rough in the rest of the body.

5. When you are satisfied with the basic shape, change the color of the sketch ink to red by altering hue and saturation, and create a new layer. Then using a black-colored brush in the new layer, tighten up your lines. Do not add all the belts, pouches, and straps yet (**FIGURE 5.5**).

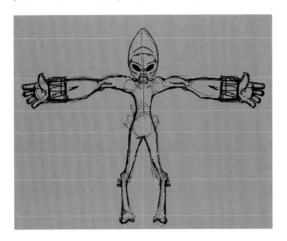

FIGURE 5.5 Add clean dark lines to the sketch.

6. With your lines tightened and the drawing pretty much done, pick which side you like better, the left or the right. Using the marquee selection tool, delete half of the character. Duplicate the layer you have been working on and flip it horizontally. Line up the two images, and merge down the new layer.

   This is done so that the body has no variation from the left to the right. Also, when modeled, the 3D artist will model only half the body, and then duplicate and mirror it, and reattach the two halves, just as you did. So it is good to represent it as a mirrored image from the beginning

7. Now add any detail that is side-specific, such as a draped belt or a pack that is only on one hip. You can create a layer under the layer with the line work and add tone to better define volume if that helps you (**FIGURE 5.6**).

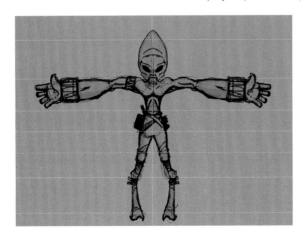

FIGURE 5.6 The mirrored alien drone illustration with custom detail.

8. Save your file and hide the layers pertaining to the front of the character. In the square next to the concept drawing, create a side-view drawing. This will be easier because it has no arms and only one leg.

9. Begin with the head, once more noting where the chin is in relation to the eyes and mouth. Also try to match the angle. As you can see, the neck was almost nonexistent in the front view but quite prominent in the side view (**FIGURE 5.7**).

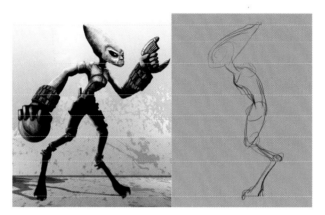

FIGURE 5.7
Roughed-in side view of character.

10. Continue sketching in the side-body volume until you have a good idea where you want to go with the character. Remember, this is just a drawing. If you find that something works well in the side view that was not present in the front view, feel free to go back and change the front view. You are by no means locked into anything.

11. Again, just as you did with the front view, change your sketch ink to red and create a new layer. On that new layer, lay down your finished line work (**FIGURE 5.8**).

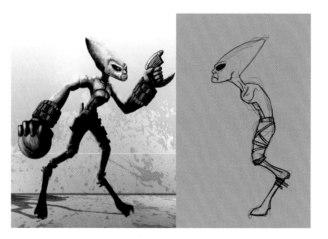

FIGURE 5.8
The right side of the alien with cleaned-up dark lines.

12. Add any custom details to the character you may feel it needs. Try to make sure that the detail you add makes sense in combination with your front view. You can also add tone here if you like (**FIGURE 5.9**).

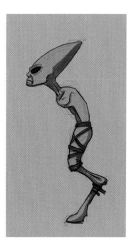

FIGURE 5.9 The finished side view.

13. Save your file and hide all the side-view layers. You are now going to add a back view.

14. Duplicate the front view and move the layer to the top of the stack. Rename it *back* (**FIGURE 5.10**).

FIGURE 5.10 Rename the layers.

15. Flip the new back layer horizontally so it lines up with the other drawings you have made. Remember, this view is looking at the character from the opposite side.

16. Using the Brush and Eraser tools, modify the front image to appear as if you are looking at the character from the rear. Erase the face and back details, as well as some of the area of the hands. Fix the legs, erasing around the ankles and darkening the area below the knees.

17. When you are happy that you have accurately drawn the character from behind, add the custom details, making sure that you keep track of belts, pouches, and bracelets (**FIGURES 5.11** and **5.12**).

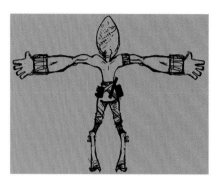

FIGURE 5.11 The back view of the alien.

FIGURE 5.12 The full alien turnaround.

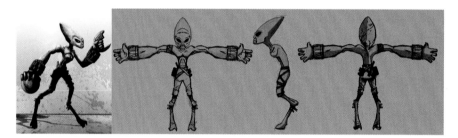

Now that you have a finished turnaround, you can go a few different ways to get it into a 3D space. You could break up the image into its individual pieces, save each view as its own file, and then apply those images to planes in the 3D environment. Or, you could just apply the whole image to one plane and duplicate it. When you need the back view instead of the side view, simply slide it into place. **FIGURE 5.13** shows what the character looks like with a bit of transparency added to the planes so you can still see the grid lines.

FIGURE 5.13 The alien modeling guides in place.

Creating Maps for a Console Character

Most people who have some idea how a console game character is mapped think a character is modeled, and then its texture is added and you're off to the pod races.

If only it were that easy. Console models go through numerous mapping passes to look as good as they do. Here is a typical pipeline for the creation of a console character's map.

First, you need to address the model itself. Because these kinds of maps are mapped to very specific locations on the model, you need to create the geometry of the model. This means that every buckle on the coat, every shoelace, every bullet in the clip must be defined. "Fine," you say, "I can do that." Remember when we discussed poly counts in Chapter 4, "Creating a Mobile Game"? Well, those rules of poly conservation apply here as well. You do get to use more polys on a console model, but unfortunately, as with all things, more is never enough.

The quality of the character model in a console game is so high that the number of polygons needed to pull off that detailed look tops out the engine's capabilities and it becomes the poor little engine that couldn't. In the console world, we are talking about millions of polygons instead of thousands. So what to do? Well, there is a pipeline for that.

Step 1: Create the model

Build your 3D model to the maximum specifications allowed to you by the engine (**FIGURE 5.14**).

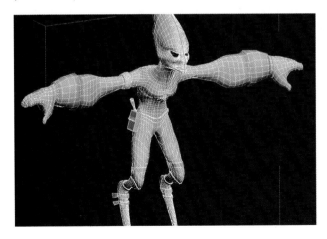

FIGURE 5.14 The alien model in 3D space with UV cuts.

Step 2: Unwrap the UVs

UV maps are the 3D versions of skin or paint. During the 3D modeling process, you apply a 2D image to a 3D model's surface. It essentially "flattens" and separates the 3D surface to allow you to paint on it in programs such as Photoshop.

Unwrapping UVs is definitely an art unto itself. Many tools are available to do it, but in the end it is the skill of the unwrapper that makes or breaks it. Basically, you take the UV map or maps you have applied to the model, and cut and flatten them to form a sort of texture atlas. This allows you to hit that optimal processing ratio you learned about in Chapter 4 (**FIGURE 5.15**).

FIGURE 5.15 The UV map of the alien model.

Step 3: Create a normal map

Normal maps are much like texture maps, except instead of representing color, they represent the way light is reflected off the model. So the idea is to build two models. One has a poly count in the thousands, and another has a count in the millions. Think of polygons as the pixels of the 3D world. The more you have, the higher the resolution, and hopefully the better your model will look. The models have to be nearly identical for this to work. There is a threshold where process falls apart, but it is great for making the previously mentioned buckle on the coat, shoelace, and every bullet in the clip.

The goal of a normal map in games is to apply the render information that the computer uses for the higher poly count models to the lower poly model in a map form. This attempts to make the lower poly count model look as if it is just as detailed as the higher count model, but without any of the overhead of an extra million polygons.

To do this, you open your lower poly model with the UVs unwrapped in a 3D sculpting program such as Mudbox or ZBrush and build out the detail. Usually you work in layers, keeping the lower-res model on layer one and the higher version several layers up. When you are done with your modifications, you can then in-program generate and apply the normal map from the higher-res model to the lower-res model for export. The files can also be saved separately and implemented in your 3D software or in the games engine (**FIGURE 5.16**).

NOTE It is important to keep a copy of the lower- and higher-res models— never save over your lower-res version.

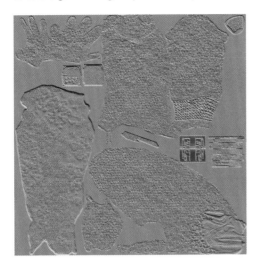

FIGURE 5.16 The alien normal map.

Step 4: Create a texture map

Creating texture mapping for a character uses the same process you used with the crate in Chapter 4 but is a little more complicated. Because you have unwrapped the character's UVs, you should have a nice flat surface to work on. These are generated in one of the 3D programs and exported as a TIFF or PNG, or any number of other file types. You can then detail it in Photoshop. However, make sure you are using the UV maps from the higher-res model so you can see where the details are.

Step 5: Create a specular map

Specular maps highlight a surface's shininess and color, although the maps themselves are black and white. The whiter the map is, the shinier the surface will be. A dark map will have less shine. These maps are used mainly for giving model surfaces a different reflective property—think of cotton as opposed to metal.

Step 6: Bring them all together and tune

Now that you have all the pieces, you can reassemble them in your 3D program and export them to the engine. Unfortunately, the engine and the 3D program do not always see eye to eye. The result rendered in your 3D program may not look like the rendering in the game engine. So you may need to play with the settings to get the desired effect. Fortunately, with all the maps separate, you can adjust them individually in Photoshop until you get the appropriate results.

EXERCISE 11: MODIFYING A NORMAL MAP

Normal maps are generally created in 3D software, so what could you do to them in Photoshop? Well, unfortunately, maps do not always come out of the 3D software the way you intended, and a little love from Photoshop can go miles toward making your normal map work. Here is an example of a normal map that has been purposefully pushed too far to create errors for you to fix.

Be aware that fixing normal maps in Photoshop should be kept to a minimum. The process of creating a normal map yields a very specific set of colors that represent directional vector values in the 3D world. Altering them in the 2D world can change those values. Even though you may think visually, while painting away the bad bits you may be obscuring the results you were after (**FIGURE 5.17**).

With that understanding, the first thing you should do is look at the whole image. Generally, issues that appear in one section often become problems in other areas. If you can alter the values and then regenerate the map without those problems, you should do it.

Let's say you did that and are now under the gun to create a quick and dirty fix. You first need to eliminate the deep cuts on the edges of the main area, as those will show up on the model as a deep trench or a raised area (**FIGURE 5.18**).

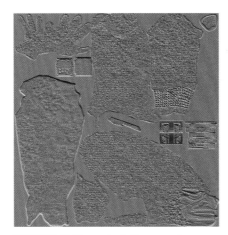

FIGURE 5.17 The pushed alien normal map.

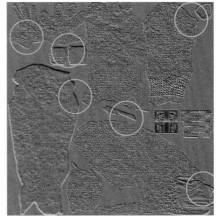

FIGURE 5.18 The problem areas of the alien normal map.

1. Open the "CH5_Alien Normal Map" file from the Resources folder, and create a new layer called *fix*. Select the Clone tool with a soft-edge round brush.

    As stated before, it is important that you try to use only the colors from the scene and not create new ones.

2. Begin with the lower area of the clothing because that has the largest issue. Stamp the Clone tool on the original layer in the area just to the side of the line you are fixing. This should keep the values in the same range. In the fix layer,

begin working around the shape. Remember that when you need to stamp a clone source, you do so on the original layer and then all your new work goes onto the fix layer (**FIGURE 5.19**).

3. You will have to go back and forth between the layers many times. It is just part of the process. Make sure, however, that you do not overwrite the original layer. You can see the finished shape in **FIGURE 5.20**.

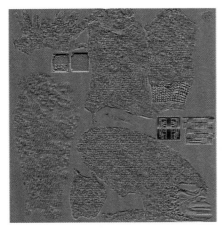

FIGURE 5.19 Fixing the first map shape.

FIGURE 5.20 The finished shape.

4. Do this for all shapes on the map, except the little square ones in the middle. You will deal with those in a minute.

   With that done, you are ready to tackle the little square box that is the hip pack. What you want to do here is make sure that the letter and the dents are raised; but it looks as if there is a bit of confusion near the letters, so you will carefully use the Clone tool to clean it up a bit.

5. Choose a hard brush for the Clone tool, and very carefully work the edge of the lettering. You may need to zoom in quite a bit. It is very important not to get sloppy here (**FIGURE 5.21**).

FIGURE 5.21 Fixing the hip pack.

Now that your map is all cleaned up, you can test it on the character for errors. Most of the time, the map would already have been applied to the character and be sourced in a folder. You would then simply update the file in the folder to update the character (**FIGURES 5.22** and **5.23**).

FIGURE 5.22 Cleaned-up normal map.

FIGURE 5.23 Normal map applied to character in 3D with no texture added.

EXERCISE 12: CREATING A TEXTURE MAP FROM AN EXPORTED UV TEMPLATE

In this exercise, you will create a texture map from an existing UV map.

Identifying the Parts

The first step in creating a texture map is to identify and separate the body parts. Hands and heads (things with skin) are usually grouped, and materials that are similar, such as the sleeves and the front and back of a shirt, are also grouped. Everything will be flattened in the end, so there are no rules; but it is helpful to have a system because this process can get quite complicated. When you first open a UV template exported from a 3D software, it looks a bit like someone has run over your model and that it was made of chicken wire. Don't be afraid, it is supposed to look like that. You are looking at the cut-up and flattened version of the model. Each polygon is represented by one of those little squares. They have been strategically cut to hide seams and to use natural breaks to minimize the tip-off that you are looking at a flat image projected onto a model.

1. Open the "CH5_Alien UVs" file from the Resources folder. First, you need to invert the color of the image so you are working with black lines on a white background. You can desaturate it if you like (**FIGURE 5.24**).

2. Now identify and separate the body parts to separate layers. **FIGURE 5.25** is an example of how you might do so. Red is skin, blue is clothing, and green is for props.

3. Hide the props and the clothing layers. Create another layer above the skin layer and name it *skin color*.

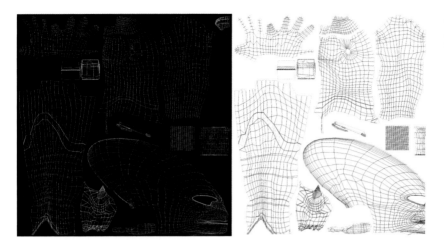

FIGURE 5.24 The original and the inverted UV template.

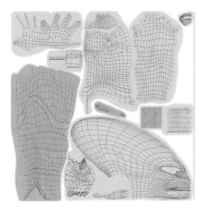

FIGURE 5.25 UV template groups.

Creating the Skin Texture

Creating a skin texture is an art unto itself, and there are more methods than skin cells in your body. That said, let's explore one possible method. Our alien, as shown in the concept drawing, is a reddish color. So it would be a good idea to start off with a bit of red fill.

1. On the skin layer, select the skin sections with the Magic Wand and then fill the skin color layer with a dark red color. Turn down the opacity of the level so that you can see the grid lines a little (**FIGURE 5.26**).

   Keep in mind the scale of the pieces in the map. The head is scaled up in comparison to the leg and the chest. If you were to just use one brush for the whole map, you would get huge spots on the head and tiny ones on the body. Remember to use a bigger brush on the head and hands, and smaller brushes on the torso and arms to get a uniform spotty look.

FIGURE 5.26 Add UV red color to the skin sections.

2. Create a new layer, and using a soft-black scatter brush, paint in a bunch of black splotchy shapes. With skin, the name of the game is random variety. Because you are going to be lighting this in the engine, you are concerned only with skin color and texture, so do not apply shading (**FIGURE 5.27**).

3. Create a new layer, select a white color, and repeat.

4. Create another layer, select a bright red color, and repeat.

5. Adjust the opacity of all three layers. In **FIGURE 5.28**, we have black at 56%, and white and red at 32%.

FIGURE 5.27 Add black splotchy bits but do not apply shading.

FIGURE 5.28 Add white and bright red colors, and adjust the opacity.

6. Create a new layer, and choose a black color with the scatter brush. With the brush opacity and flow both set to 100%, randomly scatter some black around. With the layer selected, choose Filters > Filter Gallery > Stained Glass. Set the Cell Size to **10**, the Border Thickness to **5**, and the Light Intensity to **10**. Click OK, and you have instant scales. Change the layers blending mode to **Multiply** and lower the layer's Opacity to **75%** (**FIGURE 5.29**).

FIGURE 5.29 Instant scales.

7. Create a new layer and name it *texture*. Fill the entire layer with a medium-gray color. Yes, the whole square. In the Layer editor, right-click the layer, and choose "Convert to Smart Object." You are doing this because you may need to adjust the filters later and this will make it easier to do so.

8. Choose Filters > Noise > Add Noise and set Amount to **120**, and Distribution to **Gaussian**. Also choose Monochromatic. If the noise looks generic, you can create another noise pattern on a separate layer, then change it to a different frequency or scale and set it to Multiply with a low opacity (**FIGURE 5.30**).

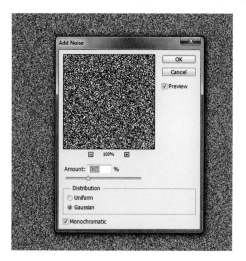

FIGURE 5.30 Add noise to the gray square.

9. With the layer selected, choose Filters > Stylize > Emboss. Set the Height to **3** and the Amount to **86** (**FIGURE 5.31**).

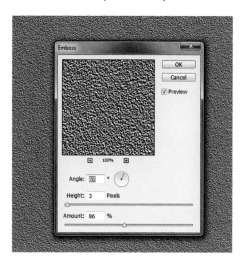

FIGURE 5.31 Add the Emboss filter to the layer.

10. Use the Magic Wand to select the extra bits of gray and delete them. Change the layer blending options to Soft Light. Collect your layers into a layer group and name it *skin*. Save your file (**FIGURE 5.32**).

FIGURE 5.32 First pass at creating skin texture.

Creating the Clothing Texture

Creating clothing is a bit easier than creating skin. The concept illustration simply has some blackish pants, so it is up to your discretion where to go with it. So let's go with black leather material that is slightly battle-worn. This choice is also versatile in case the alien decides to go clubbing between invasions.

1. Begin by locking or hiding the skin layer. Using the Magic Wand, select the clothing areas, and create a new layer called *clothing color*. On the new layer, fill the selected areas with an off-black color.

2. Create a new layer and name it *clothing splotch*. Select a white color, and use a scatter brush to splotch up the area.

3. With the Eraser tool and the same brush, erase portions of the splotch, changing the brush size as you go. Go back and forth like this a few times until your pattern fills the area and looks random (**FIGURE 5.33**).

FIGURE 5.33 Create a random patter with white splotches.

4. Duplicate that layer and name the new layer *clothing texture*. Return to the original layer and set its Opacity to **7%**.

5. From the filter pull-down menu, choose the filter gallery, and choose Texture > Texturizer. For the type of texture, choose Burlap and set Relief to **35** (**FIGURE 5.34**).

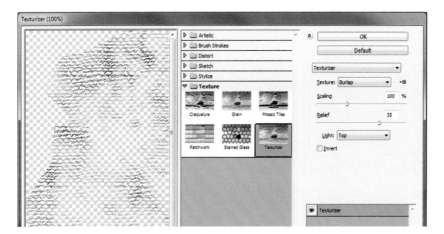

FIGURE 5.34
Texturizer settings.

6. Choose Image > Adjust > Brightness Contrast and darken it up a bit. Reduce the Opacity to **35**.

7. Create another layer and call it *color bits*. Use a scatter brush to add earth tones such as browns and greens. And just as you did previously, add white splotches in a nice random pattern (**FIGURE 5.35**).

8. Go to the layer and change its blend mode from Normal to **Color**. Reduce the layer opacity to **35** (**FIGURE 5.36**).

9. Collect your clothing layers into a group named *clothing*.

FIGURE 5.35 Create a new layer called color bits and add earth tones.

FIGURE 5.36 Switch layer blend to color and reduce opacity.

Creating the Prop Texture

Creating the prop texture is done very much in the way you created the crate texture in Chapter 4. You have identified the props in the map and added the wrist covers that initially were part of the arm. Now it is just a matter of coloring them.

1. Use the Magic Wand tool to select the prop pieces. Then create a new layer called *prop color* and use dark gray (close to black) to fill in the selected areas. **FIGURE 5.37** shows a map of the props.

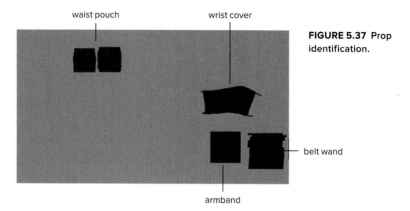

FIGURE 5.37 Prop identification.

All of these props are going to be predominantly black, with the exception of the armband, which looks like silver in the concept sketch. This is good, because you can make one material for most of the items and apply it to all four.

2. Create a new layer called *prop texture*, and fill it with a medium-gray color. Choose Filters > Noise > Add Noise. Set Gaussian to about **12%**, and then choose Gaussian Blur.

3. Choose Filter > Render > Lighting Effects, and set up a spotlight to shade the gray area to look like **FIGURE 5.38**. Note that in the figure a second spotlight was added to light the props on the left side of the page.

FIGURE 5.38 Add a light filter on the prop textures.

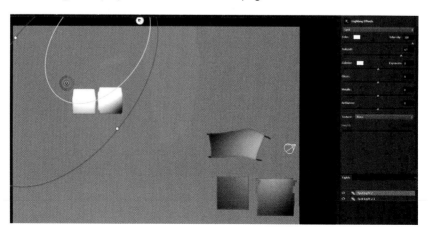

4. Create a new layer named *cover paint*. Fill it with a black color. Choose Filters > Noise > Add Noise. Use Gaussian at about **12**%. Then choose Gaussian Blur.

5. Choose Filter > Render > Lighting Effects, and set up a spotlight to shade the black area. Don't forget the second light.

6. Duplicate the UV template, and move the new file to the top of the stack. In the Blend mode, turn on Multiply. This will allow you to see the geometry you are working with.

7. Return to the cover paint layer, and in the blending options, select Bevel & Emboss. Select Chisel Soft, and set the Depth to **62** or so.

8. Using a small scatter brush, create some scratches on the hip pack as if it had seen a little action (**FIGURE 5.39**).

FIGURE 5.39 Add scratches to the hip pack.

Most of the side and back of the hip pack won't show up, so there is no need to detail it to the extent you did on the front plate.

9. Create a new layer called *decals*, and add some alien text to the front of the hip pack. Save your file.

   Next, you will work on the wrist guards, which in the concept drawing look like a bunch of dominoes on a bracelet. This is a strange case where the wireframe can actually help you generate the desired effect.

10. In the UV template layer, choose the Magic Wand, and Shift-click all the little squares of the bracelet to select them.

11. Create a new layer under the UV template, and choose Edit > Fill > Fill with any foreground color. Make sure the color makes it easy to see the separation lines (**FIGURE 5.40**).

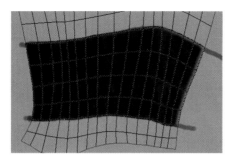

FIGURE 5.40 Select all of the little squares.

12. In the layer's blending options, select Bevel & Emboss and Gradient Overlay. Leave the gradient black to medium gray color.

13. Create a new layer and add some black splotchy bits with the scatter brush and a black color.

14. Add yet another layer and name it *buttons*. Select Bevel & Emboss, Outer Bevel, and Inner Shadow. Using a small round brush, place two dots in each square.

15. Collect all the layers for this item into a group named *wrist guard* (**FIGURE 5.41**).

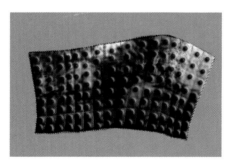

FIGURE 5.41 The finished wrist guard.

16. Return to the prop color layer, and using the Magic Wand, select the armband.

Coloring the Props

Now you will create a chrome color for the armband. It is entirely possible to assign a premade chrome texture to this object and have it mirror its surroundings as the alien walks by various objects. But that gets processor intensive, so we'll simulate the look of that reflective texture without the overhead. You'll do half with color and the other half with a specular map.

1. Create a new layer and call it *armband color*. Fill it with a blue color. Make sure you do not fill any other areas by mistake.

2. In the layers blending options, choose Gradient Overlay. Double-click the ramp to open up the gradient library. Choose the chrome style with the blue and the yellow-brown. On the new ramp, click the yellow-brown stop farthest to the left and change it to blue, as shown in **FIGURE 5.42**.

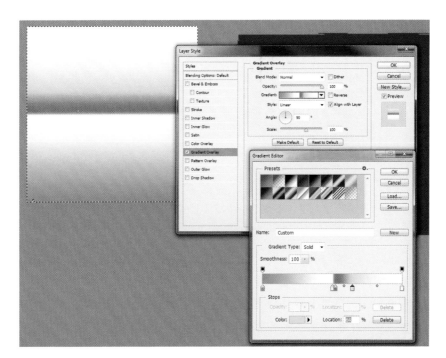

FIGURE 5.42 Create a chrome color.

Now you are going to create an alien symbol to indicate his dedication to his planet and his people, even though it will look suspiciously like the lines on a café latte to go.

3. Create a new layer called *etchings*, and once again, select Bevel & Emboss and Inner Shadow. Choose the Polygon Lasso tool. Using this tool will contribute a nice chiseled look. Create a shape on the right side of the square using the Lasso tool. Holding down Shift as you click will constrain the shape to a 90-degree direction.

4. When you have your shape, fill it with any color. With the same fill, select two colors from the background ramp. In this example, we chose blue and gold. Use the fill gradients tool to manually stripe a gradient into the fill.

5. Choose Image > Adjust > Brightness and Contrast, and adjust it so the shape is quite a bit darker. Duplicate the shape and mirror it. When you have it in place (mirrored to the original), merge it down. It should look something like **FIGURE 5.43**.

Now on to the belt wand. This is the alien's life support. It keeps a force shield around him that defends him from Earth's deadly viruses. It is made from a dark metal and has three glowing sections. It was not activated in the concept drawing.

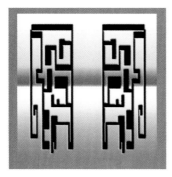

FIGURE 5.43 The finished armband symbol.

6. Turn on the UV template copy, if necessary, and create a new layer and name it *glowing bits*. Then use the marquee selection tool to select the three areas colored in blue. Fill them with your own blue color. These are going to be the glowing areas (**FIGURE 5.44**).

7. With a scatter brush, add some splotches in a lighter, slightly greener-blue color.

8. Choose Filter > Filter Gallery > Glass, and click OK (**FIGURE 5.45**).

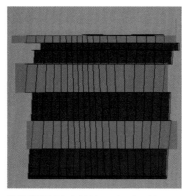

FIGURE 5.44 Add blue glowing bits to the alien's belt wand.

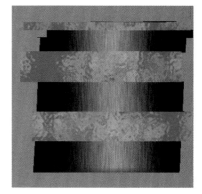

FIGURE 5.45 Add a glass filter to the blue glowing bits.

9. Create a new layer below the glowing bits layer and name it *metal*.

10. Manually apply a reflected gradient (black and gray), and make sure you do it horizontally.

11. Choose Filter > Noise > Add Noise.

12. Choose Filter > Blur > Motion Blur. Change the line to a vertical orientation.

13. With the marquee tool, select a small section of the metal texture, and cut and paste it right where it is. Then in the blending options for the layer, select Bevel & Emboss and Drop Shadow. Change the Bevel & Emboss size to **1**. This will give you what looks like a raised section.

14. Move the new raised section a little so the shading is slightly different. Then paste another into one of the other sections. Now use the marquee tool to cut out sections of the raised section to create a more interesting shape (**FIGURE 5.46**).

15. Unhide everything and save your file twice, once as a TIFF and once as a PNG (**FIGURE 5.47**).

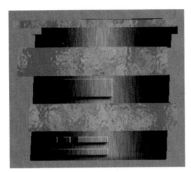

FIGURE 5.46 Finish the belt wand.

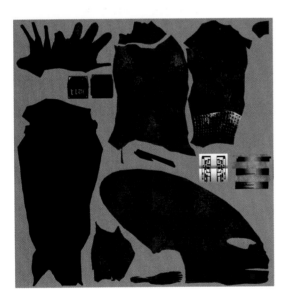

FIGURE 5.47 Texture map with all the pieces.

Detailing the Texture

Now that you have something to work with, we can really get started. The multiple layers you have used make it hard to work with the whole piece, which is why you just saved the PNG image. After applying the PNG to the character in a 3D program, we found several problems that need to be addressed.

The first problem is that using the marquee tool to frame your painting into shapes left a 1-pixel-wide area of your map uncolored in several spots. Not to worry, this is a very common occurrence (**FIGURE 5.48**).

FIGURE 5.48 Missing color due to texture misaligning.

There are two ways to fix it. Either you nudge the edge UVs in your 3D software within the color zone, or you use the Clone tool in Photoshop to bring the colored section out a little. Since this is a Photoshop book, let's do the latter.

1. Open your main alien TIFF, and collapse all the layers except for the UV template copy. You will use this as a guide.

2. Zoom into the front of the head because it may be difficult to see where the edge is (**FIGURE 5.49**).

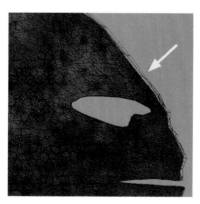

FIGURE 5.49 Missing color with UV template copy as a guide.

As you can see, you have a fairly large gap between your UV map and the color information. You need to bring the color out beyond the farthest edge line to ensure that the color covers the area. Do not worry about being sloppy, only the information within the black line is used.

3. Use the Clone tool with 100% opacity and 100% flow, stamp the source point to the left of the edge somewhere in the middle of the head. Work your way up the edge until the color is well beyond the edge all the way around. In fact, it is a good idea to do this to all the shapes; but because any issues will show up in the render, if you are pressed for time you do not have to (**FIGURE 5.50**).

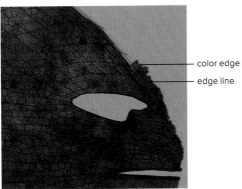

— color edge
— edge line

FIGURE 5.50 Bring color out beyond the edge of the UV.

FIGURE 5.51 Updated alien render.

That is pretty much all there is to that. It just takes a bit of time. **FIGURE 5.51** shows the updated render, which brings us to the next fix on our list.

The alien's face could use a little work. It is too uniform compared to the rest of the body. In games, it is good to have something to aim at in a bad guy. Something dramatic.

4. Open the main alien TIFF again, and zoom into the portion of the map that includes the face. Create a new layer called *face*. Pick a color (**FIGURE 5.52** uses blue) and paint in a solid section.

5. Add a highlight color and follow some of the contour lines in the UV template (**FIGURE 5.53**).

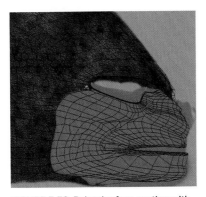

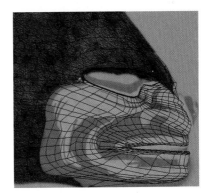

FIGURE 5.52 Paint the face section with a solid color.

FIGURE 5.53 Add a highlight color.

6. Create a new layer. Select Bevel & Emboss and set the Depth to 34. Now use the Clone Stamp tool to stamp the source into the middle of the head again. Create scales of the red skin drifting into the blue to make a better transition from the red to the blue color (**FIGURE 5.54**).

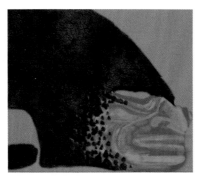

FIGURE 5.54 Add scales with the Clone Stamp tool.

FIGURE 5.55 is a close-up of the model with the refined face texture map and FIGURE 5.56 is a full-body render. There are no normal maps or specular maps applied... yet.

FIGURE 5.55 Alien render face.

FIGURE 5.56 Full-body render of the alien.

EXERCISE 13: CREATING A SPECULAR MAP

A specular map helps select the amount of light reflection that an object has in a render. It is not nearly as difficult to create as the texture map because you've already done most of the leg work.

1. Open the PNG version of the alien texture you finished in the previous exercise. Save it as *alien spec*. Choose Image > Adjustment > Desaturate and remove all the color. Remember, specular maps are black and white.

2. Choose Image > Adjustment > Brightness/Contrast, and set the Brightness to **−45** and the Contrast to **76** (**FIGURE 5.57**).

   Now you need to adjust some of the items individually.

FIGURE 5.57 Adjust the brightness and contrast.

3. Marquee select the armband area. Because it may be a bit hard to see, just make your best guess at it. Cut and paste it using Paste in Place. It is extremely important that you do not move the area around or it will not line up later (**FIGURES 5.58** and **5.59**).

FIGURE 5.58 Select the armband.

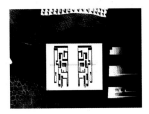

FIGURE 5.59 Armband inverted.

4. Now do the same thing to the belt wand.

5. Marquee select the hip pouch, but do not cut it. Adjust the brightness and contrast to make it very bright.

6. Using a black round brush, draw over that little blob in the upper-left corner, which is the inside of the mouth that you do not want included in this map. Remember, in a specular map, black is not shiny and white is very shiny. Your map should be looking something like **FIGURE 5.60**.

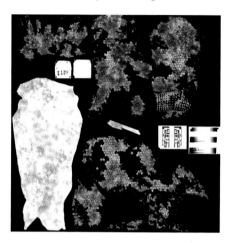

FIGURE 5.60 The specular map so far.

The large white blob on the lower-right side of the screen (the clothing) is far too bright. You do not want it to be nearly that reflective.

7. With the Lasso tool, select the blob and the little white bit above the head. Cut and paste it in place like you did with the other pieces.

8. Now, on the new layer that you created, choose Image > Adjustment > Invert. Then use the fill tool with a black color to fill in the border area. This should remove most of the white. If you have a bit of a halo, use the Brush tool to draw over the white area (**FIGURE 5.61**).

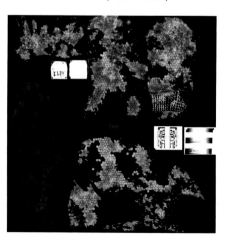

FIGURE 5.61 Invert the clothing section.

9. Return to the original layer, and use the Lasso tool to select the wrist guard. Cut and paste it into place as we have done previously. Choose Image > Adjustment > Brightness/Contrast, and select Legacy. Now push the brightness and the contrast up a bit, but try and keep some of the original shapes (**FIGURE 5.62**).

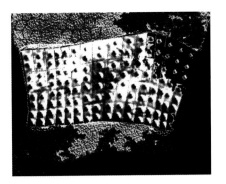

FIGURE 5.62 Adjust the wrist guard.

As you can see, the specular map can be used in quite a few ways. You have used it here to make it look as if the alien is molting and some of his scales are shiny and some are not. You have increased the reflective properties of his props so they can shine like metal, and you added a more subtle reflection to his pants to create the illusion of fabric (**FIGURE 5.63**).

FIGURE 5.63 Add texture and specular maps to the alien.

EXERCISE 14: CREATING ANIMATED TEXTURE MAPS

In this exercise, you will create an animated texture map. In games, these maps are used for effects such as static on monitors, holograms, and electricity in a cylinder. Basically, those items that need to animate but do not have a repeating sequence. Anything of this sort that requires full animation is either done in the engine using the built-in effects or as a pre-rendered sequence. Animated textures are expensive and are therefore used somewhat sparingly.

You are going to make two sequences: monitor static with a screen blip, and a hologram projection of a Wanted poster.

Creating Static

FIGURE 5.64 Create a static frame, one of six.

Monitor static is a great effect. So simple and so powerful. In this example, it signifies that in the rogue scientist's lab that you are exploring, communication has been cut off, and the systems are offline. You could execute static in a few frames of animation, but we are going to do it right. Static with a blip.

1. Create a new file in Photoshop that is 72 dpi, and 512x512 pixels. Create a layer, and fill it with a medium-gray color. Choose Filter > Noise > Add Noise > Gaussian Blur, and set it to **150%** (**FIGURE 5.64**).

2. Duplicate this layer and flip it horizontally.

3. Duplicate it again and flip it vertically.

4. Create a new layer, fill it with a darker gray color, and repeat the noise steps.

5. Duplicate this layer and flip it horizontally.

6. Duplicate it again and flip it vertically.

FIGURE 5.65 Create a blip line that is ready for animation.

   This gives you six different frames, which should be enough to allow for a good static that does not appear to repeat. In a static, you do not want to be able to recognize a repeating pattern, so if a particular section stands out, you will want to swap it out for a more nondescript section.

7. Create a new layer and name it *blip*. With the Rectangular Marquee tool, select an area that goes across the screen at about 30 points. You could also use the Line tool.

8. In the blending options, select Outer Glow. Set the Spread to **20** and the Size to **24**. Set Opacity to **90** (**FIGURE 5.65**).

9. Create another layer. Name it *blue* and fill it with a TV-screen-like blue. You may also use green or orange, depending on what planet you are doing props for. Set the layer opacity to **35** (**FIGURE 5.66**).

FIGURE 5.66 Create a new layer and add blue to create a TV-screen-like effect.

10. Choose Windows > Timeline.

11. At the lower center of the timeline, click Create Video Timeline, and all eight of your layers will appear in the timeline.

12. Move all your static images to layer 1, and rename it *static*. Shrink all the files down to two or three frames each.

13. In the layers stack, select the six static layers, and click Duplicate. Repeat this until you have 5 seconds of animation. Each new duplicate will automatically be added to the end of the timeline (**FIGURE 5.67**).

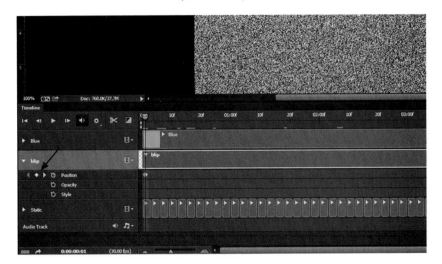

FIGURE 5.67 Timeline with layers.

14. Play your animation to make sure it has the feel you want.

15. If you are happy with the results, return to the blip layer. In the timeline editor next to the word "blip," you will see a little arrow. Click it to open the animation properties, and add a position keyframe by clicking in the little circle next to Position. Make sure that you are on the first frame of the timeline.

16. Go to the last frame and do the same thing. With the key set on the last frame, choose the Move tool, and select the blip object in the main window. Slide the object down and out of frame. In the first frame, slide it up and out of frame.

17. Play your animation, and if you are satisfied with the results, choose File > Export > Render Video. Your setting should have come from the file you created at the start, so you don't need to adjust anything. If you would like a smaller file, however, you can reduce the quality or the size. The video is rendered out as an MP4 video file (**FIGURE 5.68**).

FIGURE 5.68 Render
Video settings.

Creating a Hologram Wanted Poster

An actual hologram would have dimension, and if you wanted to fully realize that in the game world you would use 3D. What we are going to create here is a 2D hologram-looking projection, and then add it to a transparent plane in the engine. The effect will be similar to a projected computer screen, but without the 3D processing overhead.

1. Begin with the concept drawing of the alien that you used for the turnaround, and remove the background using the Eraser tool. When you have isolated the alien, cut and paste him into his own layer named *alien* (**FIGURE 5.69**).

FIGURE 5.69 Isolate the illustration of the alien.

2. Resize the image to 512x512 pixels.

3. Using the rectangle shape tool with no fill and a black stroke of 10 pts, draw a black border around the edge of the page (**FIGURE 5.70**).

4. Combine the Type tool and a good outer-space-like font, and type **WANTED** across the top of the shape. You may also add any other information, but don't let things get too wordy because this poster is just meant to add flavor, not to advance plot points (**FIGURE 5.71**).

FIGURE 5.70 Create a black, 10-pt border.   **FIGURE 5.71** Add text to the Wanted poster.

5. Create a layer under the character called *background*. Fill it with a medium-gray color.

6. Save your file. Select all the text layers and the border layer and merge them. Choose Image > Adjust > Invert. You only worked in black at first to better see what you were doing.

7. Select the alien layer and choose Image > Adjust > Hue Saturation. Near the bottom, select the Colorize check box. Set Lightness to **80** and Saturation to **70**. Click OK (**FIGURE 5.72**).

FIGURE 5.72 Adjust the hue and saturation.

FIGURE 5.73 Add a fluorescent-green layer to the poster.

FIGURE 5.74 Use the Polygonal Lasso tool to cut a slice out of the top of the image.

8. Create a new layer and name it *green*. Fill it with a fluorescent green color, and set its blend to Multiply (**FIGURE 5.73**).

9. Merge all the layers except for the empty bottom layer. Duplicate the layer seven times using the same method you used to duplicate the static in the previous exercise. Name the first two layers *main* and *main1*.

10. Select the main1 layer. Choose the Move tool, and press the arrow keys on your keyboard to move the image 1 pixel to the left. Main and main1 are going to be your alternating main frames. You offset them by 1 pixel to keep the image alive because this is supposed to be a projected image.

11. Hide both of the main layers, and move down to the third layer. Using the Polygonal Lasso tool, cut a slice out of the top of the image (**FIGURE 5.74**).

12. Repeat this in the next three images, following the cuts down the page.

13. Hide those layers. Name the seventh layer *pop*. Use the Eraser tool and a scatter brush with Opacity and Flow set to **100%** to erase some sections of the image, while leaving enough to be able to tell what your hologram is. This will be used as a buffer frame for transitioning between "no image" to "full image" (**FIGURE 5.75**).

FIGURE 5.75 Use the Eraser tool and a scatter brush on the poster image.

14. In the layers blending options, select Outer Glow. Make the color a lighter version of the green in the image. The rest of the frames should work pretty well with the default settings (**FIGURE 5.76**).

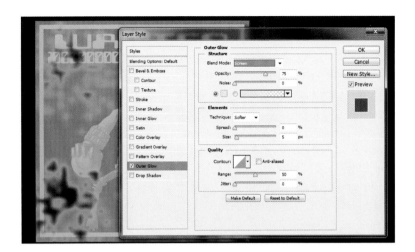

FIGURE 5.76 Add an outer glow to the image in the blending options.

15. Add this blending option to the slice layers by right-clicking the pop layer, and from the options menu, choosing Copy Layer Style. Then right-click the destination layer and choose Paste Layer Style.

Creating a Hologram Wanted Poster Animation

You are now ready to make your animation.

1. Choose Window > Timeline > Create Video Timeline (**FIGURE 5.77**).

FIGURE 5.77 The animation timeline for the Wanted poster.

2. In the timeline, on the main1 track, shorten the first purple box to 1 frame by grabbing the edge of purple box and sliding it over.

3. Do the same to the purple box on the Main track, and drag the purple box up to the main1 track and place it next to the first purple box.

You can tell how many frames a section is by looking above the lines at the frame indicator. If you need to zoom in, that function is near the bottom of the window as a slider with an image of a mountain.

4. Duplicate both of those purple boxes and line them up until you fill the timeline to the 5-second mark.

5. Reduce the purple boxes in all the tracks containing the layer 3 images to a 2-frame duration and drag them to one line below the main1 track, placing them in order.

6. Reduce the pop track to 2 frames as well.

7. In the timeline at the 1-second mark, select the latter half of the frames and slide them over 18 frames. Skip 10 frames and insert another 18-frame blank spot. Trim the line at the 5-second mark.

8. Slide the cut layers into the middle of the first 18-frame blank space. Duplicate those layers and slide them into the second blank space.

9. In the pop track, slide the bar to the space between the main layers and the cut layers. Duplicate the layer and move the new bar to the other blank spot. (**FIGURE 5.78**).

FIGURE 5.78
The timeline.

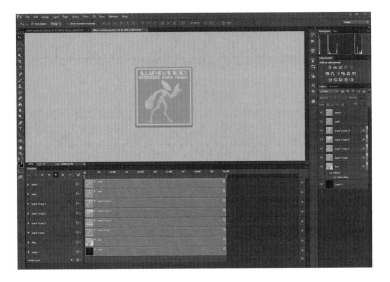

10. Choose File > Export > Render Video and render the file. Keep all the default settings and name it *Alien Wanted Poster*.

This animation would now be assigned to a plane in 3D software and exported into the game. Players would encounter it in a room or in front of the police station. It could be as big as a billboard or as small as a laptop monitor. That is the beauty of a texture. Just make sure you don't outsize your resolution and end up with an animated checkerboard.

CREATING MARKETING MATERIALS

It seems that no matter what game you are working on, once you are neck-deep in the final throes of a game, someone from the marketing department will visit your desk and ask for a week's worth of work to be delivered in two days. Oh, and it's the highest priority.

Marketing a game is hard to do without a game to market. This is why marketing never kicks in until the end of the development cycle. Even so, no one enjoys the rush work. The bulk of the marketing work an artist is required to produce ends up being *hero shots*, poses of a character that make you want to buy the game. Should be a no-brainer, right? You have tons of animations of all the characters. Just pick one and render it.

Well, this would be fine except that the texture in the game is 1024x1024 pixels, and the marketing people making the giant 12-foot-high banner for the convention booth need an image that is 8192x8192 pixels. That is a lot of stretching for something that hundreds of thousands of people are going to be seeing. What to do?

I hope you were listening when you were told to make your texture twice as big and reduce it. But even that is only a quarter of the size needed. So you have to manually up-res the image. You rescale your 2048x2048 texture up to 8192x8192. Once you have the larger file, tidy up the lines. Blurring will occur with the up-res, so it will be easy to see what needs work. This job is not for the amateur because it takes a seasoned pro to competently do this. Most of the time, it is easier to just rebuild the scene using larger textures (**FIGURE 5.79**).

FIGURE 5.79 Example of edge that is blurred in up-res.

Figure 5.79 is a pretty extreme case. Most of the time marketing is looking for art for Web banners and pop-up ads and screenshots. Oh, they love screenshots.

Once again, securing screenshots sounds straightforward. You play the game, you find a scenario that is cool, you press a few buttons, and it saves an image file. But that is only how it begins. More often than not, the screenshot is not perfect out of the box. Either a distracting element appears in the shot or marketing loves it, but "could you get it from a little to the right, or could we take down the glare on that window?" Screenshots released to the public rarely remain untouched.

EXERCISE 15: CREATING A PERFECT SCREENSHOT

In this exercise, you are going to fix up a screenshot for distribution to the gaming press.

1. First, you need a screenshot. That's easy enough. Fire up your demo version of the game and play through until you hit the target area. Your insider knowledge of the game allows you to set up the perfect scene, and you press a screen-capture key to send a PNG to your screen-capture directory. Open that file in Photoshop or go to the Resources folder and open the "Screenshot" file (**FIGURE 5.80**).

FIGURE 5.80 Take a
screenshot from the
game.

FIGURE 5.80 Take a screenshot from the game.

The marketing people liked the shot, but they would like to have a character in it and get rid of the development icons. So, first you need to take care of the dev icons, the light, and the triggers.

2. Select the Clone tool with a soft round brush.

3. Create a new layer called *fix* and stamp the clone source on the crack between the floor and the ceiling, just to the left of the big trigger. Follow the line in the floor as best you can. You may need to restamp at some point (**FIGURE 5.81**).

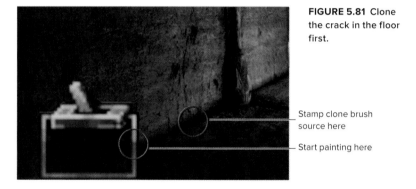

FIGURE 5.81 Clone the crack in the floor first.

Stamp clone brush source here

Start painting here

4. When you get the floor line set, restamp your source on the wall and finish your cover-up (**FIGURE 5.82**).

FIGURE 5.82 Cover up
the trigger icon.

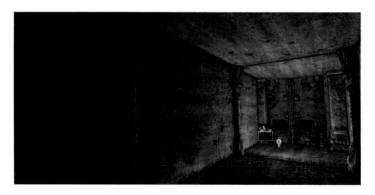

FIGURE 5.82 Cover up the trigger icon.

5. Now repeat the process for the back trigger. But this time, start with the vertical line on the wall. Work your way down the wall almost to the floor, and then move your source to an edge on the floor to finish. Because the wall door seam has a dark shadow, we cloned the rightmost side of the left door into the corner. This pass covered up the light and the far trigger (**FIGURE 5.83**).

FIGURE 5.83 This pass covered up the light and the far trigger.

Now you need to add the character into the shot. If you had access to the game assets, you would find a good animation of the character you wanted and render out just one frame that matches the lighting of the scene. We have done that for you, so all you need to do is open the alien file and place it into position.

Because the alien's eyes use in-engine procedural animation, you will have to also paint them in. You have not seen the animation in the game, so just know that it is yellow and glowing.

6. Create a layer under the alien layer, and paint in an alien eye starting with a dark brown around the edges and working your way up to a bright yellow-white. Add the pupil and a bit of highlight, and you are good. Since we were in there already, the example includes some work on the nose, teeth, and mouth folds (**FIGURE 5.84**).

FIGURE 5.84 Add color and highlight adjustments to the alien.

All that work for one screenshot? Yep, that and for about ten more screens by the end of the day. The real kicker is when you have put in all this work, bent the fabric of the universe to get a good shot, and weeks later you see it in a magazine with the text added (**FIGURE 5.85**).

FIGURE 5.85 The final alien banner ad.

CHAPTER WRAP-UP

In this chapter, we explored creating assets for console games. It is a good thing we were only speaking of Photoshop assets, or we would have been here quite a bit longer.

You learned the finer points of working with a normal map, the colorful job of creating a texture map from a UV template, and how to create a specular map. All these skills are used daily on a console game production, and now you are now in the know.

You also learned how Photoshop and 3D programs can work together, and in certain circumstances, fill in for each other. In fact, the interaction of Photoshop and most 3D software is so ingrained in the industry, that exporters and various other hooks have been incorporated into the newer releases of 3D programs. The companies that make these add-on utilities are now almost as big as the main developer.

Console games are considered the top of the heap when it comes to art and talent. The strides that are made in the name of console gaming not only benefit the games industry, but countless others as well. If you want to work at the top level of the games industry, and invent cool new things, console gaming development is where you want to be.

6

TIPS AND TRICKS FOR PHOTOSHOP

This chapter reveals some functions in Photoshop that you never knew you needed. You may already have made a few discoveries, such as animating in the timeline window or using inner glow as a stroke tool, but Photoshop just keeps on giving. You will start by making your own brushes and end somewhere over the rainbow.

NOTE To access the resource files and videos, just log in or join peachpit.com and enter the book's ISBN. After you register the book, links to the files will be listed on your Account page under Registered Products.

UNDERSTANDING PHOTOSHOP BRUSHES

A Photoshop brush is really just a predefined shape that is used by the Brush tool to define an application of color or tone or to remove properties. The brush, once defined, can be altered in many ways by changing opacity, repetition, feathering, and scale and many other parameters.

Photoshop installs with a number of useful brushes, and because it is an open system, you may also download brush sets from third-party vendors or create your own (**FIGURE 6.1**).

FIGURE 6.1 Photoshop brushes installed with Photoshop.

The types of brushes you use can make a huge difference in your work. If you were limited to only the hard, round brush, Photoshop would not be nearly as robust as it is. The scatter brush, the spray brush, and even the leaf brush all add a tremendous amount of diversity to your painting.

Because the Photoshop community is inventive and generous, you can find a huge amount of content about brushes—along with customized brushes—that you can download from the Internet, some of it shared by famous digital illustrators. There are so many brushes out there, you could use a new one every day for ten years and still only scratch the surface.

So with all the free brushes available, you should never need to make one of our own, right? Wrong! It is not enough to use the Photoshop brushes of others. You must also know how to craft your own (just in case.)

Creating and Modifying Custom Brushes

Before you can modify an existing brush, you should really take a look at the properties of the preset brushes available in Photoshop.

If the Brush window is not open, choose Window > Brush to open it. Make sure you have the Pen tool selected. Choose the most common brush: the hard, round one.

Notice that when you select the Brush Tip Shapes box, the brush's attributes are displayed, as well as an example of the brush's results. Think of this as the Blending

Options for brushes. You can create almost any effect you could ever dream of here
(**FIGURE 6.2**).

First things first. We have a Wacom Cintiq, and some of the settings we are going to
talk about are meant for use only with a tablet. If you do not have the function we are
speaking about, consider purchasing a tablet; they are wonderful tools and you will
not regret it.

Brush Tip Shapes

Most of the settings in the Brush Tip Shapes panel are self-explanatory, so let's start
off with a setting that changes things up the most. The little window with the bullseye
is commonly called a gizmo and is used to alter the shape of your brush. The white
dots are handles that you can drag to change the shape of the brush. The little arrow
on the tip is the rotational handle. Drag these around to change the stroke example
(**FIGURE 6.3**).

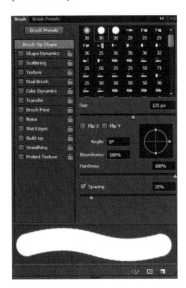

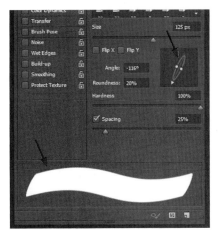

FIGURE 6.2 Photoshop brush attribute
options.

FIGURE 6.3 Photoshop brush-tip modifier.

The next item to pay attention to is the *spacing slider* at the very bottom of the menu.
It controls how many times per stroke the shape is stamped. A setting of 1% leaves no
spacing between shapes, but the higher the setting, the farther the spacing between
the shapes. Crank it up to 190% and see what happens. You get a stippling brush.

Shape Dynamics

Shape Dynamics is very good for creating things like trees full of leaves. It allows you
to add a dynamic quality, such as rotation, to any of the brushes you have created.
Rotation, for example, has the effect of spinning the brush as you use it.

Move the Angle Jitter slider to 21% and look at the stroke preview. This is with spacing still highlighted in brush-tip options. Reduce the spacing to see a different look (**FIGURE 6.4**).

FIGURE 6.4 Angle Jitter slider in action.

Each of these modifiers can change the brush pretty dramatically; and when combining them, you can get you lost very quickly. I recommend that you change one aspect, test it, and only after you are sure of the results, add another modifier. This will allow you to reverse your changes if things go sideways.

Scattering

True to its name, this modifier scatters the brush shape within a radius as you move your brush tool around. The Count variable controls how many shapes appear, and Count Jitter controls the offset placement of those shapes.

Texture

Texturing allows you to paint a line that contains a pattern, just like the Texture function in the Blending options.

To see the effect in the preview, you have to crank the settings. Pick a pattern, and then set Scale to **60**%, Brightness to **–27**, and Contrast to **100**. Set the Mode to **Multiply**, the Depth to **100**%, and the Depth Jitter to **28**%. Now you can see it. Because of the way this function adds its texture, it is best to do so in the Blending Options. You will get the same results without all the dialing in of settings (**FIGURE 6.5**).

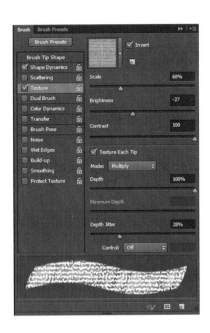

FIGURE 6.5 Add texture using the Angle Jitter slider.

Dual Brush

The Dual Brush is just like a regular brush but twice as good. First you choose a brush, and then you click the Dual Brush tab and choose a second brush. The first brush is used as a mask, and the second brush provides the fill. You get all the adjustment choices you would in a normal brush times two. As a result, using Dual Brush can get quite confusing. So what is a Dual Brush good for? It makes one heck of a dandelion (**FIGURE 6.6**).

FIGURE 6.6 Create a dandelion using the Dual Brush.

Color Dynamics

This brush works by altering the color saturation or brightness of the chosen brush.

Choose the maple leaf brush. Go into Brush Tip Shape and extend the spacing to **108** so you can see the individual shapes. Then in the Color Dynamics bar, set the Hue Jitter to **42**%, the Saturation and the Brightness to **0**, and the Purity to **100**%.

Now drag your brush around a page and see that the color of the leaf changes from shape to shape. If you lower the Hue Jitter, the colors change less. If you increase the jitter, the colors will use a wider spectrum. So if you were trying to make a yard of fall leaves, a Jitter of 18% would be good. If you wanted to make a crazy feather boa, then a Jitter of 80% would be better. Of course if you adjust the spacing on the brush tip to a number like 5, it will help create a tighter pattern (**FIGURE 6.7**).

FIGURE 6.7 Color Dynamics with maple leaves and feather boa.

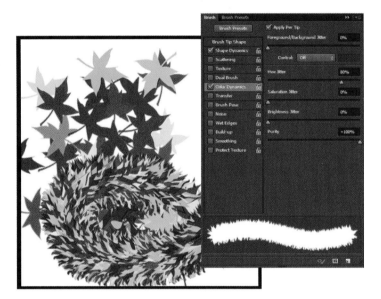

Transfer

The Transfer brush options determine how your paint will change over the course of a stroke.

Brush Pose

This function allows you to achieve stylus-like effects by setting parameters for Tilt, Rotation, and Pressure. These options will override any pressure controls assigned in the brush preset.

More brush options

Below is a list of the options that you can't change. You are only allowed to turn them on or off.

- **Noise**—Adds random noise to the brush. So instead of applying noise to the screen, it applies it only to the paint.
- **Wet Edges**—Works like the water droplet or the watercolor filter except it applies the wet watercolor effect to the brush stroke.
- **Build-up**—Applies gradual tones to an image and mimics an airbrush's paint flow.
- **Smoothing**—Smoothes the curves of your stroke while painting.
- **Protect Texture**—Ensures that the chosen texture is used for all brushes.

EXERCISE 16: CREATING A BRUSH FROM AN IMAGE

Now that you are familiar with some of the brush functionality, you can create your own brush and do so from any image. As stated before, learning brush creation is an important step in being a competent digital illustrator. Remember that old saying, "The right tool for the right job."

1. Open a new file that is 2500x2500 pixels. Using the Fill tool, color the background **red** or **pink**, but not white.

2. Create a new layer called *brush*.

3. Create or choose an image, and make sure the image is **black** with a transparent background. If your image is sampled and it has a color, the colors are converted to grayscale when you save it. We have chosen this image of a dapper guy in a top hat. We have also cut away the background portion of the image, which made it easier to see against the red background layer (**FIGURE 6.8**).

FIGURE 6.8 Dapper guy in a top hat.

4. Using the Magic Wand tool, select the image. Fit the image into the view plane as tightly as possible.

5. Choose Edit > Define Brush Preset. Name the brush, and click OK. Your brush will appear at the end of the list (**FIGURE 6.9**).

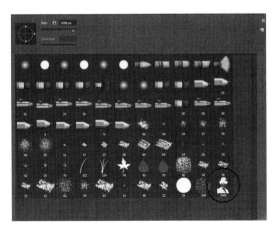

FIGURE 6.9 Our brush in the brush list.

6. Select your new brush and choose a **black** color. Create a new file with a white background and stamp the image once. There is your dapper guy. Now draw with the brush. Notice that the whiter an area is in the brush, the more transparent it is when applied (**FIGURE 6.10**).

FIGURE 6.10 Our brush as a paint tool.

The brush tool is not meant to be a photo stamp. It really just puts down the predefined shape in whatever color you choose.

Making Useful Brushes

Creating a brush for the dapper guy in a top hat was a lot of fun, although not extremely useful when it comes to illustrating images for games. But now that you know how the brush editor works and how to save your own brushes, you can make some amazingly useful brushes.

Here are four photos of items that might make good brushes. In their present state, they will not cut it as brushes because their shadows and square frames will not translate well to a brush stroke. They need to be cleaned up (**FIGURE 6.11**).

FIGURE 6.11 Original images to be used as foundations for new brushes.

Because the branch is an image against a white background, it should be easy to cut out, but the shadow will need to be removed, as it will read as a positive image in the brush.

The wood is the most challenging image of this group. To make a good brush, you would need to isolate the darker parts of the grain. That means increasing the contrast, manually selecting the dark bits, and then turning the selected parts into a brush.

The square frames of the pebbles will give you a hard edge, which is not desirable. So following the contour of the rocks, erase in an irregular pattern so that when you stamp the image, you are able to do a bit of overlap to hide the seam.

The five rocks are the easiest of all the images to turn into a brush. Just cut away the white bits, erase the shadow, and you are good to go.

It may take a little work, but the results will save you hours down the road. Try drawing a tree leaf by leaf. Before you finish a single branch, you'll be reaching for your leaf brush. These brushes also can work well for textures that have nothing to do with the original images, such as tree bark or dirt maps, or human skin (**FIGURE 6.12**).

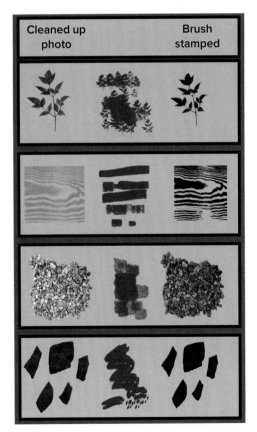

FIGURE 6.12 Cleaned-up images and final brushes.

FIGURE 6.13 The Actions tab in Photoshop.

THE BATCH AND THE IMAGE PROCESSORS

Batch processing in Photoshop applies a process or editing procedure to a number of files at once. The repeated action can include any number of functions, either custom recorded or chosen from the Actions menu.

To effectively work with this set of tools, you need to understand the parts of the batch-processing system.

Actions Tab

Actions are recorded processes that have been performed on files. Photoshop installs with several preset actions. When you record a custom action, it is automatically added to your collection of actions. To open the Actions tab, choose Window > Actions (**FIGURE 6.13**).

As you can see in Figure 6.13, the tab includes an eclectic collection of actions. The highlighted area in the Image Effects section named Neon Nights is expanded to show all the portions of the function set that will be run on a file when this action is applied.

The Batch Processor Editor window

The Batch editor allows you to choose a folder and perform the chosen action on the image files it contains. It has options for redirecting processed files to other folders, along with numerous renaming options. To open this editor, choose File > Automate > Batch (**FIGURE 6.14**).

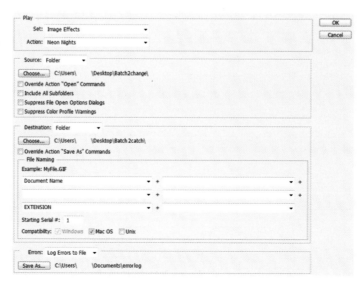

FIGURE 6.14 The Batch Processor window.

Image Processor Window

The Image Processor window is a lot like the batch window but with a few more nuts and bolts. It offers the same batch processing and redirecting options, and fewer renaming options, but includes some reformatting and resizing options. All of these can be custom recorded into a new action (**FIGURE 6.15**).

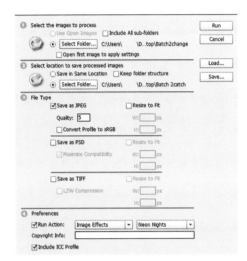

FIGURE 6.15 The Image Processor window.

New Action Recorder

The New Action recorder is the tool you use to record custom actions. To do so, open one of the files you would like to change. Then from the Actions tab Options flyout menu, select New Action. A window will open, and the record button and various naming options become available (**FIGURE 6.16**).

Pick a set (what you would like to do to the image), and name your new action. If you desire, you can assign a hot key and a color to identify the new action in the stack. Click Record and perform the actions on your file. Click Stop, and save the new action (**FIGURE 6.17**).

Your new action is saved in the group list of actions you selected and ready to use in either the Batch editor or the Scripts editor.

FIGURE 6.17 The New Action recorder. Well, it is not new, but it is called new, as that is its name.

FIGURE 6.16 The Actions tab options button.

EXERCISE 17: MODIFYING A GROUP OF FILES USING A CUSTOM ACTION

You are going to alter the color of your test images using a filter, and then save the procedure as an action and apply it to the rest of the images using the Image Processor.

1. First you need to have a number of files in a folder. Create a folder on your desktop called *Batch2change*. Fill the folder with ten images (**FIGURE 6.18**).

FIGURE 6.18 Create a new folder with ten images of a Tiki cartoon.

2. Open the original image file, and choose Actions > New Action.

3. Name the action *Tiki Neon*, and drag it into the Image Effects folder of the Actions tab. Click Record.

4. Choose Filters > Filter Gallery. In the artistic section, choose Neon Glow.

5. Set the Glow size to **−24** and the Brightness to **50**. Make the color **blue**.

6. Click OK, and in the action record tab at the bottom of the window, click the Stop button. Your action is saved.

7. Close your image file, but do not save it. Saving it would double the effect on the image.

8. Choose Files > Scripts > Image Processor (**FIGURE 6.19**).

FIGURE 6.19 The Scripts menu.

9. Select the Batch2change folder, and then create a destination folder called *Batch2catch* (**FIGURE 6.20**).

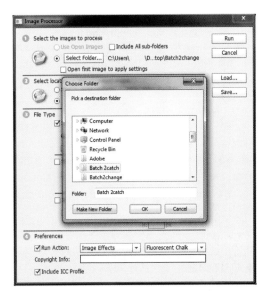

10. You are going to be saving these as JPGs, so select that check box under file type.

11. In Preferences, make sure you navigate to the Image Effects section, and then choose Tiki Neon (the action you just recorded).

12. Click Run. Photoshop will open, process, and close the files in the folder automatically.

    If you go to the Batch2catch folder, you will see that all your files have been altered by the action you created. This custom action can be applied to any image (**FIGURE 6.21**).

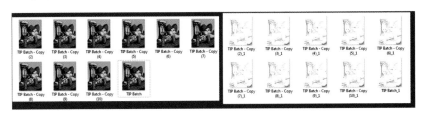

FIGURE 6.21 Before and after running the action on the files.

WORKING WITH 3D IN 2D

If Autodesk Maya and 3ds Max can have font generators and vector tools, it shouldn't be so surprising that Photoshop also has a 3D tool.

If you are familiar with 3D software such as the two applications named above, then working in Photoshop's 3D tool will be similar to what you know. Its 2D/3D workflow is connected in the layer system and you have become familiar with it.

Photoshop's 3D Editor

Photoshop's 3D workspace allows you to create and manipulate 3D objects. It has the ability to open numerous premade 3D objects, and enables you to manipulate those images and their texturing and lighting. It will also allow you to extrude a 2D image into a 3D shape, which is really handy when applying a 3D effect to text. Finally, you can also import 3D models created in other 3D applications.

Once you have placed a 3D model on a layer, you can switch between 2D and 3D using all the familiar 2D Photoshop tools. In **FIGURE 6.22**, you can see a very simple example of a 3D doughnut in a 2D environment.

FIGURE 6.22 An example of a 2D-3D composite image.

The 3D Editor Workflow

NOTE Mesh is the word used to describe a 3D object.

The workflow in 3D editor starts off like any regular Photoshop endeavor and then makes a slight left turn. You still need to create a new file, and you still need to create a layer stack. But once you reach the 3D window, things get different. You are given the option to create one of five mesh types: 3D Postcard, 3D Extrusion, Mesh from Preset, mesh from Depth Map, and 3D Volume.

After you have created or imported a mesh, you have a 3D layer stack. These layers are actually a subset of a normal layer set, with one set per 3D object in a normal layer. Once in the 3D layer stack, you can manipulate various aspects of the object's world. The first layer enables you to change aspects of the environment, which include the lights and shadows in the scene, how they are projected, and what colors they project (**FIGURE 6.23**).

The second option in the tab adjusts how the object is displayed while you are working on it. The options are similar to those in most 3D software and allow for viewing in modes such as Bounding box, Normals, Wireframe, and a slew of less familiar presets such as Sketch Grass and Sketch in Thick Pencil. Until you get your 3D "legs," just use the default setting.

The next layer sets your current view. Much like a camera, the layer dictates whether you are looking through a perspective view or an orthographic view, the field of view, and the depth of field. It even has nifty options for creating a stereo view just in case you have some 3D glasses lying around.

The next layer includes texture and material options for the 3D object that you created.

At the very bottom of the stack, you have a layer of lighting options for the object/scene. Clicking this layer displays the lighting gizmo in the scene (**FIGURE 6.24**).

You can move your object around in space using one of the 3D mode tools: Rotate, Roll, Drag, Slide, or Scale. In the Properties tab, you can select the coordinate's icon and type in numerical coordinates (**FIGURE 6.25**).

FIGURE 6.23 The Environment options tab.

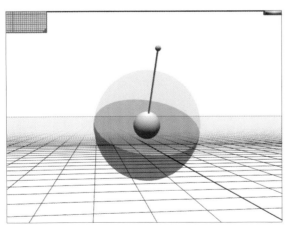

FIGURE 6.24 The lighting gizmo.

FIGURE 6.25 Numerical input for coordinates.

Like all good 3D packages, Photoshop includes an object gizmo that allows you to perform any of the previously mentioned functions by dragging object handles and interface elements (**FIGURE 6.26**).

FIGURE 6.26 Object manipulation gizmo.

When you are done manipulating your object and adding textures and lights, you can return to normal 2D mode and edit the image as you normally would modify a 2D drawing.

EXERCISE 18: CREATING A 3D OBJECT FOR A SCENE WITH A 2D BACKGROUND

You are going to create a 3D object in a scene and match it to its environment using the tools in the Photoshop 3D editor.

1. Open a file that is 3200x2400 pixels. If you have not already downloaded the resource files to your computer from your Account page, make sure to do so now. Then open the included background image, Chpt6_3DBG, or use a similar image of your own.

NOTE In most 3D packages this shape is known as a torus.

2. Create a new layer. Then choose Window > 3D. Make sure your source is set to the selected layer. Select the oval for Mesh from Preset, and choose Donut.

3. Click Create. Photoshop will place a giant donut in the middle of the screen. Notice the ground plane, the move gizmo, and the alt view also are now visible.

FIGURE 6.27 Donut with manipulation gizmo.

TIP Remember, to see the 3D tools, you must have the 3D layer and the Move tool selected (**FIGURE 6.27**).

4. Drag the rotation handle to rotate the object 90 degrees in the Z-axis. You can also do this by typing numbers into the mesh coordinates (**FIGURE 6.28**).

FIGURE 6.28 Donut rotation handle on gizmo.

The outer bar is the rotation grab point.

5. Drag the X-axis arm to rotate the torus 30 degrees.

6. Using the Move and Scale tools, position your donut slightly to the right of the middle of the screen, and raise it up until the donut and the shadow do not touch. This will give the torus the appearance of being in mid-bounce (**FIGURE 6.29**).

FIGURE 6.29 Donut in
mid-bounce.

7. In the 3D layer stack under donut, click the Donut Material layer to open the Materials options in the Properties area. Click the Materials preview button, the little arrow next to the image of the shaded ball. Select Fun Textured (**FIGURE 6.30**).

8. A larger menu of premade materials appears. You could also download a larger pack from Adobe. The one used in the example is a plastic-looking texture with small holes. The red color comes from the Diffuse channel of the material, and you will adjust that shortly to better match the environment (**FIGURE 6.31**).

FIGURE 6.31 The Materials
picker button.

FIGURE 6.30 Click the
Materials picker button.

9. Set the Shine to **50%** and the Reflection to **100%**. Click the box next to the numbers to open a dialog box, and choose New Texture. Open the Chpt6_3DBG file.

   Doing so will give the impression that the donut is reflecting its background. If this were animated, the effect would not work, because the reflection is locked to the object and would move as if it was painted on. In this static image, however, the effect looks good.

10. Set the Roughness to **0**%, the Bump to **10**%, and the Opacity to **100**%. Finally, set the Refraction to **1.5**. These values are just the aesthetic choices we made. It's fine if your visual preference varies a bit.

11. Select the 3D layer Infinite Light 1, and choose the Move tool. Move the light so it appears to be coming from above and to the left of the donut. Use the shadow as a guide (**FIGURE 6.32**).

FIGURE 6.32 Infinite Light tool.

12. From the 3D modes tab, choose Rotate. With the 3D object tool selected, click the ground plane. Rotate the ground plane a little forward so it looks like the perspective grid is going downhill relative to the contour of the background image.

13. Now return to the regular layers and duplicate the 3D layer. A little cube will appear in the bottom corner to identify it as a 3D layer. Create a new layer under the first layer and merge them. Leave the duplicate 3D layer alone but turn off its visibility. We turned off visibility in order to retain the original 3D file but still be able to convert the 3D file to a regular file. This enables us to operate on it in 2D. Create another layer above the merged layers, and name it *grass*.

14. Zoom in to the shadow of the donut. It's not looking so good because it did not include simulated grass for the Ray Trace shadows to interact with. You need to do a little clean-up in the form of some erasing and painting.

15. Choose the brush tool with a brush tip that looks like a couple of reeds. (It's #134 in our palette.) Select a color from the background just in front of the shadow. Set the Opacity to **85**% and make the size of your brush equal to the size of the grass in the image. Begin painting over the near edge of the shadow so it looks as if you are looking through the grass at the shadow.

16. Return to the collapsed layer with the shadow. Select the Eraser tool with a round, soft brush (our size was 20) and set the Opacity to **55**%. Erase small, uneven bits of the far edge of the shadow to make it look as if the grass is uneven where the shadow is cast.

17. Finally, using the Clone tool with the small reed brush, stamp the Clone tool on the current layer; and then in the grass layer, set the Opacity to **60**%. Now lightly paint over sections to blend it in a bit (**FIGURE 6.33**).

FIGURE 6.33 Before and after fixing the shadows.

Before   After

The 3D object creation of Photoshop is a very useful suite of tools. It gives you the opportunity to replicate objects that would take hours to create with the 2D brushes. Even if you just use 3D as a starting point for your work, which many artists do, you will increase the speed of your creations, and speed is money.

EXERCISE 19: CREATING AND MANIPULATING 3D TEXT ON A 2D BACKGROUND

The 3D text generator in Photoshop allows you to extrude any font into a 3D object. Once extruded, the object can be manipulated in 3D to add materials, edge bevels, materials on the edge bevels, lighting, and a whole bevy of other properties (**FIGURE 6.34**).

FIGURE 6.34 Example of extruded text.

Creating the Background Plate

You are going to turn a 2D shape into a 3D shape, and then do the same to some text to generate a piece of signage that you might find in a game.

1. Open a new file that is 3000x1500 pixels.

2. Create a new layer and call it *shield*.

3. From the Custom Shape tool collection, select the chevron. Stretch it out on creation or by using the Transform function after creation. Either way, make sure it fits in the space (**FIGURE 6.35**).

4. Choose Edit > Transform Pat > Flip Vertical.

5. Create a smaller shape and drag it to the bottom of the first shape. The first shape is shown in gray to illustrate how the second shape fits, but they will both need to be black for the next step (**FIGURE 6.36**).

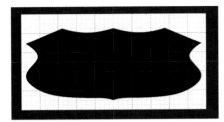

FIGURE 6.35 Create a chevron shape from the Custom Shape tool collection.

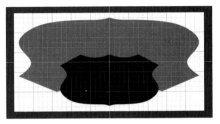

FIGURE 6.36 Create a second chevron shape and move it into place.

6. Merge the two shapes and the empty layer into one layer. This should give you a large, dark raster (non-vector) image.

7. Go up to the 3D tab and choose "New 3D Extrusions from selected layer." This will create a 3D shape (**FIGURE 6.37**).

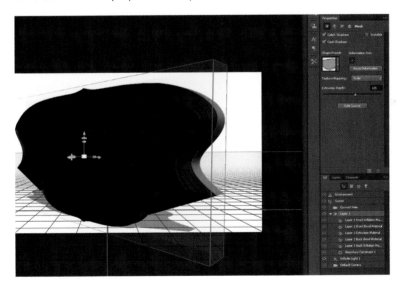

FIGURE 6.37 The chevron shape extruded into a 3D shape.

8. With the topmost layer selected in the 3D layer stack, the properties will show the Extrusion Depth. Set it to **120**.

9. Above the slider is the Shape Preset box. Click the little arrow to open it, and choose the Bevel Frame icon on the top, at the far left. You could also choose one of the bevel caps by going to the Properties tab and switching from the mesh properties to the cap properties (**FIGURE 6.38**).

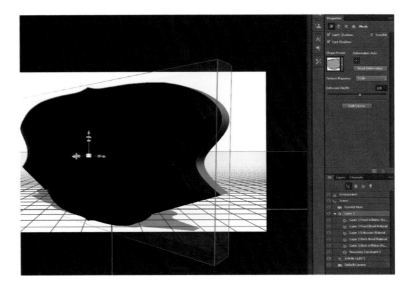

10. Below the main layer in the 3D layer stack, you'll find the individual sections of the extrusions. As you click down in the stack, you will notice that the different sections are highlighted on the model. You will now select and apply materials to the individual pieces.

11. Select the first layer (front inflation). In the properties, you will see a box next to the Diffuse setting. Click that box and change the color to **red**.

12. Go down one layer and turn that box to **yellow**, and in the next layer to **green**. This will allow you to see the breakdown of the model (**FIGURE 6.39**).

FIGURE 6.39 Beveled caps with simple diffuse colors applied.

Now that you have identified the parts, let's assign different materials to the pieces.

13. Select the first layer, and click the folder icon to the left of the Diffuse box. Choose to replace the texture, and when prompted, navigate to "American Flag on wood.tiff," and click OK. This is one way to assign materials and textures. Change the red box to **white** so your highlight isn't red, and click OK (**FIGURE 6.40**).

FIGURE 6.40 American flag texture.

14. Move down to the next layer (front bevel material). Double-click the preview sphere, and choose Metal Gold. If you do not see Metal Gold, click the Settings icon and choose Metal. When it asks you what you would like to do, choose Append, and Metal Gold will be added to your default texture set. (**FIGURE 6.41**).

    Repeat this procedure for the other layers to create a gold frame. You can assign other materials, but they won't show up because they are in the back. Save your work because this is a pretty heavy file and it may crash less robust computers.

Creating the Text of the Sign

You will now make the text portion of the sign. It will consist of two parts: the name of the town and its population.

1. The name of our town is POOKA HOOLA. So choose the Text with the Palatino Linotype font set to **85 pts**. Create a layer above the chevron, and type the name of the town in capital letters using a **black** color.

2. On a different text layer, enter **POPULATION 220** in **30-pt** type.

3. Select the Pooka Hoola layer, and from the main menu bar, select the Warp Text icon and choose Arc. Set it to **+20**.

4. Now just as you did previously, select the Pooka Hoola layer, click the 3D button, and choose the "New extrusion from selected layer." Set the Extrusion Depth to **275**, and from the Shape presets, choose Bevel.

5. Select the Pooka Hoola Front layer, and choose Metal Gold again. Then go down a layer, and choose Metal Copper. Go down another layer, and choose Metal Brass. This will give a fancier look and aid you in shading.

6. Return to the 2D layers, and select the POPULATION layer. Apply "New extrusion from selected layer" to it, thereby turning it into a 3D object. Set the Extrusion Depth to **90**.

7. This time instead of picking from the Shape Presets, in the Properties tab, click the Cap icon to open the Cap Contour library. Here you can choose a contour to set the shape that the edge bevel will take. You could also create your own with the contour editor by double-clicking the contour image. Leave the Angle at 45 degrees and set the Strength to **23%** (**FIGURE 6.42**).

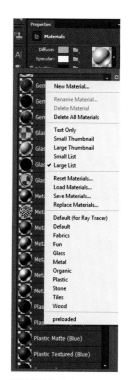

FIGURE 6.41 Appending your materials library.

FIGURE 6.42 The Cap editor.

8. Set all the layers to a metal gold color.

9. Select the main population layer, and near the top of the Properties tab, deselect Cast Shadows. You will make your own shadows later. Also turn off the shadows in the Pooka Hoola layer.

10. In the 2D layers, add drop shadows to the two 3D layers. (Yes, that works.) Increase the Distance value a bit and make the Opacity **50%** (**FIGURE 6.43**).

FIGURE 6.43 Text and background plate together.

The Sign Ornament

As you can see, you have a big empty space in the middle of your sign. This could be used for many things, such as a picture of the town or a catch phrase. You are going to fill it with two blue metal cutouts of dogs.

1. Locate a silhouette of a dog. Either draw it or use a photo; but you are going to extrude it, so make sure it is in silhouette.

2. Apply "New extrusion from selected layer" to turn the dog silhouette into a 3D object. Set the Extrusion Depth to **15**.

3. Select the front layer to access the Materials options. Click the little arrow next to the sphere preview, and choose No Material.

4. In the Diffuse section, click the file icon and navigate to the provided image, Metal Blue Scratched, which is an image of some scratched blue metal. You can use a different image if you prefer one of your own.

5. Set Shine to **80%** and Bump Map to **35%**.

6. Now go back to where you just chose the No Material map, and choose New Material. Create a new material and name it *Metal Blue Scratched* (**FIGURE 6.44**).

FIGURE 6.44 Create a new material.

This will save your material in the library, in case you want to use it again later (which you do).

7. Apply that material to the rest of the dog layers. Make sure you turn off Cast Shadows.

8. Return to the 2D layers, and duplicate the dog layer.

9. Transform and flip the image horizontally to become a mirror image. You will be prompted to create a *smart object*. Choose Yes (**FIGURE 6.45**).

FIGURE 6.45 Image with dogs.

This is really just the beginning of this image. If you were making an asset for a dystopian-future retro city with a dark secret, you would add age marks and distress marks, just as you did in Lesson 4.

NOTE In keeping with the times, Photoshop has also included a whole section on 3D printing.

THE HISTOGRAM, LEVELS, AND CURVES: A GRAPH TO ADVENTURE

A histogram is a graph that shows the distribution of data in an image as peaks and valleys. By adjusting those peaks and valleys, you adjust the distribution of data and alter the appearance of the image. Using histograms, you can see the adjustments of many different parameters, such as hue and saturation, contrast, luminosity, and percentages of RGB (red, green, blue).

Yes, those parameters can be adjusted in the Image > Adjustments settings. But when the preview image is not displaying the result you are looking for, you can open up a histogram and see what the math says about it.

Histograms are just another way to display image information, and just as an animator can tell what is wrong with an animation by looking at the function curve, artists who use histograms can diagnose image problems from a histogram, gaining information that adjustment sliders do not offer.

Where Can You Find the Elusive Histogram?

Histogram is one of the window options. Choose Window > Histogram to display a small window with a very colorful graph in it (assuming you have the color channel open). Notice that you also have the histogram icon in your expanded tool panel. In the options tab, you can select the check box to "Show all channels" (**FIGURE 6.46**).

FIGURE 6.46 Histogram window with expanded channels.

Levels

The Levels editor is like a histogram with options. It has a window displaying the input histogram, and just below is a slider with three handles (from left to right): Dark, Midtone, and Brightness. Let's see what they do (**FIGURE 6.47**).

FIGURE 6.47 Levels window with expanded channels.

Drag the Brightness handle toward the middle. As you do this, the brightness in the image increases. This is because you are weighting the image in favor of the brightness control. Notice that the middle handle also moves as you slide Brightness. This is the auto-adjustment for the midtones, and it does its best to try and keep up. Now slide the Brightness handle back.

Slide the Dark handle to the right and it does pretty much the same thing, except that this is the dark handle, so the image is weighted toward the dark side (**FIGURE 6.48**). (Insert *Star Wars* joke here.)

FIGURE 6.48 Levels window with Jedi and Sith settings.

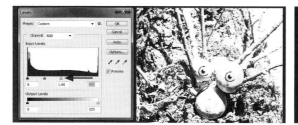

Levels are great for adjusting those light and dark aspects of your image. Adobe realizes that these can be difficult things to dial in, so Photoshop makes things easier with a few features to help you on your way.

At the top of the Levels window is the presets pull-down menu, which includes many interesting looks all worked out for you. You only need to choose one and the handles in the input window magically jump to the perfect locations for the chosen preset.

In addition to the Presets, clicking Auto button motivates Photoshop to try its best to fix the image based on a secret code passed down from the da Vinci days. Or a fairly smart algorithm. Yeah, I am pretty sure it is one of those (**FIGURE 6.49**).

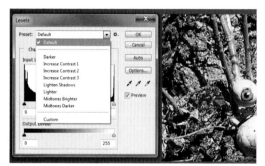

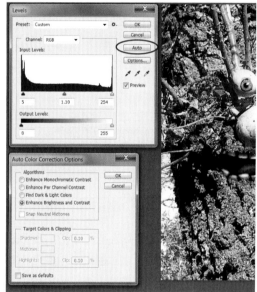

FIGURE 6.49 Auto Color Correction Options.

Speaking of algorithms, you also have presets for the Auto Color Correction Options. They do some pretty interesting things, but the coolest thing they do is this:

Select your image, and make sure you have all the artwork on one level. Open the Levels editor, and choose Auto. From the Options menu, choose Enhance Monochromatic Contrast. Then, in the color section, turn Highlights and Midtones to **chartreuse** (**FIGURE 6.50**).

Then return to the Levels input graph, and drag all three to the middle (**FIGURE 6.51**).

What does this make? Only the coolest T-shirts ever, perfect for your next big game convention.

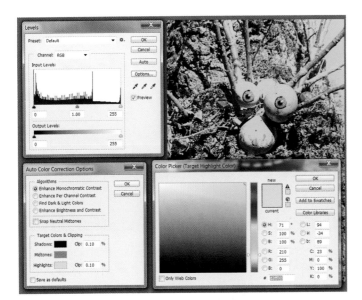

FIGURE 6.50 Choose Enhance Monochromatic Contrast from the Auto Color Correction Options presets.

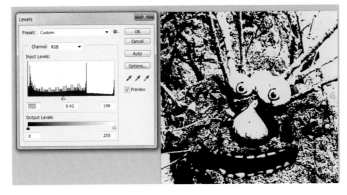

FIGURE 6.51 Contrast adjusted in Levels.

Curves

Curves are the slightly smarter cousin to Levels that allow you to manipulate the tones of an image, and selectively stretch and compress the values by adding stops along the spline (the little dotted line that crosses the graph diagonally) and directly manipulating the curve, thus giving you a greater level of control (**FIGURE 6.52**).

The graph can be a little confusing at first, and you should have the histogram window open when you are working with curves so you can keep an eye on the levels.

The Curves editor lives in a couple of places. One place is next to the Levels editor in Image > Adjust > Curves. The other place is the Adjustments area when you switch to a Photography Workspace or open Adjustments from the Window menu. Choosing Image > Adjust > Curves directly affects the layer you are working with, but if you

FIGURE 6.52 The Curves editor.

choose the function from the adjustments area, it will add an adjustment layer. Adding an adjustment layer is a bit safer because you won't alter your original.

To get a feel for how Curves works, you need to open a test file such as Ent.tiff, but any image will do. Open your file, and in the adjustments area, click Curves. A new layer will appear along with Curves editor.

In the Curves editor, notice a line running diagonally from the bottom corner to the top. Try dragging the top end point of the diagonal line to the left. Notice that the image and the histograms change.

Now drag the point straight down, and back to the right. You can see the profound effect this has on the image. The points on the end of the diagonal line allow you to adjust the black (bottom-left) and white (top-right) values in the image, that is, the maximum highlight on top and the maximum shadow on the bottom (**FIGURE 6.53**).

If you click the line between the two dots, you get the midtone handle. Dragging this handle up creates brighter midtones, and dragging this handle down creates darker midtones, just as with the end points (**FIGURE 6.54**).

This is how you manipulate the curve, but it is not how most artists use the tool. The preferred usage of this tool is to click the Auto button (#1), which makes adjustments to tone and color based on Photoshop algorithms for optimizing an image. Auto doesn't always does a great job, but it is great for pointing out a possible fix for your image. And since this is Photoshop, you also have a slew of preset ranges to choose from (**FIGURE 6.55**).

Nothing is stopping you from dialing in the image on your own, however, or choosing a preset and then manipulating its curve. It is all up to you and your artistic sensibilities.

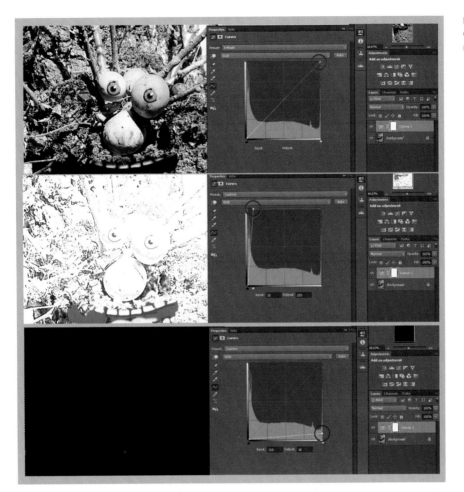

FIGURE 6.53 The
Curves editor
manipulation.

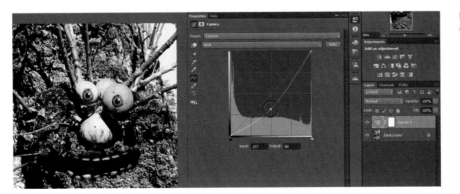

FIGURE 6.54 The
Curves editor midtones.

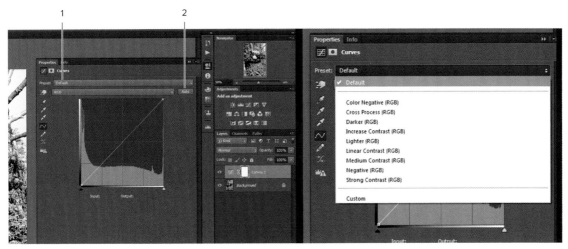

FIGURE 6.55 The Curves editor presets.

FIGURE 6.56 The Adjustment window with all of the presets applied.

Learning the Rules

All this flexibility seems great, but there are some rules. First, the Curves editor maintains the hierarchy of tonal range. If you have one pixel that is brighter than another pixel, it will still be that way after an adjustment, though maybe not as bright.

Secondly, when you are making some pixels brighter, other pixels will become less bright. Everything is a trade-off with the Curves editor. Think of it as having a finite amount of adjustment. You can weight your pixels one way or the other, but the entire image will adjust to compensate for the changes.

Thirdly, don't go all crazy pants. Using the Curves editor is tricky, and the best adjustments are tiny adjustments. If you swing the spline too far, your image goes bad very quickly. Always pretend you are defusing a bomb when making Curves adjustments, because any wrong move could blow up your image.

Adjustment Layers

Adjustment layers were mentioned in the Curves section, but we should explore them briefly just in case they are new to you. An adjustment layer is a layer with a modification applied that directly affects that layer, and sometimes the layer below it.

What is the advantage of an adjustment layer? The big advantage is that you are never directly altering the original layer. If it is an image of a bird, the adjustment layer will alter it by making it monochromatic, or whatever, but the original bird remains untouched; whereas if you were to run a filter or a modification on it, such as desaturation from the Image/Adjust menu, you would be changing the actual image.

The Adjustments window in Photoshop includes a bunch of presets (most of which we have already covered). In **FIGURE 6.56**, you can see all of those adjustments applied.

SECRET "INSIDER" FUNCTIONS

Photoshop includes some cool functions that don't really fit into any particular section and are too short to get their own section. However, we use them enough to include them here.

Circle Pattern Hot Key Trick

If you need to duplicate a layer and repeat a previous function on it:

1. Draw your image (**FIGURE 6.57**).

2. Copy it and paste it (**FIGURE 6.58**).

3. Then press the "magic button" key combo—Win+Ctrl+Shift+Alt—and press T repeatedly to paste and move your new layer by the amount you translated it the first time.

What is this function good for? Making cool circular patterns (**FIGURE 6.59**).

FIGURE 6.57 Draw a circle pattern.

FIGURE 6.58 Copy and paste the circle pattern.

FIGURE 6.59 Circle pattern 2, created using a hot key.

Making Stylized Caricatures

Many games require a stylized look for a celebrity, and creating them can be a challenge. It not only requires you to have a mastery of illustration, but a mastery of caricature as well. So here is a quick fix that makes the Liquify filter your new best friend.

The Liquify filter is more like a suite of tools that nudge the pixels of an image in some way. It includes a Pucker tool, a Bloat tool, a Forward Warp tool, and a Push tool. These allow you to mutate an image without losing the nuances of its subject.

1. Obtain an image of the celebrity you wish to modify and choose Filters > Liquify.

2. Using the Forward Warp tool, drag the subject's head up in the frame (**FIGURE 6.60**).

FIGURE 6.60 Use the Forward Warp tool to move the head.

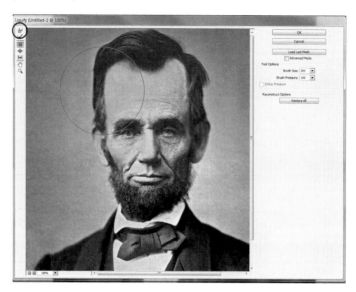

3. With the Pucker tool, and beginning with his mouth, start stamping the tool around until the subject has a tiny mouth and neck (**FIGURE 6.61**).

FIGURE 6.61 Use the Pucker tool to alter the mouth and neck.

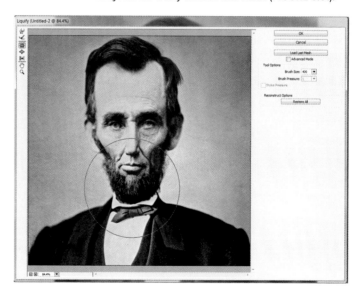

4. With the Bloat tool, work on the eyes to make them just a little oversized (**FIGURE 6.62**).

FIGURE 6.62 Use the Bloat tool to manipulate the eyes.

5. Finally, using the Forward Warp tool, move things around. Make the ears large by grabbing their edges and pulling them out. Make the neck thinner and longer, and drop the shadows a bit. In the example, we also repainted the neck because it wasn't visible in the original, but with the elongated neck you were able to see it (**FIGURE 6.63**).

FIGURE 6.63 Before and after modifying the image.

Creating a Clipping Mask

A clipping mask in the layers stack can be very useful. It allows you to take an image (usually a silhouette) and turn it into a clipping mask for a layer of some sort above it.

1. Create a shape in silhouette, or just pick one from the Custom Shape tools library. We chose this fleur-de-lys shape (**FIGURE 6.64**).

FIGURE 6.64 Shape tool image of a fleur-de-lys.

FIGURE 6.65 Color image of dirt.

FIGURE 6.66 Dirty fleur-de-lys pattern.

2. Create a new layer and add a color. We added this image of dirt (**FIGURE 6.65**).

3. Make sure you have the dirt layer selected, and choose Layer > Create Clipping Mask. Boom! You now have a dirty fleur-de-lys. We added a gray background so you could see it better (**FIGURE 6.66**).

Applying Content-Aware Scaling

Content-aware scaling is a method of scaling that does its best to not stretch your image too much when you need to scale your image in a non-uniform dimension. Working on a game, you are often called upon to create backgrounds, and some-times the reference photos just don't match up to the space you intended to fill. So what do you do? You add a bit to one side or the other and use information within the image to fill in the gaps. **FIGURE 6.67** is an image that is not quite long enough. The green area denotes the area you need to fill. Simply scaling the image would stretch it out far too much. So we use content-aware scaling.

FIGURE 6.67 A beach image in need of content-aware scaling.

1. Select your image as you normally would to scale it.

    As you can see, the modifier did a pretty good job with the nonlinear items in the scene, but the rectilinear items are all messed up (**FIGURE 6.68**).

FIGURE 6.68 Modifying the image resulted in irregular rectilinear lines.

2. You can alleviate some of this using a Selection Save. Use the Lasso tool and select most of the area of the image above the sand (**FIGURE 6.69**).

FIGURE 6.69 Use the Lasso tool to select the area above the sand.

3. Choose Select > Save, and name your selection *Beach wood*. Deselect the image.

4. Repeat the scaling process using the Content-Aware scale function. Do not press Enter to finish.

5. In the Protect tab, from the pull-down menu, choose the selection you previously saved (**FIGURE 6.70**).

FIGURE 6.70 Select the saved selection set.

6. Press enter, or double-click to engage the scale. This should give you a cleaner image in which the brunt of the stretching was applied to parts of the image where it would be less noticeable (**FIGURE 6.71**).

FIGURE 6.71 Before and after applying the Content-Aware scaling function.

Using Plug-Ins

Few people realize the huge number of third-party plug-ins available for Photoshop. Professionals in different fields, other software developers, and even enthusiastic nerds love making their own inroads to the software, so tons of great additions are available for Photoshop.

Most plug-ins come with instructions and are easily downloaded and installed from the creators' websites. If you are unsure if you need a plug-in or not, ask yourself this question: Is what I am doing a pain in the butt? If your answer is yes, then someone else has probably felt that way and written a plug-in to help ease the pain.

Adobe has devoted a whole section of its website to plug-ins, called the Adobe Photoshop Marketplace (**FIGURE 6.72**).

Here you will find all sorts of strange and wonderful Photoshop add-ons. It is also a good place to sell your plug-ins if you so desire. Adobe has a great developer agreement and even allows you to host the download and sales of your work from your own site.

FIGURE 6.72 The Adobe Photoshop Marketplace.

Speeding Up Your Workflow Using Hot Keys

Photoshop supports hot keys, and as you would expect, they make tasks go a lot faster. In the Window tab, choose Window > Workspace > Keyboard shortcuts to see all the shortcuts that Photoshop has to offer (**FIGURE 6.73**).

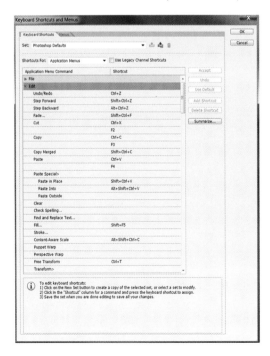

FIGURE 6.73 The Photoshop hot-key list.

Some shortcuts are specific to certain tasks and you will never use them, but others will save you loads of time. Here is a quick list of some of the more useful ones used in making game art:

[:	Decrease brush size
]:	Increase brush size
Control+T	Quick image scaling/rotation/translation
Control+N	Open the options for creating a new file
Control+C	Copy selection or file
Control+V	Paste image file from the buffer
Control+Print Screen	Take a screenshot and store it in the buffer
Caps Lock	Toggle between precise and normal cursors
Control+Alt+Drag (on the canvas)	Change the brush diameter
Control+Alt+Command+Drag (inside canvas)	Change the brush hardness
Shift+Drag	Constrain the brush to right angle
Click, move cursor, then Shift+Click	Draw a straight line from the first click to the second click
Alt	Switch to Eyedropper tool to select color
X	Switch foreground and background colors
F	Toggle Screen modes
Z	Choose Zoom Tool
T	Choose Text tool

CHAPTER WRAP-UP

In this chapter, you learned some of the more esoteric functionality of Photoshop. You spent some time creating custom brushes and using batch processing. You explored 3D modeling and looked into the use of histograms and hot keys. Even if you never use the tips and tricks discussed, you may have opened your eyes to what is possible in the outer fringes of Photoshop use.

7

HOW TO PROMOTE YOURSELF USING PHOTOSHOP

It is great that you can now do fantastic things with Photoshop; but if you can't sell yourself, you'll find it difficult to find work in the games industry. In this lesson, you'll leverage the skills you've acquired to present yourself in a way that lets everyone know why they should hire you.

To get an art job in the games industry, you must have a multipronged strategy that usually consists of a resume, a portfolio, and a reel. These need to support whatever type of artist you are (or want to be) and sing your praises as the best in that field.

YOUR RESUME

NOTE To access the resource files and videos, just log in or join peachpit.com, and enter the book's ISBN. After you register the book, links to the files will be listed on your Account page under Registered Products.

A resume, curriculum vitae, or CV is your first point of contact with most potential employers, so it is important that it communicates the information that you intend. It is quite possible to write a resume that lists all of your deeds and talents, yet still misrepresents you because of the words you have used or the way you have listed things. This is why you should develop your resume following some sort of format.

There are many different theories on how a resume should be written and what format it should be. You will notice also that the style ebbs and flows with the times. With all these factors to consider, you should do loads of research before you commit to the final version; it will literally be the difference between getting or not getting a job.

YOUR REEL

Not everyone needs a reel. In fact, unless your work involves movement (animation or the like), you are best advised to keep your reel static. (We are talking to you, modelers with turntables.)

Reels are essential for animators, cinematic guys, scripters, effects artists, and even level builders. Any output that involves motion should be represented in a showreel format.

The preferred length for the average game artist reel is around 2 minutes. The reel should be labeled with the name of the game (if any), the date it was created, and the nature of your contribution.

You will also need an opening or title page that includes your name, the name of the reel (such as My Animation Reel), and your phone number and email address. This opening is sort of the business card of the reel, so after a hiring manager looks at your work, she can contact you easily. You should also place a similar segment at the end.

A title can be created simply using video-editing software such as Adobe After Effects or Camtasia Studio, which have built-in text generators. But with your skills in creating 3D titles, you might want to create something a little more interesting. Remember, that title sequence is the first thing employers see when they watch your reel.

EXERCISE 20: CREATING TEXT OVERLAYS FOR YOUR REEL

How to assemble your reel could become a book on its own, but let's assume that you already know what you are doing. You have 10 animation clips cut together to show your prowess as the world's greatest animator. You are going to need 10 segment IDs (one for each clip), a title, and an end card. The video size you are working with is 720x480 pixels. We chose that because the resolution is high enough to see everything, yet still it produces files small enough to stream without errors. Now that you know the parameters of the reel, you can begin.

Because the text appears in every cut, it is important to enforce some sort of homogeny over the text system. Consistent text styles will make sure that the people are looking at your work and not distracted by reading. So, you should create a visual link between your title card, your cut IDs, and your end card. Whether the common element(s) is a color, or a font, or a placement on the page, it must be consistent throughout the reel.

1. These 10 screenshots are 720x480 pixels. They are put together on one page, with one frame for the title card and one for the end frame. They are the first frames of each of our cuts in the animation reel. We did this so we could find a good place to locate the text in all the shots (**FIGURE 7.1**).

FIGURE 7.1 Animation reel proof sheet.

2. Beginning with the second frame (the one with the roses), choose the Type tool, and type the information for that cut. We have decided to place the text in the lower-right corner and align it to that side. We also chose a white font with a slight black stroke (**FIGURE 7.2**).

FIGURE 7.2 Text on proof sheet.

3. Once you have one frame done, you can duplicate the text layer and similarly align it in all of the screen captures to test if that positioning will cover any of the action in the frames. Using the guides is highly recommended (**FIGURE 7.3**).

FIGURE 7.3 Multiple text on proof sheet.

4. Now retype the individual information for each layer to match its image.

5. Create a new file and call it *ID master*. Make it 720x480 pixels, and be sure that it has a transparent background.

6. Select the first text layer from the original file and drag it into the new "ID master" file. Save it with a name that suggests the subject, such as "*rose animation.png*." Repeat this for all 10 of the ID tags, resulting in 10 unique ID files.

With this part of the job completed in Photoshop, you can then import the images into a video program, such as After Effects, to generate your reel and overlay these title images on your animation. If you find that you do not like the text or it is too bright, you can return to the original text files and rework the text formatting. Save the revised files over the old ones and they should pop up with the changes. All you need to do is render your reel file (**FIGURE 7.4**).

FIGURE 7.4 Animation and overlay in Adobe After Effects.

Creating a Title Card

Now you are going to make a title card, which at this point should be child's play for you. You'll use a combination of a Photoshop 3D background object and transparent 2D lettering with some glowing smoke effects. In truth, this task might be better done in After Effects, because we would have access to a similar set of effects as in Photoshop but with the additional ability to animate them. But in this Photoshop book, we will learn how to create a static version.

1. Open a new file that is 720x480 pixels, and in the Shape library, choose the shape file that looks like home plate (**FIGURE 7.5**).

2. Choose another shape that looks like a radioactive symbol, and position it in the middle of the home-plate shape (**FIGURE 7.6**).

FIGURE 7.5 Choose a shape that resembles home plate.

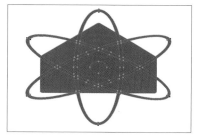

FIGURE 7.6 Choose a second shape that looks like a radioactive symbol.

3. Now create four ellipses and place them as shown in **FIGURE 7.7**. Scale the bottom shape to fit. (The ellipses are shown in a darker color here to show placement.)

FIGURE 7.7 Create four black spheres.

4. Create a new layer and merge all the shape layers. In the 3D panel, choose "New 3D Extrusion from Selected Layer." Set the Extrusion Depth to **0.7**, and pick the cap shape called **Rounded Steps**.

5. From the Resources folder, select the Stone Granite material, and set it to the whole shape, but exclude the main front area (the front inflation). For the front material, choose the folder option next to the Diffuse material, and then the Load material option. Load the Black Moss Rocks texture from the Resource folder (**FIGURE 7.8**).

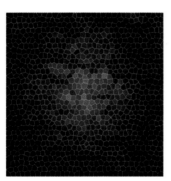

FIGURE 7.8 Select the Black Moss Rocks texture.

6. Click Render, and when the render is completed, return to the 2D layers and save the file twice: once as a TIFF with all of the 3D information, and once as a PNG with a transparent background. Call the new PNG file *Text BG* (**FIGURE 7.9**).

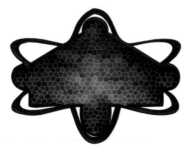

FIGURE 7.9 Create a new PNG file called Text BG.

7. Close the TIFF, and open the PNG. Create a new layer. Choose the Type tool, and in a **112-pt** font, type your **name** across the front of the shape. (We used the Palatino font with a red color.) In Blending Options, turn on Outer Glow and set the Stroke to **1 pt** in an **orange** color (**FIGURE 7.10**).

8. Duplicate the layer you just made and change the color of the font to **green**. Using the Type tool, change your name to your **email address**. Reduce the font size to **31 pts** and center the new text just below your name.

9. Duplicate your email address and change the text to your **phone number**. Resize it to **45 pts** and keep it the same color. Move it into place just below your email (**FIGURE 7.11**).

FIGURE 7.10 Type your name on a new layer.

FIGURE 7.11 Add your email address and phone number.

10. Duplicate the layer with your name and change the color of the font to **blue**. With the Type tool, change your name to a description of this clip. In this case, it's Animation Reel 2014. Change the font size to **112 pts** and center the new text just below your name. Choose Create Warped Text > Arc. Check the box for Horizontal, set Bend to **–12**, and Vertical Distortion to **+4**. Once again, save the file as a TIFF and a PNG. Open your proof sheet file and test it against the opening card (the very first square with the purple and the scratches) (**FIGURE 7.12**).

FIGURE 7.12 Check the text on the title card.

Creating an End Title Card

The end title card could be a couple of different things. You can bring up the purple scratchy background again and, in the same text treatment you used for your name, simply type *The End*. Or as you are about to do, you could reorganize the opening text and add The End to the layout.

1. Reopen your title card file. Duplicate your name layer, and move it up a bit.

2. With the Type tool, change the text on the new layer to THE END. Change the font size to **150 pt.**

3. In your name layer, reduce the font size to **90 pts** and change the color to a **green** similar to that of the email and phone number (**FIGURE 7.13**).

FIGURE 7.13 The final text on the title card.

EXERCISE 21: YOUR PORTFOLIO

Your portfolio is a collection of images that are representative of your work. So if you are a concept artist, you should include concept drawings, and if you are a story art-ist, you should include storyboards. Whatever your art type, the intelligent organiza-tion of your images is crucial.

How do you pick which images go into your portfolio? You start off with the famous ones. If you have images that are easily recognized as being from a well-known game, they will buy you miles of street cred. The people who hire artists are look-ing for someone who can do a particular job. If you have already done that job for someone else and you can show graphic proof, your chances of getting hired greatly improve.

1. Begin by creating a folder called *my work*. Collect all your work from its various locations and copy it into the folder. Don't worry about naming it at this time.

2. In Photoshop, create a file that is 1024x960 pixels, which is the average screen size of a Web page. Fill it with a slightly dark gray color. Save your file with the name *gray template* (**FIGURE 7.14**).

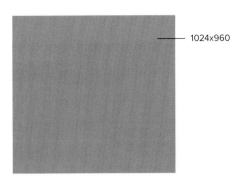

1024x960

FIGURE 7.14 The gray template file.

3. To homogenize your image size, copy and paste your images into the template file and save them out individually, giving them names that are representative of what they are. If the images are too big or too small, scale them to fit into the safe zone that you created with the guides.

You should have between 15 and 20 art pieces to work with, all of them exactly the same size. This should show a good slice of your talents. If you have art from different types of work—such as some UI examples as well as concepts and storyboards—they should all fit into the template.

In **FIGURE 7.15**, you can see that images in the first row are uncropped. Images in the second row are cropped, and images in the third row are thumbnails, which are image portions. When you click on them in a website, they expand to show the full image.

FIGURE 7.15 Create a template file showing multiple examples of your work.

Creating and Organizing Content for Your Website and Portfolio

Long gone are the days of sending your DVD around with a dapper resume and smart marketing package. The games industry is extremely competitive and moves at breakneck speed. Therefore, you should be prepared to send your information (resume, reel, and portfolio) to hiring managers as soon as possible after finding a job you would like to apply for. If you wait for days, the position is often filled before you even get a chance to apply.

To this end, we are going to prepare the content created for this chapter for publishing to a website, which is the fastest way to allow people to see your work.

The first step in creating your own Web page is to browse the Internet and see what other people have created. Doing so will fill your head with cool possibilities of what can be done. Incorporate what you think is cool about a site into your own site. It is kind of like the mood board exercise you did in Chapter 2, "Pipelines for Games."

Next, you can get an idea of where people like you are being hosted. A ton of free website-creation software is out there, each with its own little quirks. If you find a site you like and it was made using a particular set of tools, chances are you can also make a site using those tools. If you can't readily see what tools were used for the site, you can always write and ask the author what they were.

In the next exercise, you will use Photoshop to create a wireframe of your website's homepage, and then fill it out with content. You will then slice it up and spit it out as an HTML file.

EXERCISE 22: PORTFOLIO WIREFRAMES

You should know from looking at the various websites you just researched that a homepage sets the tone for how its creator is perceived by the viewer. To this end, some elements must be included on this page of your portfolio website. The most important of these is your name. It should be the first thing people see when your site pops up. This way whoever is looking for you can easily see that they have found who they were looking for.

Recruiters at larger companies often review hundreds of portfolios a week. So if your portfolio is hard to read or missing a crucial element, they will get cranky with you. Trust us, you do not want the person holding the keys to your dream job angry at you for stupid formatting issues and bad fonts on your website.

1. Begin by opening a new file in Photoshop that is 1000x960 pixels at 72 dpi. Make sure it has a white background. You are making it this size so the math is a bit easier to deal with.

2. Turn on your rulers, if necessary. Left-click the ruler bar and change it to pixels.

3. Choose the Shape tool with no fill and a **black** stroke of **3 pts**. Create a box that is 100x900 pixels. This will be the area where your name lives. Center the box in the frame. It may be helpful to use the guides here. You can input the size numerically on the top bar.

4. Type your name into the slot almost as big as the area will allow. Align it to the upper-left side of the box. Do not worry about the fonts at this time.

5. In the same box, type your title. We have reduced the size of our name and aligned the title to the left side, but it can live anywhere in that box (**FIGURE 7.16**).

FIGURE 7.16 Add an area in the box for your name and title.

6. Now you will create the main view window. Create another shape that is 100x900 pixels. This is where your eye-catching art will live. You can later decide what art to use and how it will behave. Right now, you will just allocate a space for it (**FIGURE 7.17**).

FIGURE 7.17 Create another box to showcase your art.

Now you will add areas for buttons, for both the site navigation and for your personal information. This is where you will place links to social media and other websites. Create another long box about 10 pixels above the area where your name is. Make it 50x900 pixels. You can duplicate the name box if you like, and then modify its size on the options tab.

7. Duplicate the box you just made and move it below the art area about 30 pixels. It should look something like **FIGURE 7.18**.

FIGURE 7.18 Create a new box for link buttons.

8. Create a small rectangle that will represent a button for the navigation menu. Make it 140x30 pixels, and then copy and move it across the bar. The number of buttons you make depends on how many other areas you plan to have on the site. Center them vertically in the bar, and justify them to the right. Space them about 10 pixels apart.

9. Type the names of the different areas in the buttons.

10. Copy three of the buttons. Move them down to the social screen and place them to mirror the upper area.

11. Type the names of the links into those buttons.

   Although this is a pretty standard portfolio front-page layout, it does contain all the information you will need to offer. You were really just making a map of what you need to include. If you wanted to resize, reorder, or even change the shapes of the buttons, that's fine. However, you now have something to work with (**FIGURE 7.19**).

FIGURE 7.19 Add names to the navigation buttons.

End Title Card

Now that you have a homepage, you can easily create the three other pages listed in the navigation area. You just need to modify the homepage layout a bit. Similar layouts are great for continuity when navigating from page to page on the actual site. It is important that you don't move navigation buttons around, and by copying the same page three times, you can be assured that they do not move a pixel.

1. Save your homepage file as *Home Page* so it corresponds with the navigation tabs.

2. Save it again as *Animation*, and then twice more as *2D Art* and *Biography*. This will give you four duplicate files.

3. Open up the Animation file, and near the bottom of the layout, remove the social buttons. Although they are good to have on the homepage, they are distracting when trying to showcase your work.

4. Now type the word **ANIMATION** and right-justify it above the art window.

    Generally, when presenting animation, you will post your clips to a site such as YouTube, and then embed a link to the clip on your site. If that sounds complicated, it isn't. On a host site, you'll find easy-to-follow instructions. However, our reel clips are 720x480, which is slightly larger than the area you have to work with.

5. No problem, just stretch out the art area to encompass the video area. However, do not move the side wall, just stretch it in height to **540 px**. This will create a nice framework for the video. The video box should be centered and about **140 px** from either side of the page (**FIGURE 7.20**).

FIGURE 7.20 Create a page for your animation reel.

6. Now open the 2D Art page and remove the middle social button and all of the social text. Create a rectangle shape that is 190x175 pixels. Create a gallery that is 2 units high by 4 units wide. These will contain the thumbnail views of your 2D work. When you click the thumbnails, they will expand to display the full-size images that you saved earlier.

7. In the social area, type the words **PREVIOUS** and **NEXT**. Put one box on the far left, and drag the word PREVIOUS into it. Slide the other box over to the left, and drag the word NEXT into it. These will be your scroll buttons for the gallery (**FIGURE 7.21**).

8. Open the Biography page, but this time do not remove the social buttons. They will actually enhance this page. Create a rectangle shape that is 270x460 pixels, and place it on the right side of the screen. Add the words **YOUR BIOGRAPHY** to it.

9. Duplicate the rectangle and change the dimensions to 340x270 pixels, and add the words **YOUR IMAGE** to it. In the example, we also changed the color.

10. Above the Biography square, create a new box that is 445x460 pixels. Type the word **RESUME** in it. This will be the link to your resume.

    You will want to write a personal work-related statement about yourself as well as take a good picture. It is important that people have a face to associate with your artwork (**FIGURE 7.22**).

Now that you have all your pages mocked up, you can put them together and see how the flow works.

FIGURE 7.21 Create scroll buttons for your 2D art page.

FIGURE 7.22 Create a biography page.

FINALIZING THE LOOK OF YOUR WEBSITE PORTFOLIO

Now that you have identified all the items you will need to build your portfolio and defined the layout of these items, you can start to design the look and feel of you site. Part of what you're judged on is taste, so you should factor that into your design. If you have any questions about your taste, you should ask a colleague or experienced professional to look at your portfolio (not your mom).

The look of your site can vary greatly, even two people who do the same job and have the same style of work can have radically different-looking sites. It really all boils down to how you would like to represent yourself.

In **FIGURE 7.23**, you can see the same information presented in two different styles. Both presentations have the same buttons, the same layout, and the same gallery with the same art. The only differences are the fonts, the backgrounds, and the colors. Even though you may have your site architecture worked out in a wireframe, you can see that there is still a long way to go to make it your own.

FIGURE 7.23 Two different styles of the same page.

EXERCISE 23: CREATING ASSETS FOR YOUR WEBSITE PORTFOLIO

We are going to pretend that we had a meeting with ourselves and decided that we wanted our portfolio look to be a sort of artistic shabby retro thing. Don't worry, we were quite excited with the decision. We will begin by creating an appropriate background.

Before you begin to design, walk around with your phone or camera looking for a cool background. Because of the style we chose, we are looking for something with a bit of visual history that has some good neutral space where the text can live. When you find the perfect subject, frame it and take several pictures of it. Make sure you move around a bit while shooting. You never know what will work best and it is good to have options. We found this old paint ladder in the backyard, with at least 20 years of paint on it. It was generally in good shape. We darkened some areas and painted out some bits that were a little distracting (**FIGURE 7.24**).

FIGURE 7.24 An old paint ladder is the background for this website.

1. Open your wireframe homepage and put the background behind all the text and boxes. Because of the photographic nature of the background, you will make your boxes using Photoshop 3D (**FIGURE 7.25**).

FIGURE 7.25 Wireframe with new background.

2. Select the art area and choose 3D > New 3D Extrusion from Selected Path.

3. Set Extrusion Depth to **150**. Under the Caps tab in the 3D properties section, select the Gaussian cap with a Width of **16%** and an Angle of **45** degrees. Set the Strength to **0**.

4. Shift-click all the materials layers to select them, and next to the Diffuse tab, click the file icon and choose Replace Texture. From the Resources folder, select the Galvanized texture, which will apply it to all of the material sections.

5. Rotate the box a tiny bit to the right to better showcase its 3D quality.

6. Using the Magic Wand, select the art box, and choose 3D > Render. This should leave you with what looks like a large piece of metal (**FIGURE 7.26**).

FIGURE 7.26 Use an image of a metal box in the area where your artwork will go.

7. In the 2D layers, select the name area shape layer. From the Resources folder, open the slide rule image and scale it to roughly the same size as the shape.

8. In Blending Options, turn on Bevel & Emboss and Drop Shadow.

9. Rotate the slide rule slightly clockwise, and drag the left side out of frame. Don't worry about the text. You will adjust it soon (**FIGURE 7.27**).

FIGURE 7.27 Use an image of a slide rule in the area for your name.

10. Import the ruler image file into the scene and scale it to cover half the social media bar. In Blending Options, turn on Bevel & Emboss and Drop Shadow.

11. Duplicate the layer and move it to cover the other half of the bar. Rotate them both slightly to be a tiny bit askew. Notice how the slide rule and the ruler colors match, and are in the warmer range to bring them forward a little and give the image a bit more depth (**FIGURE 7.28**).

FIGURE 7.28 Add rulers to the social media bar.

12. Now import the image file of the rusty yellow bar into the scene and scale it to cover half of the navigation bar. In Blending Options, turn on Bevel & Emboss and Drop Shadow (**FIGURE 7.29**).

FIGURE 7.29 Import the image of the rusty yellow bar and place it on the navigation bar.

Now that you have some of the background objects in place, you can get started on the text. Some of the text is obviously going to be tied to code of some sort, and in most website-crafting programs, the text for buttons and the like uses a limited font palette that is integrated into their system. However, this will not stop you from setting up the noncoded buttons. Ideally, whatever program you choose to build your website has enough font bandwidth to find something that matches your design concept.

13. Select your name layer, and choose 3D > New 3D Extrusion from Selected Layer. Set Extrusion Depth to **190**. Click the gray box next to the word "Diffusion" and change it to a slightly subdued **red** color.

14. Adjust the Infinite light in the scene to have an intensity of **318%** or so. Make it **red** and match the lighting direction of the rest of the items in the scene.

15. In the 2D layers, turn on Drop Shadow and Stroke. Make the stroke a **black** color with a width of **2 pts**.

16. If you are happy with the look, go to the 2D layers and do the exact same thing to the Games Specialty Artist layer that we did to your name layer, except set Color to **blue** and Extrusion Depth to **90**. Do not add a stroke (**FIGURE 7.30**).

FIGURE 7.30 Use red for your name and blue for your title.

There is a problem with doing the lettering this way. Because you made it using Photoshop 3D and added lights, the 3D portion needs to be re-rendered every time you make a change. While this can be a pain, the results are worth it, and you can later do a final render on the completed image. You can also work on a new layer above the text.

17. Create a new layer above the Your Name text layer, and call it *scuff*. In the layer's blending properties, turn on Bevel & Emboss. Set Style to **Emboss**, Technique to **Chisel Hard**, Direction to **Down**, and Size to **2**.

18. Using a scatter brush, carefully add scuff marks to the letters. Be mindful of the 3D, as the scuffs will not wrap around the text. The games specialty text is too small for this kind of treatment, so just skip it (**FIGURE 7.31**).

FIGURE 7.31 Add scuff marks to the letters in your name.

Building Buttons

With the name section in good shape, you can move on to the buttons. Buttons are available in a few flavors. One is premade and usually looks like every button you have ever seen. It has a gradation and a highlight, and if you remember, you made one in Chapter 3, "Game Asset Creation for Social Media."

These will not be your buttons. The kind of buttons you are going to make are generally the shape of buttons, but are really just images to which you can later apply some code to make them to behave like buttons. The downside is that your buttons do not scale like vector-generated buttons and they will load a bit slower, but they will also sell the look, which is what you are after right now.

1. Select the galvanized 3D Art area layer and duplicate it. Create a new layer underneath it and merge the two layers.

2. Cut out the button and paste it down again, creating a new layer that does not have all the baggage of the empty space.

3. Reduce the button size to fit roughly over the first box of the social bar, but make sure it is below the text.

4. In the Blending Options, turn on Drop Shadow and duplicate it two more times. Slide the duplicate over to cover the other two boxes. Select the middle button and flip it horizontally (**FIGURE 7.32**).

FIGURE 7.32 Add buttons to the social bar.

Now you are going to create the buttons for the navigation area. But instead of making a traditional button, yours will be cutouts in the rusty yellow bar.

5. Create a new layer just above the rusty yellow bar and call it *Nav Button*. With the marquee tool, select a shape that is roughly the same size as the animation navigation button. Fill it with a **black** color.

6. In the Blending Options, select Inner Glow. Change Blend Mode to **Normal**, Opacity to **100%**, Color to a **chocolate brown**, Choke to **100%**, and Size to **3**.

7. Now select Bevel & Emboss. Change Style to **Inner Bevel**, Direction to **Down**, and verify that Size is set to **5** (**FIGURE 7.33**).

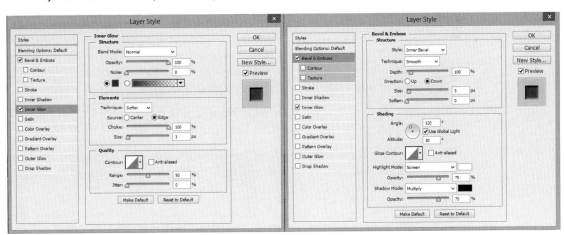

FIGURE 7.33 The Blending Options setting for navigation buttons.

8. Once you've created one button, duplicate it across the top. However, you will find that you have another issue. Now you cannot see the text because it is black on black. Double-click each text layer and change the text to **white**. Your file should look something like **FIGURE 7.34**.

FIGURE 7.34 Change the text for the navigation buttons to white.

Making an Introductory Slideshow

You now need to decide what you are going to do in the main show space. We have been calling it the art area. Traditionally, this is sort of an ad space for your work: a window with a slideshow of your work plays on a loop, so that when a recruiter is viewing your homepage, she instantly gets a taste of your talent. Then, if she is interested, she can dig deeper into your site.

This area is often accompanied by a text blurb that says something about how good it would be to hire you, and how smart you are, and how you have devoted your life to the craft and the cost of your grandma's freedom.

You are about to add both elements to the art area. The artwork won't slideshow yet, but you will get an idea of how it will look.

1. The first step is to identify the slideshow area. Create a new shape that is 450x300 pixels. This is a scaled-down 720x480 pixels. Any color fill is fine, and with no stroke. This will be the slideshow window.

2. From the Resources folder, select the "galvanized frame" file and put it over the box you created. This will be the slideshow area (**FIGURE 7.35**).

FIGURE 7.35 Galvanized frame for your slideshow.

3. From the Resources folder, open the Red Tag file and place it next to the frame on the right side. This will be the personal statement area. The tag will serve as the backdrop. Most likely, the text will be from the build software. You just need to use a font color that can be read easily. **FIGURE 7.36** shows the tag with some slug text.

FIGURE 7.36 Red tag with slug text—your personal statement.

Now that all the pieces are in place, it is important that you note a few things. First, it may look like some of the text is askew, but it isn't. Web-building software certainly allows you to adjust the rotation of text, but you did not rotate any of the button text here. This is because it is far easier to lay out and justify text if it is at a right angle.

The second thing to note is that you did skew the images that overlay the buttons. This is fine, as long as the overlay and the buttons occupy most of the same space.

FIGURE 7.37 The overlay area and active zone for the button.

However, you don't want to click a button overlay and have the button not respond because your mouse point is out of the active zone (**FIGURE 7.37**).

In **FIGURE 7.38**, you can see the original wireframe overlaid on the final homepage art. Some liberties were taken, but for the most part, this result adheres to the original design.

FIGURE 7.38 Finished homepage with wireframe overlay.

Quite often in a game studio, you will be required to submit wireframes to the engineering department so they can start working on the functionality of the page while you generate the art. This means that your final execution needs to be close to your submitted wireframe, otherwise they might have to (unhappily) redo work to match your design. But because this is your website, and if you don't like the differences, you will just be yelling at yourself.

You may be wondering about the button states. As we discussed in Chapter 3, buttons usually have two states: active and inactive. The button overlays you have created would be the inactive state, and the obvious active state would be to modify the overlays by adding a color or darkening the existing colors. The problem with that method is that it requires doubling the number of PNGs, which can get expensive. The other method is to use the website software to change the text color when the button is activated, which should provide enough interaction to identify the function as active. That method requires no extra PNGs and still reflects the interaction.

Preparing Your Page for Implementation

Now that you have all the pieces and the look is fleshed out, it's time to clean up your files and prepare them for importation into the HTML code. If you have slacked off on naming your layers, you should now properly name them, and also group layers that operate as a single piece. The text will not be included in what you are doing, so you should also collect those layers to a separate layer group.

EXERCISE 24: SEPARATING YOUR LAYERS INTO INDIVIDUAL PNG FILES

If you were working with an engineer, this is when you would save all those layers—each one is an element in your Web page—as individual, Web-ready PNGs. The names of the files would match the layers in the master file, and the engineer would have a sort of map for how to assemble your page.

Unfortunately, even without an engineer that is what you have to do.

1. Select the first layer in your stack, the galvanized frame layer. In the selection menu, choose Select All. Copy the file.

2. With the file in the buffer (you just copied it), create a new file called *galvanized frame*. It should be the exact size of the frame.

3. Paste the copied frame into the new file and delete all layers other than the one with your image on it.

4. In your Web-page master, select the galvanized frame layer. Choose Layer > Copy Layer Style.

5. In the new file, paste the layer style into the new file's layer by choosing Paste Layer Style. You will need to repeat this for any files that have FX in them. **FIGURE 7.39** shows the two files next to each other.

FIGURE 7.39 The galvanized frame layer extracted to its own file.

6. Repeat this for all layers in the file except for the text layer group.

7. For layer groups such as the Artist Name group, you need to open the group and select all the layers in the group.

8. Then with the layers selected, choose Layers > Merge Layers.

9. Now you can use the Select All Function again and create a new file. Then paste the selected file.

   The blending options for these layers were infused into the file when you merged them, so you needn't copy/paste the layer styles this time. A word of caution: Do not save your master file with this group merged. You may need access to it again later, so back yourself out of the merge before you save.

It is always good to practice efficient file storage, so while the saving will be minimal in this exercise, the following steps show you how best to save a file for the Web.

10. Choose File > Save for Web. An options window will open. The most important option is the second box from the top, on the right, which probably reads gif. Change it to **PNG-8** to create a PNG file at 8-bit resolution. The other option is 24-bit resolution.

On the left, at the top of the image plane, you'll find a few tabs, including Original and Optimized. If you click between the two, you can see how much memory you save by optimizing your saved file.

11. If you are happy that this process did not destroy your image, click Save (**FIGURE 7.40**).

FIGURE 7.40 The Save for Web tool optimizes files for the Web.

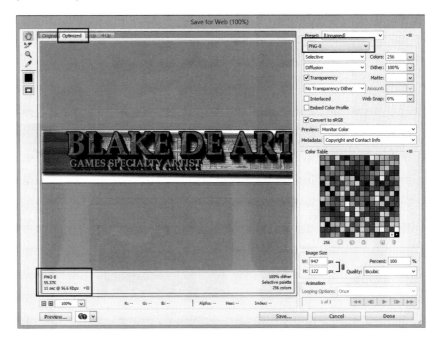

Once you have everything separated, you can use any of the hundreds of Web software packages to build your very own website. Use the master file as your map and just fill out the page with the PNG files. You can even copy and paste the text files if you are too lazy to retype the button names.

What we didn't cover in this exercise were those other three wireframe pages: Animation, 2D Art, and Biography. They will also need to be fleshed out, their pieces saved as PNGs, and then reassembled. The good part is that a lot of the pieces, like the navigation bar, can be made persistent throughout the site so you have to make those only once.

EXERCISE 25: THE SLICE TOOL AND HOW TO MAKE A QUICKIE WEBSITE

The Slice tool is not the kind of tool that the average game artist uses. It is mostly used for chopping up images and turning them into Web pages. It doesn't care about format, it doesn't care about blending options; it just dices the sections you choose into Web-ready slices. You can then apply rudimentary code such as URL links to those slices. So, if you only needed one page and wanted it to send people to a YouTube video link, this would be a good way to go.

This tool is very easy to use because it runs on the crop window technology using movement handles. To start a new slice, you just put the brush down again. Want to create windows in windows? No problem.

1. Open the final Web page you made.

2. On the toolbar, hold down the mouse button over the Crop tool until the alternative tool option appears. Choose the Slice tool. It looks like the tip of an Exacto knife. The Slice tool has several style options for how to make selections, but just leave it at normal for now.

3. Drag a slice marquee around the navigation buttons and the rusty yellow bar (**FIGURE 7.41**).

FIGURE 7.41 The Slice tool with cut sections.

Notice that when you sliced that box around the navigation menu, it turned the single slice into three slices: the one you selected, and ones to fit the space above and below your selection. You can identify the slices by the little numbers in the corners. And you can adjust the boxes by selecting and translating any of the handles.

4. Draw slice boxes around each of the navigation buttons individually. This will allow you to add separate code to each button (**FIGURE 7.42**).

FIGURE 7.42 Slice each button into its own section.

5. Repeat this procedure for each of the sections on the page. Anything that you would like to alter at some point, or that will need code, needs to be sliced into its own section. Don't worry if the Slice tool creates many little boxes. That is just how the tool works, and as you become more familiar with it, you can reduce the number by cutting more efficiently (**FIGURE 7.43**).

FIGURE 7.43 The homepage all sliced up.

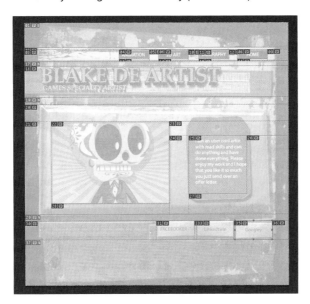

Adding Links

Code is added to the slices via the Slice Options window, which can be accessed by right-clicking the numbers in the upper-left corner of the slice and choosing Edit Slice options.

You will now add links to your navigation bar, and in order to do so, you need a place to navigate to.

1. Open the three wireframes: Animation, 2D Art, and Biography. Save each one into a folder on your desktop using the Save for Web function, and save them as HTML files.

2. On your homepage, choose the Slice tool and navigate to the animation button slice. Right-click the little number to open the Slice tool options window. In the tab for URLs, add the files you just saved as *Animation.html* (and make sure you add the html extension) (**FIGURE 7.44**).

FIGURE 7.44 The Slice
Options window.

FIGURE 7.44 The Slice
Options window.

3. Repeat this procedure for the 2D Art and Biography pages.

4. Save your homepage file as a TIFF, and then save it again for the Web. Choose
the HTML and Images option, and save it as *Home.html*.

5. From the folder in which you saved your homepage as a Web-ready file, open
Home.html. Your Web browser should open and display the page.

6. On the navigation bar, click the animation button to go to the animation wireframe. Click the back button on your browser to return to the homepage. If you
had generated buttons for the homepage on the wireframe, you could have used
those to return home (**FIGURE 7.45**).

FIGURE 7.45 All four
pages of your website.

CHAPTER WRAP-UP

In this chapter, you learned how to showcase your work and promote yourself using Photoshop as an integral tool in that process. You explored the importance of having a concise, directed resume that is easy to read, and how to make it convenient for recruiters to contact you.

You also created title and end pages for your reel, and learned a bit about how to assemble a reel. Finally, you learned how to create assets to build a portfolio website.

If you master these skills and update your content frequently, you should be in good shape for applying for your dream position; and even if you do not get it, you can be assured that at least your self-promotional ducks were in a row.

Be careful. Different companies require different skillsets. It's better to present yourself for one specific job, but also be open to doing other things if asked. What you don't want is to appear unfocused.

INDEX